MICHIGAN BUSINESS STUDIES

Volume XVIII   Number 3

INSTITUTIONAL HOLDINGS OF COMMON STOCK, 1900–2000

History, Projection, and Interpretation

Robert M. Soldofsky

BUREAU OF BUSINESS RESEARCH • GRADUATE SCHOOL OF BUSINESS ADMINISTRATION
THE UNIVERSITY OF MICHIGAN

Copyright © 1971

by

The University of Michigan

All Rights Reserved
Printed in the United States of America

PREFACE

Economists, historians, political theorists, lawyers, and other social scientists have been attracted to the study of the concentration of economic and financial power in American society. Perhaps the best-known and most influential of these studies was published in 1932, *The Modern Corporation and Private Property,* by Adolf A. Berle and Gardiner C. Means. Their statement of the extent of economic concentration in the United States and the separation of corporate ownership and control is especially important because it has strongly influenced a wide range of disciplines as well as the popular views of the structure of the American economy.

Other scholars who were concerned with economic and financial concentration are not so well known to the general public because they either wrote in the earlier part of the century or addressed themselves to limited audiences. For example, the name of William Z. Ripley of Harvard University, whose articles and books did much to bring about the establishment of the Securities and Exchange Commission, is virtually unknown to present-day economic and financial technicians. A. A. Berle acknowledges that a part of his studies of economic and financial power were directly inspired by William Z. Ripley.

Unfortunately, the attention of young financial economists appears to be directed almost solely to important technical and professional problems such as capital budgeting techniques for business enterprises, performance analysis methods for portfolios of securities, methods of computing yield and risk on real assets and securities, and the relationships between the change in the money supply and the performance of the economy. Since about 1960 the advent of the computer on university campuses has encouraged the assault on a range of economic and financial problems by providing a growing arsenal of tools. Both the problems themselves and the education of students are continuing to be restructured in order to utilize the latest and most powerful computers. The many requirements for education in economic theory, behavioral sciences, mathematics, and statistics have been crowding out historical studies and discouraging a professional concern with broad public policy issues in cognate fields.

There are nevertheless hopeful signs of a revival of interest in the broader issues of society. A review of the papers being read at the annual meetings of the American Economic Association indicates concern with the economics of health, poverty, pollution, race relations, and other problem areas. A paper prepared by two mathematical economists, Burton G. Malkiel and Richard E. Quandt, on "The Moral Dimension of Investment Policy" was received too late to be referred to in the text of this monograph.* Their major concern is with the problems that universities face when they own securities in a company whose operations are seen as being morally objectionable by some part of the university community.

The actions of important groups in our society indicate continuing public concern with growing concentrations of financial power. On July 28, 1968, a joint resolution of Congress authorized and directed the Securities and Exchange Commission to study the investment practices of institutional investors. Congress authorized $875,000 for this study, which was to have been completed by September 1, 1969, but has not yet been released. Additional funds have been appropriated to finance the completion of the study.

A *New York Times* article on October 11, 1970, by H. Erich Heinemann pointed out that at the end of 1969 the commercial banks with the five largest trust departments controlled $69 billion in trust assets, and the ten largest trust departments controlled $102 billion. Describing the major concerns of bankers expressed at the annual meeting of the American Bankers Association at Miami Beach, Heinemann wrote,

> The question is simply this: Do the major commercial banks, largely through their trust departments, possess excessive economic power? If so, have they abused this power, and what, if anything, should Congress do about it?

I have read studies of the growth of the common stock holdings by financial intermediaries as they have been published over almost two decades. Detailed information about the ownership of common stock by each of the financial intermediaries except trust departments of commercial banks has been available through scattered sources. A study of the growing concentration of ownership of individual stocks was clearly beyond the resources available to an individual researcher until some information about the trust department holdings became available.

*Burton G. Malkiel and Richard E. Quandt, "The Moral Dimension of Investment Policy," Research Memorandum No. 8, Financial Research Center, Princeton University, 1970.

PREFACE

I knew that I could gather together the basic data for the total market value of common stocks beginning about 1900 and that some portfolio concentration data were available from about 1935. Given data points for a number of years, it seemed feasible to make projections to the year 2000 for the total market value of stocks, for stock holdings of the financial intermediaries relative to the total market value of stocks, and for the individual corporation portfolio concentrations ratios. Not only did I want to project these three major components to the year 2000, but also—and more important—I wanted to interpret the financial and societal consequences of what I found.

In 1967 and 1968 both events and some things I read encouraged me to start the project which has resulted in the present monograph. For example, the summer, 1967, issue of *Daedalus,* which was devoted to the theme *Toward the Year 2000: Work in Progress,* excited my imagination. This volume contained twenty-three articles by a very distinguished and varied group of scholars and reported several round-table discussions in which most of these scholars participated.*

In July, 1968, the names and amounts of the largest holdings of common stock by the trust departments of the leading commercial banks were published by Representative Wright Patman's Subcommittee on Domestic Finance, Committee on Banking and Currency, as a part of its continuing investigations into the activities of commercial banks. The publication of this trust department information made my project appear to be feasible.

The University of Iowa made graduate students available to help collect and process the scattered information about the institutional holdings of common stock. I had carried on some correspondence with corporate pension fund managers and with state and local pension officials in conjunction with other projects, and additional correspondence was undertaken for this common stock project. A 1969 Old Gold Summer Fellowship award provided by the Old Gold Foundation of the University of Iowa gave me an uninterrupted period of eight weeks during which the monograph could be written.

A number of people assisted me in various parts of this total undertaking. A colleague, Leon Pearce, wrote the collection and sorting programs at an early stage of the work. Several able and conscientious graduate students, Kenneth Crepas, Donald Jud, and Dewey Woodall, collected and facilitated the processing of the data and also assisted me in seeking meaningful relationships between the characteristics of the individual common stocks and the observed distribution of portfolio concentration ratios. Professors Thomas Pague and

*Included among the contributors and participants were Daniel Bell, Herman Kahn, Martin Shubik, Daniel Moynihan, Erik H. Erikson, Margaret Mead, David Riesman, and Eugene V. Rostow.

Hyman Joseph gave badly needed assistance, suggesting techniques that might be used in seeking statistically significant relationships and in interpreting the results. Professor Edith Ennis and Mrs. Cheri Loftus of the Bureau of Business and Economic Research, University of Iowa, assisted me in the initial editing of the manuscript; and Mrs. Rosannah C. Steinhoff, Senior Editor, Bureau of Business Research, Graduate School of Business Administration, University of Michigan, and her associates, Mrs. Kathleen Schoonmaker and Mrs. Teresa D'Arms, were extremely helpful in putting the manuscript into its final form. Mrs. D'Arms also indexed the work.

The completeness, accuracy, and intelligibility of this study have depended greatly on the cooperation of the people named and on others who ably assisted in various stages of the work. Any errors of omission and commission are my own.

None of the persons who worked with me are in any way responsible for the projections of the common stock holdings to the year 2000 or for the interpretation of the results. The projections to the year 2000, the several recommendations for legislative reform, and the suggestions for the continuing institutional developments in the voting of common stock* and for the private control of business corporations are the outgrowth of my calculations and reflections on these topics. I bear the sole responsibility for constructing projections on the basis of what may seem to some to be a very simple methodology, using implausible future growth rates and absolute magnitudes for the institutional ownership of common stock, and for recommending naïve—or maybe in some opinions harmful—legislative changes concerning limitations on and publication of information about the stock holdings of the trust departments of commercial banks. Finally, the suggestion that the monetary rewards and voting rights be separated when the portfolio concentration for a common stock reaches some predetermined point and that the voting rights be placed in the hands of a new institution may be viewed as foolish, revolutionary, or even worse.

However, I see the suggestion for creating a new institution, the Stockholders' Voting Council, as being essentially conservative—conservative of the

---

*Princeton University has very recently created a Council of the Princeton University Community to recommend to the Board of Trustees what should be done about the ownership of securities or the voting of shares in companies that have received attention because some of their activities have been alleged by some group to be undesirable. This Council includes administrative officers, faculty members, undergraduate and graduate students, research, library, technical and other staff, and alumni representatives. This development is consistent with the Stockholders' Voting Council discussed in Chapter VI of my study.

many traditional elements in our inherited value system. The best parts of our evolving society must be adapted in the effort to bring tensions such as those resulting from technological change and imperative ecological requirements under the workable control of a stable, but responsive, political system. No political party or political system is likely to be stable enough to win broad public support unless it makes notable advances in improving the quality of life for all of our citizens and sustains a minimum level below which no citizen's living conditions should be permitted to fall.

R.M.S.

Iowa City, Iowa
January, 1971

CONTENTS

I	Major Developments	1
II	Investment Companies	11
III	Noninsured Corporate Pension Funds	36
IV	Insurance Companies and State and Local Pension Funds	54
V	Growth of Stock Ownership by Financial Intermediaries to the Year 2000	73
VI	The Expected Growth of Portfolio Concentration Ratios and the Societal Responses	105
	TABLES	155
	FIGURES	220
	INDEX	223

TABLES

1. Portfolio Companies in Which Investment Companies Held an Influential Interest 155
2. Total Assets and Stock Held by Investment Companies 156
3. Two Estimates of Investment Company Assets 157
4. Rates of Growth of Stock 158
5. Estimates of Market Value of Corporate Stocks by Series 160
6. Size Distribution of Assets of Mutual Fund Companies 163
7. Concentration Ratios for Assets of Mutual Funds 164
8. Net Assets of Ten Largest Investment Company Complexes 165
9. Concentration Ratios of Mutual Fund Groups 168
10. Investment Company Size and Potential Ownership of Portfolio Companies 169
11. Portfolio Concentration for Largest Corporations 170
12. Ranking of Thirty Portfolio Companies by Amount of Institutional Investment 172
13. Increases in Protfolio Concentration Ratios for Holdings of Investment Companies 174
14. Changes in Portfolio Concentration Percentages for Fifty Highly Concentrated Companies 175
15. Inner Structure of Portfolio Concentration Percentages for Large Investment Funds and Investment Fund Groups 178

16. Detailed Structure of Ownership Concentration by Investment Companies—Northwest Airlines. 181
17. Portfolio Concentration Percentages for Investment Company Complexes. 182
18. Assets of Noninsured Corporate Pension Funds. 183
19. Corporate Stock Owned by Institutional Investors 185
20. Historical and Projected Growth of Private Retirement Plans 187
21. Corporate Pension Fund Assets by Size of Fund. 188
22. Asset Size of Corporate Pension Funds Held by Firms with Largest Assets 189
23. Investment and Portfolio Concentration Practices and Rules for Noninsured Corporate Pension Funds 190
24. Attitudes of Corporate Pension Fund Administrators toward Portfolio Concentration Problems. 191
25. Assets Administered by Trust Departments of Commercial Banks. 194
26. Distribution of Voting Rights in Common Stock Held by Trust Departments of Commercial Banks 195
27. Frequency Distribution of Percentage of Common Stock Held in Leading Corporations by Forty-Nine Banks. 196
28. Stock and Total Assets of Life Insurance Companies 197
29. Common Stock and Total Assets of Fifteen Largest Life Insurance Companies 198
30. Contributions of Highly Concentrated Insurance Companies to Concentration Ratios. 199
31. Stock and Total Assets of Property and Casualty Insurance Companies. 200
32. Common Stock and Total Assets of Fifteen of the Largest Property and Casualty Insurance Companies 201
33. State and Local Pension Funds 202

34. Stock and Total Assets of Fifteen Largest State and Local Pension Funds. 204
35. Frequency Distribution of Common Stock Maximum Percentages Authorized for State Pension Funds. 205
36. Common Stock and Total Assets of Nine Large Foundations 206
37. Common Stocks and Total Assets of Seven Large University Endowment Funds. 207
38. Gross National Product Projections. 208
39. Projected Market Values for Stock Holdings of Financial Institutions. 209
40. Stock Diversification Patterns by Type of Financial Intermediary and Size Class 210
41. Companies Cross-classified by Market Value of Common Stock and Portfolio Concentration Percentage. 212
42. Portfolio Concentration Multiple Regression Experiments. 213
43. Known Portfolio Ratios above 20 Per Cent 214
44. Known Concentrated Holdings of Airline Common Stock by Financial Intermediaries 216
45. Difference between Market Percentage of Total Investment and Portfolio Concentration Ratios 218
46. Stockholder Pyramids for Two Very Large Corporations. 219

FIGURES

1. Growth of GNP and total market value of stocks, 1909-2000 220
2. Stock holdings of financial intermediaries relative to total market value of stock 221
3. Portfolio concentrations, 1952-2000. 222

I

MAJOR DEVELOPMENTS

Public, governmental, and academic concern with business size, mergers, operations of the money and capital markets, and the power of financial institutions has come in waves since the beginning of this century. The present rising tide of economic, social, and political problems has integral, financial aspects. The main focus of this study is on the concentrations of stock ownership of individual corporations in the hands of rapidly growing financial intermediaries—primarily investment companies and commercial banks. An analogy that compares the growing public awareness of this problem to the spectacular bore of a rising tide may be even more apt than the analogy with waves. The rising tide at the mouth of a sheltered river may be held back for some time by a seaward sandbar. The pressure of the rising tide continues to build up until it overcomes the barrier and rushes upstream with a roar that symbolizes its power.

Some of the events that have shaped our economic and financial organization took place before the beginning of the twentieth century. Organizational structure, as conceived here, includes both the regulations and the regulatory agencies of state and local government, as well as what is usually called private enterprise. The development of other financial organizations—notably the banking system and stock exchanges—has an important role. The concurrent growth and public acceptance of ancillary skills such as accounting and actuarial science has occurred, along with the growth in size and complexity of business, finance, and government. Attempts to categorize some of these organizations and their related professional societies as private or public is not helpful. The growth of these professional skills and the force of professional associations have interacted with changes in and the growth of governmental and private aspects or phases of the financial infrastructure.

Major changes and developments in financial institutions can be appreciated only if ten-, twenty-, or even thirty-year panoramas are brought into focus. The brief sketches given in the following pages of some of the changes and organizations important to this study are intended to suggest such a wide viewpoint. Many readers will have more detailed knowledge of some changes; others will recall having studied some of them; but few persons are likely to have an intimate or detailed knowledge of each of them. These changes and developments are not automatic. They are accompanied by social trauma, personal travail, and individual leadership. When social, political, and economic tensions about a specific issue intensify over a period of years, legislative and other proposals are suggested to reduce or overcome the problem; and public and private actions result in new laws and other classes of institutional change. The prospect of continuing growth of common stock ownership in the hands of banks, investment companies, and state and local pension funds to the year 2000, which is the concern of this study, is causing such tensions to build.

Mergers and the size of business units

The late nineteenth-century populist reaction to the power of railroads and the attitude of the big businesses of that day led to the passage of the Interstate Commerce Act of 1887 and the Sherman Anti-Trust Act of 1890. Despite the latter act, business units continued to grow in size through various pooling and combination plans, as documented in such works as John Moody, *The Truth About the Trusts* (1904); William Z. Ripley, *Trusts, Pools and Corporations* (1905); Gustave Myers, *History of Great American Fortunes* (1910); and Arthur R. Burns, *The Decline of Competition* (1936). In 1909, United States Steel Corporation had $1,820 million of notoriously watered assets. Standard Oil was second with assets of $372 million, and only sixteen other corporations had assets of more than $100 million. The Clayton Act of 1914, the trust busting of Attorney General Thurman Arnold in the late 1930s, and the investigations of the Temporary National Economic Committee just prior to World War II are some of the historical responses to the size and concentration of power in business units. The concentration of wealth in the two hundred largest corporations was impressed upon the public consciousness by the work of Berle and Means in 1932. There has already been an investigation of the conglomerate merger movement that started in the late 1960s; this new merger movement, which has different dimensions in a changed context, will result in specific legislation in due time.

At the end of 1968, nine corporations had assets above $10 billion, and by the year 2000 several firms will have assets above $100 billion.[1] Nevertheless popular and legislative action has demonstrated fear, resentment, and hostility toward giantism and concentrations of power in private hands, and this attitude is likely to continue.

Banks, insurance companies, and stock markets

The National Banking Act of 1863 established an inelastic currency system; in fact, the money supply under this system tended to contract in periods of financial crises and thereby intensified rather than ameliorated these crises. In 1896, three years after the financial panic and depression of 1893, the American Bankers Association meeting in Baltimore suggested a new plan to remedy the currency system. In 1897 a meeting in Indianapolis sponsored by the Chamber of Commerce and the Board of Trade suggested a plan that was the direct forerunner of the reserve currency plan embodied in the Federal Reserve System. The financial crisis of 1907 made the need for revision of the banking system so immediate, obvious, and intense that a National Monetary Commission was established by Congress in 1908. Preparation of the legislation began at once. In 1913 the bill, which included the results of numerous compromises, was enacted establishing the Federal Reserve System.[2]

In 1905 the famous Armstrong Committee investigation into the life insurance industry was authorized by the New York legislature, and in 1910 the same state directed that a corresponding but less well-known investigation of the property and casualty insurance companies should be carried out by the Merritt Committee.[3] As a part of the political infighting prior to the establishment of the Federal Reserve System, the Pujo Committee—named after Congressman Pujo of Louisiana—was set up in 1912 to investigate the Money Trust which centered in New York City.

The public offerings of securities and the operations of the stock exchanges, as well as the leading financial institutions of the day, came under both public pressure and state and federal government scrutiny before World War I.[4]

Rise of public accountants and their role

During the same period that industrial enterprises, banks, insurance companies, stock exchanges, and investment banking were under investigation, the public accounting and actuarial professions were emerging. The first professional accounting societies were established in the 1880s,[5] and the Wharton School of Finance and Economy was founded in 1881 in Philadelphia by a $100,000 gift from Joseph Wharton.

After several years of effort, a law recognizing and licensing public accountants was passed in 1896 in New York. Similar laws were also passed in Pennsylvania (1899), Maryland (1900), and California (1901). The passage of a 1 per cent federal franchise tax on corporate net profits in 1909 triggered the adoption of public accounting laws in five more states that year. The passage of the Sixteenth or Income Tax Amendment to the Constitution in 1913 was the apparent reason why seven more states passed laws for the licensing of public accountants in that one year. By 1913, 31 states had passed such laws, but not until 1921 did Indiana, New Mexico, and New Hampshire, the last three states without such legislation, pass their C.P.A. laws; twenty-six years elapsed from the date of the first public accounting statute in New York in 1896 until all states in the Union had similar laws.

The political and economic events recounted here and other pressures led the New York Stock Exchange (NYSE) in 1914 to ask corporations whose stock was listed on that exchange to publish quarterly income statements. By 1932 only 730 of the 1,198 NYSE listed companies published quarterly reports, and another 308 companies published only annual statements.[6] The remaining listed companies apparently did not publish any income statements. Even when statements were published, their quality was dubious because of the absence of any accepted accounting standards. Public accountants and academicians, among whom the Harvard economist William Z. Ripley stands foremost, worked to have the situation remedied in the 1920s and early 1930s. Except for railroads and other miscellaneous utilities, there was no requirement for audited statements and no force behind the standards that accounting associations tried to establish.

The efforts of the NYSE to establish standards for financial statements in the early 1930s and the events that eventually led to provision for such authority in the Securities Exchange Act of 1934 are retold in a Twentieth Century Fund study. In the late 1960s the development of the conglomerate merger movement, the interest of the Federal Trade Commission, the activities of the Antitrust Division of the Justice Department, the desires of the professional security analysts and the financial organizations they represent, and the goals of the Security and Exchange Commission (SEC) itself have resulted in pressure on large corporations to publish financial information for their major divisions. These pressures undoubtedly will result in the publication of increasingly detailed divisional statements for widely held corporations during the next thirty years.

The number of public accounting certificates issued annually has grown dramatically. Until 1902 more certificates were issued each year under waivers, as additional states gave "grandfather" rights to practicing public accountants, than on the basis of examinations. By 1913 only 2,265 certificates were issued in the entire country. In the latter part of the 1920s the certificates issued annually passed the 1,000 level. They exceeded 2,000 for the first time at the end of World War II (1946) and reached a peak of 4,386 in 1951.

Growth of the actuarial profession

The Actuarial Society of America was founded in 1889 and had 101 members in 1895. The actuarial examination was first given by the society in 1897. "This innovation was one of the most important steps in the history of the organization and has been largely responsible for its rapid growth and development."[7] The American Institute of Actuaries was organized in Chicago in 1909 to accommodate persons employed in the South and Middle West. The Casualty Actuarial Society was founded in 1914 under the leadership of Dr. Isaac M. Rubinow,[8] but it has never had as many Fellows as the other societies, which were composed primarily of those working with life insurance problems. This society, which had 11 charter members when it was founded, had 151 Fellows and 123 Associates in 1949, and 230 Fellows and 202 Associates in 1967.[9]

Even though actuaries think of their profession as being most like that of accountants in professional outlook and responsibility, they have not sought to be examined and licensed by the state or federal government although this subject was studied by actuarial committees in 1924 and again in 1958.[10]

In 1949 the Society of Actuaries was formed by the merger of the Actuarial Society of America and the American Institute of Actuaries; at that date the new society had 673 Fellows and 401 Associates. By 1969 the numbers had grown to 1,866 Fellows and 1,569 Associates. The most spectacular growth took place among that subgroup known as Consulting Actuaries.[11] The increased number of actuaries and especially of consulting actuaries is attributed to the rise of corporate pension funds.

Other aspects of the financial infrastructure

The development of industrial organization, financial institutions, and means to provide more and better public information based upon known, objective standards is perceptible only in time spans of twenty years or more. Within such periods ideas, concepts, processes, and institutions that were once only dreams and hopes of individuals and organizations have become embodied in the fabric of business, financial, and political organization. Things that to younger people seem to have existed forever as a part of the financial scene have arisen and become accepted within the lifetime of our senior citizens.[12]

A trivial but interesting example is the ratio of current assets to current liabilities. These terms were not used until the last decade of the nineteenth century, but by the 1920s financial and accounting writers used them as though they had always existed.

Both undergraduate and graduate students in business and economics are startled when they first learn of the problems and growth of the public accounting profession. Yet the growth and development of accounting is an essential part of the higher level of business and economic organization as it now stands. The Securities Act of 1933 and the Securities and Exchange Act of 1934 established another part of our financial infrastructure. The administration of these two acts by the SEC, which was created by the 1934 Act, would have required the development of something like the skill of public accountants if it had not already existed.

The SEC is now one of the several organizations that have been seeking to have corporate income statements published on a divisional or product basis. This concern for publicizing more of the detailed results of business operations is a response to the growth in size and complexity of business units. The rapid and highly visible conglomerate merger movement, which joins widely diverse business activities under one central management, provides a firm basis upon which to make the argument for divisional financial reporting.

Security analysts, who are trying to emerge as a distinct professional group, are in favor of such reporting. In 1944 the Financial Analysts Federation began the publication of the *Financial Analysts Journal.* The Institute of Chartered Financial Analysts was formed in 1959. In 1963 charters were first granted by written examinations covering accounting, economics, financial analysis, portfolio management, and ethical standards; in that year 263 charters were granted. During six years of operation 2,243 charters have been granted, and 3,000 additional persons are registered as candidates.[13] Actuarial firms and Chartered Financial Analysts are part of the proliferating structure of professional organizations and individuals developing along with financial and industrial organization. The American Finance Association, which is the primary academic organization for this discipline, was organized in 1939; its major publication, the *Journal of Finance,* was started in 1945. The National Association of Securities Dealers, the North American Securities Administrators, and the SEC represent quasi-private, quasi-public, and public organizations associated with these developments. The existence of all these various groups will contribute to pressures that will result in divisional financial reporting—perhaps in the 1970s.

The purpose of recounting these developments in finance is to focus attention on the underlying changes in institutions, organization, and concepts that take place over a span of several decades. The changes in financial organization that will be occurring during the next thirty years are rooted in and built upon what has gone before, and upon the trends that are observable to all. Just what form the legislative controls over the concentrated institutional ownership of common stock will take is not known. Now, before the greatest concentrations of stock ownership by the trust departments of commercial banks, diversified investment companies, and state and local pension funds occur, society has more options than it will later have to shape these developments in a way that is consistent with the best of our deeply rooted value structures and the onrushing technological and environmental changes.

Other governmental and academic students of the financial scene have focused their attention on other aspects of the global problems of financial organization and processes. Currently the organization of the stock markets to facilitate the exchange of very large blocks of stock is a leading concern. The resolution of this problem relating to the operational efficiency of markets is important to the existing exchanges, stock brokers, financial intermediaries, and the general stockholding public. The question of appropriate fee schedules is closely related. Portfolio turnover or churning by some financial intermediaries may be contrary to the best interests of those who are concerned with the cost and performance of a fund; such churning is under surveillance as a possible area of malpractice. The very meaning of liquidity and auction markets, as these terms are used in the security business, is very likely to be reexamined.

These topics and others, such as the role of the specialist on the floor of organized stock exchanges, merit the serious examination that is being given to them. At other times and places the author has joined such discussions and will continue to do so. However, the thrust of the present study is different and more far reaching: the concern here is with direction of the organization for the control of business by primarily private persons and financial intermediaries. The direction or shape of such private control of business will influence the nature of the governmental response and the quality of business performance in the public interest.

Plan of this study

This study is largely devoted to the historical development of common stock ownership by each of these financial intermediaries. Such individual narratives are interesting in their own right, but their purpose is to highlight the extent to which portfolio concentration has already taken place and indicate the forces that will push these concentrations continually higher in the coming decades; they also suggest some of the legislation needed to direct these continuing changes into channels of orderly development that are consistent with what I believe our basic values to be. At least one of the suggestions in the final chapter may appear to be radical or revolutionary by some, but I see it as being essentially conservative and well within the path of our evolutionary development as a nation and as a society.

NOTES

[1] These nine corporations are, in order of size to the nearest $0.1 billion of book value: American Telephone and Telegraph ($37.6); Prudential Insurance Company ($25.1); Metropolitan Life Insurance ($24.6); Bank of America ($21.3); Chase Manhattan Bank ($17.8); First National City Bank ($17.5); Standard Oil of New Jersey ($15.2); General Motors ($13.3); and Equitable Life Assurance ($13.1). Note that six of these nine corporations are in the financial industry. The assets of commercial banks do not include their trust department assets. Four banks held over $10 billion each of such assets at the end of 1967, as shown in Table 25.

[2] See the final section of Chapter VI for a description of the composition of the boards of directors. Henry Parker Willis, *The Federal Reserve System* (New York: Ronald Press, 1923); Paul M. Warburg, *The Federal Reserve System: Its Origin and Growth* (New York: Macmillan Co., 1930); J. Lawrence Laughlin, *The Federal Reserve Act: Its Origin and Problems* (New York: Macmillan Co., 1933). Each of these three authors played an important role in the origin, conception, structure, and development of the Federal Reserve System.

[3] See Chapter IV, "Life Insurance Companies" and "Property and Casualty Insurance Companies" for further details and references.

[4] The first state "Blue Sky" law, intended to help protect investors from fraudulent promotions, was passed by Kansas in 1911. Included in the federal Postal Fraud Laws of 1909 were prohibitions against the use of the mails for the fraudulent sale of securities or even distribution of misleading information about securities, but the administration of these sections of the law was ineffective. Merwin H. Waterman, Wilford J. Eiteman, *et al., Essays on Business Finance* (3d ed.; Ann Arbor, Mich.: Masterco Press, 1957), pp. 143-44.

[5] Most of the facts for this sketch of public accounting are in James Don Edwards, *History of Public Accounting in the United States* (East Lansing, Mich.: Bureau of Business and Economic Research, Graduate School of Business Administration, Michigan State University, 1960).

[6] Frederick W. Jones, "Corporate Accounting and Reporting," chap. xv of Twentieth Century Fund, *The Security Markets,* Alfred L. Bernheim, ed. (New York: Twentieth Century Fund, 1935), p. 590.

[7] "Address of the President, Arthur B. Wood: Uniformity of Life Insurance Legislation in Canada," *Actuarial Society of America: Transactions* (New York: Actuarial Society of America, 1925), pp. 1-20. This address also sketches the history of major British and European actuarial societies up to that date.

[8] Dudley M. Pruitt, "The First Fifty Years," *Proceedings of the Casualty Actuarial Society* (New York: Casualty Actuarial Society, 1965), pp. 148-81. Isaac M. Rubinow was trained as a physician, but did not practice medicine. He left actuarial work by World War I and migrated through several other careers.

[9] Information from yearbooks published by the Casualty Actuarial Society.

[10] Reinhard A. Hobaus, "Professional Status of Actuaries," *Conference of Actuaries in Public Practice: Proceedings, 1962-1963* (Chicago: Conference of Actuaries in Public Practice, 1963), pp. 284-98. See also references cited therein.

[11] V. E. Henningsen, "Society of Actuaries—Its First Twenty Years" (paper presented at the annual conference of the Society of Actuaries, Nov., 1969).

[12] One of my teachers was Isaac Lippincott (1879-1959). He wrote *The Economic Development of the United States* in 1921 and was a witness to developments that to me are historical events.

[13] Institute of Chartered Financial Analysts, *The C.F.A. Program* (Charlottesville, Va.: Institute of Chartered Financial Analysts, 1969).

II

INVESTMENT COMPANIES

This chapter will discuss the development of investment companies since about 1929, and of investment company regulation as it is related to the ownership and concentration of control of common stock of portfolio companies. The extent of publicly available information on topics of concern to this study will also be indicated; and statistical evidence will be presented to show the size of investment company holdings compared with other institutional holdings and the total market value of equity securities and terms of extent of their ownership of individual portfolio companies.

The two major types of investment companies are the open-end investment company (mutual fund) and the closed-end investment company. The mutual fund is continually offering new shares to investors and redeeming or buying back existing shares from investors on demand. The redemption price is the net asset value per share of the mutual fund shares at the time of redemption. The net asset value fluctuates exactly with the prices of the assets held by the mutual fund. A closed-end fund offers new securities only occasionally, and its outstanding shares are traded in the stock markets. This market price fluctuates independently of the net asset values of the closed-end shares themselves.

Almost all mutual funds are diversified—as that term is defined in the Investment Company Act and in the Internal Revenue Code—in order to obtain the tax advantages available to them. Two major aspects of diversification are: (1) not more than 5 per cent of the investment company's assets can be invested in the securities of one issuer; and (2) not more than 10 per cent of the outstanding voting stock of one company can be owned. (Exceptions are discussed below.) About 45 per cent of the total assets held by closed-end companies are owned by the diversified type of company.

Background of 1940 Investment Company Act

The Investment Company Act of 1940 undoubtedly has played an important role in the steady and spectacular growth of the total assets held by investment companies, from about $2.1 billion in 1940 to about $60 billion at the end of 1969. In relative terms the stock held by this one type of financial intermediary has increased from about 2.3 per cent to about 6.7 per cent of all marketable stock.

The origin of several relevant sections of the Investment Company Act is worth relating, since the details apparently have never before been pieced together. Part of the intricate tale and some of the infighting among powerful contestants go back to the Revenue Act of 1936. Besides being essential to a full understanding of parts of the present regulations, a knowledge of the origins of the present diversification rules will help readers to understand and accept the changes recommended in Chapter VI.

The 5-10 rule

The Investment Company Act of 1940 requires that 75 per cent of the assets held by an investment company calling itself "diversified" conform to the requirements noted above; that is, it may not have more than 5 per cent of its assets or 10 per cent of the voting stock in any one issue in its portfolio. An exception to this restriction is the ownership of government securities. Under the terms of the "free pool" provision of section 5, up to 25 per cent of the assets need not be so diversified. However, several states, including Ohio, Wisconsin, and California, apply the 5-10 rule to all of the investment company's assets.

The Internal Revenue Code is less restrictive than the Investment Company Act in that it permits a free pool as large as 50 per cent of the investment company's assets. As long as an investment company complies with these diversification rules, pays out at least 90 per cent of its interest, dividends, and short-term capital gains, and meets other provisions of the tax law, it is subject to special income tax provisions. The investment company itself is subject to income taxation on the elements of income named only to the extent that they are not paid out to its shareholders. This provision has generally resulted in 100 per cent distribution of interest earned, dividends, and short-term capital gains. The owners of investment company shares pay income taxes on the income they receive, as though they had received the income directly. This "conduit" theory of taxation was incorporated into the Revenue Act of 1936 in order to avoid taxing income a third time.

During the 1940 hearings on investment trusts and investment companies prior to the enactment of the Investment Company Act, the investigators were somewhat surprised to learn that there was no legislative history for the 5-10 rule.[1] The problems faced by the investment companies during the 1920s and during the Great Depression, and the novel tax developments during Roosevelt's first term as president are the main elements of this background.

The investment company movement did not get strongly under way in the United States until 1920. By the end of 1929, the assets of all types of investment companies had grown from almost nothing to $7 billion. Along with this rapid growth numerous abuses and dubious features developed.[2] The investment company industry was dominated in the 1920s by the closed-end type of company. The market prices of their shares rose well above the prices of the underlying securities held. Furthermore, many of these closed-end companies used leverage to increase their ability to purchase equity securities of their portfolio companies Many closed-end companies did not survive the Depression, and investors owning shares in them suffered severe financial losses.

The SEC investigations were especially concerned with the control of portfolio companies by investment companies. This control could come about through the majority ownership of the voting stock, through working control maintained with only a minority of the voting power, or through indirect company claims. The SEC study looked into such matters as the extension of bankers' influence and the techniques of obtaining or ensuring control through such means as participation in the original organization of the portfolio company, purchase in the open market, exchange offers, and control through two or more investment companies. According to this documented study, direct or indirect control of portfolio companies had many implications for portfolio companies, investment companies, and the economy. More than twenty case studies of control in a variety of industries were presented. Table 1 summarizes a part of the original portfolio concentration data.

In 1924 the first two modern open-end investment trusts were started: the Massachusetts Investors Trust (MIT) and the State Street Investment Corporation. The next year Incorporated Investors, another mutual fund, was founded. All three of these mutual fund companies were located in Boston. In 1929 the largest mutual fund was Incorporated Investors; but in 1936 the largest was MIT, which had assets of $130 million by that date and accounted for about 25 per cent of all mutual fund assets.

1936 corporate income tax[3]

Economic recovery measures recommended by President Roosevelt included forcing corporations to pay out all their current earnings in the form of dividends. Any earnings not paid out were to be taxed at a high penalty rate. The Revenue Act of 1936 largely rejected the President's strong urging but did adopt an undistributed profits tax with rates ranging from 7 to 27 per cent. This measure was so bad that the tax rate was reduced in 1938, and the measure was repealed entirely in 1939.

After President Roosevelt sent his 1936 tax reform recommendations to Congress, Paul C. Cabot, William Tuder Gardiner, and Merrill Griswold, the leaders of three of the largest mutual funds, were very active in seeking special relief for their organizations and for owners of mutual fund shares. These funds all had their headquarters in Massachusetts.[4] They talked with James Landis, then Chairman of the SEC, and sought his help in gaining tax relief; but he could express no opinion at the time because the SEC was about to undertake a detailed study of the investment trust industry. Mr. Griswold wrote a letter about the special tax problems of the mutual funds to President Roosevelt, and numerous conversations were held with Treasury officials. On May 5, 1936, Senator Walsh of Massachusetts introduced a memorandum on the subject before the Senate Committee on Finance.

During May, 1936, a great debate was occurring in the Senate Finance Committee about the details of the proposed Revenue Act and especially about the famous section on the taxation of retained earnings. The deliberations and proposed amendments were reported daily in the *Wall Street Journal.* Congress was hurrying toward an adjournment date, tentatively suggested as June 5. On June 3 the tax bill was still uncertain, and Congress planned a three-day recess. The President tried to break the deadlock on the tax bill; he is reported to have wanted a balanced budget.

On June 5, the revenue bill was being debated on the Senate floor. An amendment offered by Senator Walsh and adopted with virtually no discussion defined a "mutual investment company" and included the following as a part of that definition:

> *Provided,* That at no time during the taxable year subsequent to a date 30 days after the date of the enactment of this act (1) more than 10 per cent of the gross assets of the company taken at market value was invested in stock or securities or both of a single corporation or of any group of corporations. . . . and, (2) at no time during the taxable year the company owned, directly or indirectly, more than 5 percent of the outstanding stock or securities or both of any corporation.[5]

The issue of *Business Week* that appeared a few days later reviewed the amendment and its implications and then commented, "New York and Chicago blame it on smart Boston Boys."[6]

The tax relief provided for "mutual funds" did signal the sharp relative decline of the nondiversified and of closed-end investment companies. In 1929 the mutual funds were very small relative to the other investment companies, but by 1940 the assets of the mutual funds were almost one-third as large as those of the other types of investment companies and by about 1951 they were equal in size. Now they are very clearly dominant in the investment company industry. At the end of 1968 the assets of the four major types of companies were:[7]

	Millions
Open-end diversified	$61,476
Open-end not diversified	506
Closed-end diversified	3,751
Closed-end not diversified	4,629

A 5-10 rule was included in the Internal Revenue Code prior to the SEC investigation of the industry and seems to have no other precedent. The reasonableness of this formulation and the more restrictive 5-5 rule included in the original draft of the Investment Company Act, S. 3580, which after modification became the Investment Act of 1940, were discussed to some extent in the SEC investigations. Mr. Paul Cabot, who is still associated with the State Street organization, wrote in response to my question about the basis of the provision in the Revenue Act of 1936 which gave tax relief to a minimally diversified investment company:

> You asked what was the thinking on the original limitations that appeared in the Revenue Act of 1936. In the first place I think you will agree that without some corrective tax limitation, such as was passed in 1936, the taxes on investment trusts would have been prohibitive and in all probability would have killed the business. The big argument for the investment trust, then and now, is that it performs a service for the person of limited means in that he can get by this means a reasonable diversification with expert management. Obviously, in seeking this legislation we wanted to keep it as unrestricted as possible and at the same time we obviously had to agree that some degree of mandatory diversification was in order. This concept also went to the point of view of some reasonable limitation on the acquisition by an investment company of undue control of portfolio companies.
>
> It is my best recollection that the Treasury Department was on the side of somewhat stricter limitations, whereas the industry was on the side of somewhat less limitation, and the figures arrived at, which still pertain, represent a reasonable compromise between the two.[8]

Investment Company Act of 1940

Three specific aspects of the SEC's 1936-40 study of investment trusts and investment companies have interesting bearings on the goals of this study: (1) the original proposal on limiting the investments made in portfolio companies and the related discussion, (2) the application of these limits to individual investment funds rather than to groups of funds managed by a single control group or complex, and (3) the proposal to limit the assets of a single fund to $150 million.

The 5-5 proposal. Section 5b (1) of the original bill[9] referred in its definition of a diversified investment company to "an amount not greater than 5 per centum of the value of the assets of such management company and to not more than 5 per centum of the outstanding voting securities of the issuer." In the hearings before a subcommittee on interstate and foreign commerce,[10] Mr. David Schenker, Chief Counsel for the SEC investment company study, and a number of representatives from the investment company industry addressed themselves to the question of the appropriateness of these restrictions. Most of these hearings took place in April and June, 1940.

Mr. Schenker responded to a question from Senator Wagner, chairman of the hearings at that time, and defended this part of the proposed bill as follows:

> Also, a diversified investment company is a company which can only have one class of securities outstanding, and it does not control or own any voting securities issued by another investment company. That means a diversified investment company is a company which diversifies its investments, has a simple capital structure, and does not turn over its portfolio excessively. There is the added reservation, however, that if they feel that they can contribute capital to industry up to 15 per cent of their assets, they are not subject to the provision that they cannot own more than 5 per cent of the securities.
>
> That, to our mind, at least conforms to what the popular concept and our concept of what a diversified investment company is. It should be diversified. It should be an investment. It should not be speculating. It should have a simple capital structure. It should not be pyramided on any other investment company.[11]

At another point in his discussion of the classification of investment trusts, he commented:

> This question was regarded by the Staff as complicated. There was a great difference in the minds of the staff between diversified trusts and nondiversified trusts. [Given the 15 per cent free pool]...it would be quite

possible to own 100 per cent of a number of companies providing the total value of each holding was not in excess of 5 per cent of the trust's assets.[12]

Many of the leading persons in the investment company industry—including Merrill Griswold, Hugh Bullock, and Raymond D. McGrath—addressed a part of their testimony to the proposed diversification rules. Later, academicians discussed these rules in learned journals. On April 15 Merrill Griswold, Chairman of Massachusetts Investors Trust, made this statement about the control of business units by mutual funds:

> Regarding this argument of undesirable concentration of control, we wish to point out that the basic theory of the mutual fund prevents any such fund from acquiring control of any business. Quite the contrary, such trusts do not invest more than 5 per cent of their funds in the securities of any one company and can invest in no more than 10 per cent of the outstanding securities of any one company.[13]

Mr. Hugh Bullock, vice-president of the well-known Calvin Bullock firm, gave little credence to those who stressed the fear that mutual funds would acquire control over portfolio companies:

> To be sure all this [the possibility of control of portfolio companies] is highly theoretical, because a compilation covering 51 investment companies prepared by *Barron's* showing the stocks jointly held by 18 or more investment companies as of the close of 1938 indicates that in only four cases do the combined holdings of the 51 trusts account for more than 10 per cent of the stock of the corporations in question.[14]

Raymond D. McGrath, executive vice-president of General American Investors, was one of several men who advocated increasing the reservoir or free pool to 25 per cent and increasing the limitation on the holdings of a portfolio company's stock to 10 per cent because of the relatively high information costs related to the search for and surveillance of investments in small corporations. He observed that "10 per cent has been regarded in a number of other acts as the dividing line between a casual investment and an investment tinged with the power of control."[15]

Professor Bosland addressed himself to this same question in 1941 after the 10 per cent figure was included in the Investment Company Act as finally approved in 1940:

> Since ownership of over 10 per cent of the voting control of the voting stock is presumptive evidence of control under practically all recent legislation and since working control is found in many cases where less than 51

per cent of the voting stock is owned, it is apparent that many of the concerns were organized primarily for control rather than for investment.[16]

Investment company groups or complexes. Those persons who drafted Senate File 3580 and industry representatives testifying at the hearings understood that the definition of diversified investment companies applied to each individual fund and not to two or more funds that might be managed by the same group or same persons. Mr. Griswold spoke forcefully and broadly on this topic.

> If it is feared that a group of open-end trusts under the same management might conceivably obtain control of other corporations through their combined holdings—this I should like to say is one of Mr. Frank's ideas—any such possibility can easily be prevented without arbitrarily limiting even the size of the group. For instance, (1) a maximum could be placed on the percentage of ownership in any corporation that can be held by any group of companies under the same or affiliated management, or (2) an individual director could be prevented from serving on all the boards of investment trusts which between them controlled more than a specified percentage of the stock of any corporation.
>
> That is not against the law now. It is not in the bill, but it is entirely acceptable to us.[17]

Mr. Hugh Bullock viewed corporate control by a management group as being rather far fetched in 1940, but the question is serious in 1970. Mr. Bullock said:

> I have heard of one other highly theoretical objection, to wit, that if the same group managed several investment companies, they might have too much influence over some companies whose shares were included in all trusts' portfolios. For example, assume that 10 trusts managed by the same people, each owned 5 per cent of a corporation's stock. This group would then control the portfolio company.[18]

The extent to which some investment company groups or complexes hold stock in portfolio companies is discussed toward the end of this chapter.

$150 million limitation on size. Mr. Merrill Griswold made some of his most critical comments about the part of the proposed bill limiting the size of a diversified investment company to $150 million.

> The bill for Federal regulation of investment companies proposes that trusts which maintain diversified portfolios shall be arbitrarily limited to a maximum size of $150,000,000. Higher and lower limits are also set for other types of investment companies. In addition, by preventing the same group of individuals from serving as a majority of the board of directors of more than one trust, the bill limits the amount of funds under any one management.

As reasons for these provisions for limitation of size, the bill states that the public interest is adversely affected when investment companies:

1. Attain such great size as to preclude efficient management; or
2. Attain such great size as to have excessive influence on the national economy.

I do not know what facts, if any, the SEC may have discovered in the course of its investigation that would tend to bear out either of the above contentions. My own experience and observations have convinced me that neither contention is justified, at least in the case of diversified companies.

It is my firm belief that the reasons for size limitations, as given in the bill, are not the real reasons for this provision. I say this because such reasons are too easily disproved. I believe that the real attitude of the SEC is that size in itself is bad, and that this limitation has been imposed in accordance with preconceived social and economic theories.[19]

The Investment Company Act, when finally passed by Congress, did not include any limitation on investment company size; management companies with interest in more than one trust fund were not prohibited; the free pool was raised to 25 per cent; and the limitation on the ownership of the voting stock of a single portfolio corporation was raised to 10 per cent. This last provision was similar to that of the Revenue Act of 1936, but the free pool permitted by that act was 50 per cent. As pointed out earlier, however, the free-pool provisions in these federal laws have been made largely ineffective by many state regulations which do not permit them.

Growth and Concentration Patterns

Sources of information

The direct and secondary sources of information about size and asset holdings are both ample and conveniently available. The basic documents are the financial statements and portfolio information published regularly by the investment companies themselves as required by law. Numerous summaries have been prepared on various topics by investment services,[20] industry associations,[21] public investigations,[22] and for scholarly studies.[23] The volume, quality, and convenience of information are much better than those which can be found concerning any of the other major financial intermediaries holding common stock. Data which the student desires can usually be compiled from published information, even though the task may require some time and effort.

Growth of investment company assets

Investment company assets grew from $2.1 billion in 1940 (Table 2) to close to $56 billion by the end of 1968 as reported in Table 3. Only about 84 to 87 per cent of their assets are invested in common stock, as indicated in Table 2. The remainder is held in corporate bonds, cash and near cash items, preferred stock, and miscellaneous assets in that order. Some funds of both the open-end and closed-end type specialize in bond ownership. The relative and absolute amounts of stock owned may be compared with the total amount of marketable stocks or with the amounts held by other institutional investors. A particularly useful series is the amount of stock listed on the New York Stock Exchange (NYSE) which investment companies hold. The size distribution of the assets of individual funds and fund groups or complexes is another part of this aggregative concern.

During the 25-year period from 1940 through 1965, the market value of stocks held by investment companies grew from $1.8 billion to $41.1 billion, or at the rate of about 13.3 per cent per year, as shown in Table 4, a table that will be frequently referred to in the course of this study. The growth rate was about 16.2 per cent for the fifteen years from 1950 to 1965, about 12.9 per cent from 1955 to 1965, and 15.0 per cent for the period 1960-65. The growth of mutual funds only was slightly faster. Consistent data for the mutual funds have been published by the Investment Company Institute and are in many ways the easiest to use. According to this source, in 1960-65 the market value of stock owned by mutual funds grew at 16.5 per cent per year. The somewhat lower growth rate of 15.4 per cent per year for 1960-67 very probably reflects the general decline in the market prices of common stock during 1966 and 1967.

Even though amounts growing at 15 per cent per year double every five years, the importance of such high growth rates cannot be properly assessed until they are compared with other series for all marketable securities and with other institutional investors. Table 5 shows the total market value of all widely held corporate stock, according to three different series, the value of all NYSE listed securities, and the value of stocks listed on all United States exchange markets. The three series for widely held stocks have different values for the same year and leave numerous gaps. The growth rate for the total market value of stocks from 1900 to 1945 is approximately 5.3 per cent according to either the Raymond Goldsmith or the Irwin Friend series. The growth rate from 1900 to 1963, according to the Friend series, is 5.9 per cent.

From the base date of 1929 to 1958, the total market values have grown at 3.7 per cent according to Friend's series and at a somewhat lower 3.1 per cent according to Goldsmith's series. During this same 29-year period, the market value of NYSE listed stock grew at 5.1 per cent per year. Two reasons for this faster growth for the NYSE series are suggested. First, additional stocks are always moving to the NYSE from the over-the-counter markets and from other exchange markets such as the American Stock Exchange. In 1929 there were 1,293 listed on the NYSE; the number increased to 1,507 by the end of 1958 and to 1,700 by the end of 1967. Second, the NYSE listed securities probably included almost all of the very dynamic stocks in the country.

Growth rates using 1929 as the base year substantially understate the average growth rate because market values were still high at the end of 1929 compared with values at the end of 1933. The growth rate of NYSE listed stocks from 1933 through 1958 was 8.9 per cent. From 1929 to 1967 this growth rate was 8.3 per cent. Growth rates for the total market value of NYSE listed stocks during other periods are shown on Table 4. These data help to establish long-run growth rates for marketable stocks.

Comparative growth rates of institutional stock ownership

In comparisons of the growth rates for investment companies' common stock holdings, those of other financial intermediaries, and the total market the most convenient starting point is 1940. One reason is that fundamental changes occurred in this industry after the Investment Company Act of 1940, and the other is that data are more easily available.

From 1940 to 1960 stock holdings by life insurance companies grew rapidly—10.9 per cent per year—because of the small amount held in 1940 and because of the very rapid growth of life insurance companies' assets. During the 1960s the investment companies showed the more rapid growth in stocks held. The stock holdings of investment companies were about three times as large as those of life insurance companies in 1950 and over four times as large by 1968. The very rapid growth of noninsured corporate pension funds did not get under way until 1942, and the similar growth of state and local pension funds and holdings of common stock did not get well under way until at least 1960. The factors underlying these changes are discussed in Chapters III and IV.

The percentage of all NYSE listed stock that investment companies' holdings represent grew from about 3.9 per cent at the end of 1949 to about 6.1 per cent at the end of 1968. The market value of the NYSE listed stock held by corporate pension funds exceeded the value of investment companies' holdings in about 1965. At the end of 1968 the NYSE listed common stocks of these pension funds amounted to about 7.1 per cent of all listed NYSE stocks. Together these two types of financial institutions held some 13.2 per cent of the 22.4 per cent of NYSE listed stocks held by all institutional investors. (The absolute and relative future growth of the common stock holdings of financial institutions to the year 2000 and some of the implications of this growth are discussed in the final chapter.)

Size and concentration of investment companies and groups

Another way of viewing size is to consider the asset size of individual investment funds and groups of investment funds. The asset-size frequency distributions for investment companies have been prepared by other investigators and private investment services. The absolute and relative size of individual funds and fund complexes themselves is also an important consideration. The perspective obtained from viewing fund complexes is especially helpful in understanding the actual and potential concentration of ownership of portfolio companies by investment companies.

All parties who participated in the hearings held prior to the passage of the Investment Company Act understood that the 5-10 rule limiting investments applied to individual funds and not to fund complexes or fund groups. There were few important fund groups in 1940. Mr. Hugh Bullock called the possibility of control over portfolio companies by mutual funds "highly theoretical."[24]

At the end of 1936 the Massachusetts Investment Trust, which was then the largest mutual fund, had assets of $130.3 million. In 1952 and 1958 it maintained first place with assets of $512.4 million and $1.3 billion, respectively. In about 1960 Investors Mutual moved into the top place with assets of $1.6 billion, and it continued to hold that position, with assets of $3.0 billion at the end of 1968. The largest diversified closed-end investment company has been Tri-Continental Corporation; it had assets of $652.6 million at the end of 1968.

Meanwhile investment companies as a group have been increasing both in number and in asset size. As Table 6 shows, only five of the 118 open-end investment companies had assets of $150 million or more by the end of 1952. By the end of 1958 the number was 21, and by 1969 there were 29 mutual funds with assets of above $500 million.

The assets of both investment companies and investment company groups are highly concentrated. The four largest mutual funds hold about one third of the combined assets of all mutual funds, and the eight largest hold about one half. The extent of concentration of mutual fund assets in 1952, 1958, and 1968 is shown in Table 7. The data displayed in this table show a clear-cut trend toward a lower concentration for individual funds over this period. A much more meaningful category, however, is the extent of the asset concentration for fund groups, which shows only little decline.

The existence and legitimacy of groups of mutual funds using the same investment advisers, and even instances in which investment advisers organize individual investment companies, such as Lord, Abbett and Company and the Putnam Management Company, Incorporated, have been investigated. At least four reasons explaining the existence of such groups have been suggested. First, a greater range of potential investors may be reached because each fund in the group may have a different investment objective. For example, Keystone Custodian Funds offers bond funds, common stock funds, and most recently capital exchange funds. Common stock funds themselves have different objectives, such as growth of capital values, high current income, or purchase of "special situations." Other funds are specialized according to the characteristics of the companies such as utilities, chemical, or science-oriented companies, whose securities are purchased. Second, efficiency is increased because one marketing and research organization can serve the whole group or complex. Third, growth is in and of itself a distinct goal among organizations of each group. Slight product differentiation may increase a "firm's" market share. Extra selling effort may increase the relative and absolute amount of financial savings invested through mutual funds. Fourth, competition in the industry has led to specialization, as firms in a broad sense have struggled to maintain or increase their market share. Fifth—but this may not be a distinct reason—is the profitability of this form of financial activity. As long as the salary levels are high and the stockholders of the management companies themselves receive a high return on their investment, continuing efforts to expand the sales and services of the industry should be expected.[25] The growing financial resources of most Americans since the beginning of World War II and the continuing general prosperity have been two important and fundamental conditions leading to these developments.

The Wharton School's *A Study of Mutual Funds* identified 18 fund groups or complexes in 1952.[26] By 1958 there were 29, either formed among existing companies or newly organized. Included in these groups were 86 of the 156 mutual funds registered in 1958. Since then both the number of groups and the number of distinct investment companies have continued to grow. The ten largest fund complexes included 28 individual funds in 1950 and 52 in 1966.[27] The assets of the largest fund complex at present, Investors Diversified Services, grew from $260 million at the end of 1950 to $6,667 million at the end of 1968 (see Table 8).

The number and asset size of mutual fund groups for 1952, 1958, and 1968 are shown in Table 9, in the same form that data for individual investment companies were presented in Table 7. If the data for 1968 are exactly comparable to those for 1952 and 1958, there has been a marked decrease in the concentration of assets for the single largest, the four largest, and the eight largest fund complexes. One explanation may be the vigorous competition within the industry and an increase in the number of companies from 156 to 240, a ratio increase of .54 in ten years. Both the concentration ratios for individual investment companies and complexes of investment companies exhibited a downward pattern for the period reviewed.[28] For the future the direction of concentration ratios is so uncertain that specific projections would be foolhardy, especially when such projections are not essential for the purposes of this study. No reason exists to expect that substantial concentration will not continue.

The concentration ratios for the four and the eight largest investment company complexes are increasing relative to those for the four and the eight largest individual mutual funds. The obvious reasons are the changing competitive patterns and increasing specialization among funds.

The observed downward drift in concentration ratios should not obscure the extremely rapid relative and absolute growth in the assets held by investment companies. In absolute terms the net assets of open-end investment companies grew from $1,974 million at the end of 1949 to $52,677 million at the end of 1968; in relative terms, stock held by investment companies grew from 3.9 to 6.1 per cent of the total value of all stock listed on the NYSE. Even though the concentration of assets among the largest investment companies or groups of investment companies has decreased as shown, the largest four, eight, or twenty individual investment companies or groups now own a considerably larger proportion of NYSE listed shares than previously, and this trend toward owning an increasing percentage of NYSE listed shares is expected to continue.

The voting control that investment company complexes potentially have over their portfolio companies is much greater than it is for very large individual nongroup-member investment companies. For example, Investors Diversified Services sponsors three funds, each of which has assets well over $1 billion (Table 8). These three funds could have owned about $325 million in the securities of a single portfolio company in 1968 without violating the 5 per cent limitation on the amount of their own assets that they could invest in one company. The smallest of these three funds, the very rapidly growing Investors Variable Payment Fund, could have owned about $60 million in the stock of one company, provided that the $60 million amounted to 10 per cent or less of the company's outstanding voting stock.

At the end of 1968 there were a few hundred corporations whose common stock had a market value of $600 million or more. The three Investors Diversified Services funds could easily have controlled 30 per cent of the outstanding shares of several major corporations. At the end of 1968, six of the investment fund groups had assets of $2 billion or more. A minimal 1 per cent investment of $20 million in the same portfolio company would clearly enable two or three fund complexes to hold a very substantial proportion of a single corporation and easily more than 50 per cent of its outstanding shares. Even substantial ownership of a number of major corporations in the same industry is quite possible as a later discussion of the present ownership concentration in the air transport industry will show (Chapter V). Table 10 sets out the general relationships between investment company size and permitted investments in portfolio companies. The extent to which investment company groups actually do concentrate their holdings in portfolio companies will be reported in the latter part of this chapter.

The $10,000 million level shown in Table 10 may seem far from present-day reality, but the fact that assets of several fund complexes are growing at about 13 per cent per year means that they will clearly be much larger than $10,000 million by 1980. At the end of April, 1967, the Morgan Guaranty Trust Company administered almost $10,000 million in employee benefit accounts. Two other banks administered employee benefit accounts above $5,000 million, and fourteen banks administered such accounts larger than $1,000 million.[29] A vital concern that will be discussed in the next chapter is that there are no legislative limitations on the amount that a bank trust department may invest in one portfolio company.

Portfolio Company Concentrations

The general growth of open-end and closed-end investment companies, both absolutely and relatively, and the degree of concentration within this industry are important in their own right. However, from a slightly different viewpoint, these observations form only the background for the study of how greatly the ownership of common stock for portfolio purposes has concentrated on individual corporations.

The original SEC investigation of investment companies was concerned with the concentration of ownership of large corporations by these specialized financial companies; that is, they were concerned with what is called "portfolio concentrations." According to this early investigation, at the end of 1935 investment companies owned 10 per cent or more of the voting stock of the eighteen companies with assets of $200 million or more (Table 11). These eighteen corporations comprised one-fifth of all corporations with $200 million or more in assets at that date. As the "Comments" in Table 11 show, most of these high concentrations were the result of ownership by nondiversified, closed-end investment companies.

Four major government studies have been conducted since 1950 primarily to investigate the effects of institutional investment on stock prices, the organization of the securities markets, fees and expenses, and malpractices. These four studies, which differ in extent, depth, and direction of detail, are: *Factors Affecting the Stock Market* (1955) and *Institutional Investors and the Stock Market, 1953-55,* staff reports to Senate Committee on Banking and Currency (1956); *A Study of Mutual Funds* (1962) and *Public Policy Implications of Investment Company Growth* (1966), two reports of the Committee on Interstate and Foreign Commerce. Concern over corporate control through the ownership of voting stock has been present to some extent in each study.

The 1940 study, *Investment Trusts and Investment Companies,* developed a number of different ways of determining portfolio concentrations. Table 1 showed that in 1935 there were 106 companies in which investment companies held 10 per cent of the voting stock. Almost half of these large holdings were in the finance industry. Each of the 86 companies with assets of more than $200 million at that time were discussed separately in the report. The concentration ratios for 18 of these 86 companies were above 10 per cent and for 7 of the 86 they were above 20 per cent. However, such data are not comparable to the more recent studies because many of the investment companies were nondiversified and were organized specifically for the purpose of gaining control of operating corporations. The 1940 study also named the fifty stocks that were most popular with investment companies, popularity being judged by the percentage of management investment companies holding each stock.[30]

Thirty portfolio favorites

There are numerous ways of viewing the size, relative extent, and concentration patterns of investment companies, and the assets that they hold. Table 12 illustrates one very popular way of showing portfolio concentration in terms of the market value of the investment in a given common stock by institutional investors.[31] The rankings in Table 12 are listed in their 1964 order as they appear in *Public Policy Implications of Investment Company Growth.*[32] The 1954 and 1968 rankings were obtained from other published sources as noted at the end of the table. Even a casual study of changes in the ranking of market value of investment and percentages of outstanding common stock owned is surprisingly instructive.

Three companies were in the top ten in terms of market value of investment by institutional investors in 1954, 1964, and 1968; and nine were in the top twenty at each of these three dates. The market value of the investment for "first place" was $354 million in 1954, $897 million in 1964, and $2,026 in 1968; the market value of the first-place holder increased sixfold over a fourteen-year period. The market value of the tenth and twentieth highest investment each increased about fourfold. The increase in the market value of investment has been so rapid that maintaining or even slightly increasing the aggregate counted amount would result in a declining ranking.

In 1964 the concentration ratio for portfolio companies in the first ten places was below 10 per cent, and only five were above 10 per cent in the favorite twenty companies. In 1968 three of the top ten favorites and eight of the top twenty favorites and concentration ratios above 10 per cent. In 1964 there were no concentration ratios above 20 per cent among the top twenty, but there were three above the 20 per cent level in 1968.

Generally the ranking of portfolio companies by market value of investment is not particularly useful for the analysis of concentration ratios. But data showing the number of financial institutions holding the stock are also available from the same well-established company, and such information is of interest to institutional and individual investors. These data tend to confirm the point to be elaborated later on in Chapter V that the higher portfolio concentration ratios are not to be found among the nation's very largest corporations.

General view of portfolio concentration ratios

The 1962 *Study of Mutual Funds* prepared for the SEC shows portfolio concentration ratios for investment companies and investment company complexes. These data for 1952 and 1958, along with figures from the author's less exhaustive data for 1966, are set forth in Table 13. The number of portfolio company holdings at the 1 per cent level or above approximately doubled from 1952 to 1958 both for individual investment companies and for investment company complexes. Those numbers have undoubtedly continued to increase rapidly with the relative and absolute growth of investment companies during the years since 1958. The number of holdings in the 10-20 per cent range for individual investment companies increased from 7 in 1952, to 22 in 1958, and to 142 in 1966; the number in the 20 per cent or above range increased from 1 to 2 between 1952 and 1958, then to 26 by 1966. One may play down the importance of such a relatively large increase of concentrations in the 20 per cent plus range because of the small numbers for 1952 and 1958, but these large holdings of major companies did exist at the end of 1966. (The names of these companies and further details will be set out later in this section.) The number of 20 per cent plus concentrations for investment company complexes increased from 2 to 6 to 15 for 1952, 1958, and 1966, respectively, and they may be most important because of the obvious possibilities of voting control involved. These data do not include holdings of non-insured corporate pension funds; such data would increase the number and level of high concentration ratios.

The trend is running very strongly toward increased concentration percentages and no sophisticated analysis is needed to suggest that it is very likely to continue for many years to come. The relative rates of growth for mutual fund assets and the total stock market values displayed in Table 4 point in the same direction.

The data collected for this study show some fifty portfolio companies for which the concentration percentage is 20 per cent or more when the known holdings of insurance companies and the pension fund accounts of trust departments in banks are added to those of investment companies. An interesting and important question is the pattern by which the portfolio concentration percentages rise, fall, or fluctuate. The corporations listed in Table 14 are those with the highest concentration ratios in 1966. The 1966 percentage column is the concentration for investment companies only in that year. In the case of American Airlines, for example, the concentration ratio rose rapidly in the years prior to 1962 and has remained high through 1968. The decrease of almost five percentage points from 1966 to 1968 should be noted. The concentration percentage for Gimbel Brothers grew rapidly to a 1960 peak and has fluctuated since then. Dramatic year-to-year shifts in the percentages for some companies are seen. These shifts undoubtedly reflect the changes in the popularity of the portfolio companies; such changes presumably respond to some underlying analysis of both the short-run and long-run prospects for the dividends, income, and market prices of each stock. Changes of this kind in prospects are a major concern of institutional investors—and all stockholders— as statements received by the author from pension fund managers attest.

The number of investment companies holding stock in these portfolio companies with high concentration percentages is generally quite low as compared with the number of investment companies holding stock of the companies in which the largest number of dollars were invested (Table 12). The average number of large investment companies per portfolio company for the group with high concentration percentages in 1966 was only 13, and the highest was

40 for Polaroid. For the 30 companies in which the market value of the investment was largest in 1964, the average number of all investment companies holding each of the stocks was much larger. The highest number was 197 for International Business Machines (IBM); these 197 investment companies held $897 million of the stock. Twenty-second in this list of 30 portfolio companies was Avon Products, some $161 million of whose stock was held by 42 investment companies. This was the smallest number of investment companies holding any of this 1964 group of 30 favorite stocks. The asset size of the highly concentrated portfolio companies is also generally much smaller than that of the companies shown in Table 12.[33] The facts indicate a point that will be stressed in Chapter V: the highest concentration ratios are found among medium-sized rather than giant companies.

Inner structure of portfolio concentration ratios

Thus far, only the general concentration percentages of portfolio company stock held by investment companies have been introduced. The likelihood that institutional investors will take any active role in voting for directors or in other policy matters of their portfolio companies would seem to depend to some extent upon the diffusion of such ownership among investment companies. The fewer the investment companies or investment company complexes controlling a given percentage of a portfolio company's stock, the more likely such active participation would seem to be. In 1966 shares amounting to 20 per cent or more of six smaller corporations were owned by six or fewer of the larger investment companies. Therefore, the study of these detailed concentration patterns is extremely important.

Concentration percentages similar to those used for the study of industrial organization are shown in Table 15. This table shows the extent to which ownership of individual portfolio companies is concentrated in the hands of those investment companies that own the largest proportions of their shares. Column 3 shows the percentage of each portfolio company's stock held by that investment company which owned more of that specific stock than any other investment company; the next three columns show the cumulative ownership concentration in the hands of those funds owning the four, eight, and twelve largest amounts of the portfolio company's shares. Table 16 gives the details of this ownership structure for Northwest Airlines.

Ownership concentration percentages for portfolio companies tabulated on the basis of investment company complexes are shown in Table 15. In the case of Northwest Airlines, the eight largest investment company groups happened to own the same percentage of the voting stock as the eight largest individual investment companies.

The potential concentration of portfolio company ownership was illustrated in Table 10 in the preceding section. The actual concentration percentages for investment company complexes presented in Table 17 show six cases in which concentrations were above 10 per cent and six more in which concentrations were between 8 and 10 per cent. Four of the largest investment company complexes are included in this list. Internal policy on investment, prudence, or other considerations have evidently kept more instances of high portfolio concentration within investment company complexes from developing up to the end of 1966. None were noted in which two or more investment company complexes each held 10 per cent or more of the outstanding shares of a single portfolio company. However, Investors Diversified Services held 13.7 per cent, and Wellington Management held 7.7 per cent of Armstrong Rubber's outstanding stock; together these two investment company complexes owned 21.4 per cent of Armstrong Rubber. In four additional cases, two investment company complexes held 15-20 per cent of the outstanding shares of portfolio companies, and in ten additional instances 10-15 per cent was concentrated in the hands of two investment company complexes.

The ranking of the individual companies that have the highest portfolio concentrations fluctuates from year to year. Such fluctuations are in keeping with reasonable expectations, and such evidence as exists is shown in Table 14. The continuing marked increases in the percentage of all stocks owned by investment companies will have two results: a manifold increase in the number of concentration percentages at the present levels, and concentration ratios reaching much higher levels. Investment companies and other institutional investors could change considerably their policies toward the number of different companies' shares they hold in years to come. Related and important considerations are the information that portfolio managers have about "who else is in it with us," and the current style or pattern of diversification in relation to asset size.

Another point about portfolio concentrations was mentioned earlier: the marked increase in the number of investment companies either managed by an investment advisory service or using the same advisory service. Four investment funds in the Fidelity Group and two funds in each of three other fund complexes owned shares in Northwest Airlines. In other cases of highly concentrated ownership in portfolio companies by investment companies, similar patterns are observed. If there is a strong sentiment in the Congress, among institutional investors, individual investors, or the general public with respect to a ceiling permitting portfolio concentrations only to some level such as 10 per cent for an investment company complex, the time for action is here.

When the Investment Company Act of 1940 was passed by Congress, there were no types of institutional investors in common stock comparable in size or power to those that exist now. A tabulation of common stock held by trust departments in commercial banks for employees' benefit plans showed sixty individual instances of ownership of 10 per cent or more in large portfolio companies. (These companies were all included in the *Fortune 500* list.) The Chase Manhattan Bank held 11 per cent of Northwest Airlines, a company which has been used above to illustrate high concentration among investment companies.

NYSE and Other Measures of Institutional Ownership

The difference between the percentage of the market value of NYSE listed stocks held by investment companies and the portfolio concentration percentages reported in this chapter needs to be clarified. The NYSE estimates the market value of all shares in NYSE listed stocks held by financial institutions. This estimated value is shown as a percentage of the market value of all NYSE listed shares.

The reader should keep in mind the fact that the market value of the 5 largest NYSE listed companies (in terms of the market value of their common stock) accounts for about 18 per cent of the market value of all NYSE listed shares. The 10 largest NYSE listed companies account for about 24 per cent of NYSE market values, and the 25 largest of the some 1,700 listed stocks accounted for about 36 per cent of the total NYSE market value of listed shares. Fifteen companies are in both lists: the 25 largest NYSE stocks, and the 25 largest in terms of the market value of shares held by institutional investors. The concentration ratios for 10 of these 15 companies were below 5 per cent. The only one above 10 per cent was Polaroid, with 13.9 per cent in 1968.

The structure of market values of NYSE listed stocks and the holdings of institutional investors—so far as they are known—is such that the percentage of NYSE listed stocks publicized by the NYSE is likely to be misleading for the analysis of portfolio concentration ratios and changes in them. The mean of concentration ratios for each common stock may be below the NYSE published number. The median, or the mode of the distribution, might be much more revealing because of skewing in the distributions. More information is needed about the shape of this distribution. A discussion of the present and projected economic, political, and social implications of generally rising portfolio concentration ratios must give attention to several measures of this dispersion and its most likely direction of change. A rapidly increasing number of portfolio concentrations at 25 per cent and above is surely a matter of considerable public concern.

NOTES

[1] U.S., Congress, Senate, Committee on Banking and Currency, *Investment Trusts and Investment Companies, Hearings,* before a Subcommittee on Banking and Currency, Senate, 76th Cong., 3d sess. (Washington, D.C.: Government Printing Office, 1940), Part 3, pp. 1076-81. These six pages constitute a memorandum on this legislative history prepared by three men who played a very important role in the origin of the diversification rule as developed below. These men were Paul C. Cabot, President of State Street Investment Company; William Tuder Gardiner, Chairman, Incorporated Investors; and Merrill Griswold, Chairman, Massachusetts Investors Trust. All three of these mutual funds had headquarters in Boston, Massachusetts.

[2] For a more detailed history of early developments, see *Management Investment Companies,* a monograph prepared for the Commission on Money and Credit (Englewood Cliffs, N.J.: Prentice-Hall, Inc., 1962). A detailed study and documentation of the problems of the investment companies is included in U.S., Congress, Senate, *Investment Companies and Investment Trusts, Hearings,* Part 4, "On the Economic Significance of the Trusts."

[3] For a brief discussion and critical analysis of this issue, see Dan Throop Smith, *Federal Tax Reform* (New York: McGraw-Hill Book Co., 1961), pp. 205-8.

[4] The facts in this section are based largely upon the memorandum of the legislative history of the 5-10 rule prepared by Cabot, Gardiner, and Griswold and cited in footnote 1.

[5] U.S., Congress, Senate, *Congressional Record,* 74th Cong., 2d sess., 1936, LXXX, Part 8: 9070.

[6] *Business Week,* June 11, 1936, p. 45.

[7] *Vickers Directory of Investment Companies,* March, 1969, p. 51.

[8] Paul C. Cabot, State Street Research and Management Company, letter to the author dated Oct. 29, 1968.

[9] H.R. 10065, 76th Cong., 3d sess.

[10] U.S., Congress, House of Representatives, 76th Cong., 3d sess.

[11] U.S., Congress, Senate, *Investment Trusts and Investment Companies, Hearings,* Part 2, p. 192.

[12] *Ibid.*, p. 417.

[13] *Ibid.*, p. 501.

[14] *Ibid.*, pp. 510-11.

[15] *Ibid.*, p. 431.

[16] Chelcie C. Bosland, "The Investment Company Act of 1940 and Its Background," *Journal of Political Economy,* XLIX (Aug., 1941), 487.

[17] *Ibid.*, p. 501.

[18] *Ibid.*, p. 510.

[19] *Ibid.*, p. 495.

[20] Arthur Weisenberger and Company, *Investment Companies* (New York: Arthur Wiesenberger and Co.), published annually; Vickers Associates, Inc., *Vickers Guide to Investment Company Portfolios* (Huntington, N.Y.: Vickers Assoc., Inc.), material updated regularly; Moody's Investors Service, Inc., *Moody's Bank and Finance Manual* (New York: Moody's Investors Service, Inc.), published annually, and weekly news supplements prepared.

[21] Investment Company Institute, *Mutual Fund Fact Book* (New York: Investment Company Institute), published annually; New York Stock Exchange, *Institutional Shareownership* (New York: New York Stock Exchange, 1964). Similar NYSE studies may be expected in the future. A bimonthly newsletter, *Institutions and the Stock Market,* is prepared for institutional investors by the NYSE.

[22] U.S., Securities and Exchange Commission, *Investment Trusts and Investment Companies,* a four-volume basic SEC study, 1938-42; *Institutional Investors and the Stock Market, 1953-55* (Washington, D.C.: Government Printing Office, 1956); U.S., Congress, Senate, *Factors Affecting the Stock Market,* Staff Report to the Committee on Banking and Currency, Senate, 84th Cong., 1st sess., July 30, 1955; U.S., Congress, House, Committee on Interstate and Foreign Commerce, *A Study of Mutual Funds,* Report of the Committee on Interstate and Foreign Commerce, House, 89th Cong., Dec. 2, 1962 (prepared for the SEC by the Wharton School of Finance and Commerce and called the "Wharton Report"); U.S., Congress, House, Committee on

Interstate and Foreign Commerce, *Report of the Securities and Exchange Commission on Public Policy Implications of Investment Company Growth,* H.R. 2337, 89th Cong., 2d sess., Dec. 2, 1966 (Washington, D.C.: Government Printing Office, 1966).

[23] *Law and Contemporary Problems,* XVII (Winter, 1952–"Institutional Investments"); this issue includes eleven papers by different authors. Investment Company Institute, *Management Investment Companies* (Englewood Cliffs, N.J.: Prentice-Hall, Inc., 1962), a monograph prepared for the Commission on Money and Credit. Other monographs prepared for the Commission deal with other aspects of investment companies: Raymond W. Goldsmith, *Financial Intermediaries in the American Economy Since 1900* (Princeton, N.J.: Princeton University Press, 1958); Raymond W. Goldsmith, *The Flow of Capital Funds in the Postwar Economy* (New York: National Bureau of Economic Research, 1965).

[24] See above, p. 19.

[25] For evidence on costs, salaries, and profits, see U.S., Congress, House, *Report on Investment Company Growth,* chap. 3, "The Management Function and Its Cost," pp. 84-154.

[26] U.S., Congress, House, *A Study of Mutual Funds,* pp. 39-44.

[27] Brief sections on fund complexes are included in U.S., Congress, House, *Report on Investment Company Growth;* see especially pp. 44-50, 102-14, 294-303. However, the major concerns of this report were the fees, costs, and methods of operation of mutual funds.

[28] The 1966 report of the Committee on Interstate and Foreign Commerce states that no decrease was observed in the percentage of mutual fund assets managed by eight advisory organizations. The percentage was 52.2 per cent on September 30, 1958 (according to the Wharton Report) and on June 30, 1966. U.S., Congress, House, *Report on Investment Company Growth,* p. 30, footnote 59.

[29] U.S., Congress, House, Committee on Banking and Currency, *Commercial Banks and Their Trust Activity, Emerging Influence on the American Economy,* Vol. I, Staff Report for the Subcommittee on Domestic Finance, 90th Cong., 2d sess., July 8, 1968 (Washington, D.C.: Government Printing Office, 1968), p. 39.

[30] U.S., Congress, Senate, *Investment Trusts and Investment Companies, Hearings,* Part 4, pp. 575-77. The top ten companies on the list for the 1929-36 period, beginning with the most popular, were: General Motors, Union Carbide and Carbon, Consolidated Edison of New York, Standard Oil of

INVESTMENT COMPANIES 35

New Jersey, General Electric, American Telephone and Telegraph, American Gas & Electric, International Nickel of Canada, E. I. du Pont de Nemours, and Atchison, Topeka & Sante Fe. Some readers may be interested in comparing this list with that appearing in Table 12.

[31] Here and elsewhere these concentrations are limited to readily available public information. The amounts owned by noninsured corporate pension funds are not included. The great bulk of the pension fund dollars involved are administered by the trust departments of the largest commercial banks as discussed in Chapter III.

[32] P. 292.

[33] None of the 30 companies in the 1964 highest total investment list appear in the 1966 highest concentration percentage list. However, five of the companies in "Vickers Favorite 50" for 1968 also appear in the 1966 list. These portfolio companies are Polaroid (5), Burroughs (10), Northwest Airlines (25), Philip Morris (29), and Raytheon (33). The number in parenthesis is the rank in "Vickers Favorite 50."

III

NONINSURED CORPORATE PENSION FUNDS

Very little information about the details of individual noninsured corporate pension funds is available. Because of this fact it is worthwhile to examine the attitudes of pension fund managers toward this privacy and their views on other topics closely related to pension fund management. Most of the information given here was obtained directly from the responsible corporate officials themselves.

Almost all noninsured corporate pension funds are administered by the trust departments of commercial banks. The extent of the concentration of these funds in the hands of banks must be examined along with the attitudes of the banks toward these concentrations and their portfolio management problems. This chapter will present unique data on concentrations of holdings of portfolio companies by these funds which are administered by the trust departments.

The material about the growth of noninsured corporate pension funds, the accumulation of these funds in the major commercial banks, the attitudes of corporate pension fund administrators and trust officers, and the paucity of public information about the pension fund portfolios will lead to an important public policy question: should more data about pension fund assets held by trust departments be made available?

Growth of Private Pension Funds

The roots of private retirement plans in the United States extend back into the nineteenth century. To understand their development, it is useful to review the economic, demographic, and social movements and the specific historical events that have helped to shape the pension programs for private and public employees. Private retirement plans, the bulk of which have been established by corporations, and especially the assets or reserves accumulated to meet the obligations of the individual plans, are the direct concern of this chapter. Most of the general background statements apply equally well to pension plans for employees of state and local government whose assets are considered in Chapter IV.

The first private pension plan is reported to have been established by the American Express Company in 1875. At least four other major corporations established pension plans before 1900.[1] The first lawsuit concerning pension rights, a dispute over the contributions of a police officer toward his pension, reached the Supreme Court in 1889.[2] Pension plans grew more rapidly after 1915, and by 1930 some 2,700,000 persons were covered by private plans. However, the assets accumulated under these plans were relatively small and grew slowly (Table 18). Their assets were so small because in the late 1920s only about one third of the plans were funded at all; most were limited to bookkeeping entries.

General reasons for growth

The growth of private pension plans has been spurred by the urbanization and industrialization of the nation, by our increasing life expectancy, mobility, productivity, and by technological change. In the latter part of the nineteenth century a person at age twenty could expect to live about forty-two years longer; now the figure is about fifty-three years. Furthermore, Americans start to work later in life and expect to retire earlier than formerly. Hence the number of working years during which funds may be set aside to finance retirement income has been decreasing.

The continuing urbanization, industrialization, mobility, and other factors have increased the desire or necessity for grandparents and great-grandparents to live independently of their offspring. Both the working and retired generations seek personal and financial independence. Financial independence is viewed as being achieved by providing for one's own retirement years through savings rather than through a current transfer of goods and services as economists view the process. Financing the current transfers of goods and services according to a different outlook and method, such as taxation of current income, is quite possible; but historical developments have not moved in that direction. Americans are independent individuals, but they are also very conscious of economic insecurity and inflation.

The enlightened view of the social responsibility of business, that each enterprise itself should contribute substantially to the retirement benefits of its employees, has become accepted by executives of large businesses, labor leaders, and government officials largely as the result of a struggle that has been going on for several decades. One of the results of tying individuals to pension plans of their employers is to reduce employment mobility, but during the coming decades the drive for "portable" pensions is expected to become more intense. Of course, a basic retirement benefit is being provided for most individuals through increasing social security coverage.

Specific reasons for growth

The specific historical events and attitudes that have given rise to the growth of private pension funds include: income tax inducements and administrative definitions, starting with the Internal Revenue Code of 1921; the level of the income tax rates themselves, which made the income tax inducements important to employers; and the administration of wartime wage controls, which encouraged deferred fringe benefits such as increases in pension benefits. The definition of wages under the Labor Management Relations Act of 1947 made it the duty of employers to bargain collectively with employees on pension plans. This definition was tested in the courts and upheld in 1949 in the *Inland Steel* decision. During World War II and the Korean War the pressure of organized labor resulted in the very rapid expansion of the permitted fringe benefit increases, while wage increases were held down. After the *Inland Steel* decision, some labor unions campaigned even more forcefully for increases in pension benefits. During the earlier years, at least, pension plans were rationalized as a method of reducing labor turnover and thereby increasing productivity.

The development of the administrative provisions in the Internal Revenue Codes has been especially important. The 1921 Code exempted payments on current service into employee benefit plans, but income from trust funds was not exempted until 1926. The Revenue Act of 1928 recognized that current payments for unfunded past-service liabilities should be exempt from income taxation; but this treatment was not extended to plans funded through group annuities until 1942, when the provisions of the Code relating to pension plans were extensively revised.[3] The combination of changes in the Internal Revenue Code in 1942, the increases in the income tax rate needed to finance World War II, and the administration of wage controls all contributed to the rapid growth of pension fund assets shown in Tables 18 and 19.

Employer contributions in dollars and investment income on pension funds are all very substantial, but so is the amount of the special income tax inducements. In 1964 when employer contributions were about $6 billion and the income from the investment of pension funds came to about $2.5 billion per year, the amount of income tax relief was estimated to be either $1.2 or $3.4 billion depending upon the assumptions made. If the assumption is that without the special income tax provisions the entire $8.5 billion would have been treated as income of the employees and taxed as such, the income taxes would have been $1.2 billion; if the same $8.5 were taxed at corporate income tax rates, the income tax would be $3.4 billion.[4] The investment income received by the employees in benefits after retirement is taxed at the applicable personal income tax rates when received. This complication and others were considered in the federal income tax losses estimated above.

The 1965 Report of the President's Committee gave four reasons for the broad public interest in private retirement plans:

1. They are a major element in the economic security of some twenty-five million workers and their families.
2. They are a "significant, growing source of economic and financial power" and a source of funds for new investment.
3. They reduce the mobility of manpower especially where the portability of the pensions is absent or narrowly limited. Such limitations are undesirable during periods of rapid technological and economic change.
4. The special tax concessions narrow the tax base and place the tax burdens elsewhere. These concessions must be weighed against their costs.[5]

Funding and investment policy

The assets—reserves, in insurance terminology—of pension or employee benefit plans grow when funds actually are paid to help meet the obligations undertaken. In the 1920s only about one third of the plans funded any of their obligations. Providing the funds to meet the eventual obligations to retired workers either through insurance annuities or through irrevocable trusts is obviously of great concern to employees because of the vicissitudes of business. The time periods to keep in mind for these changes in fortune may be sixty years or more; this period covers both the working and retirement years of the employee and his beneficiaries.

Retirement plans in the form of group annuities administered by life insurance companies obviously are funded, and currently most "noninsured" corporate pension plans are also funded.[6] Life insurance plans are more widely used for smaller corporations because of their lower per capita costs of administration and because a large group of employees is needed before actuarial factors are reliable. Whether an employee benefit plan is administered by an insurance company or by a trustee—typically a commercial bank—the ultimate benefit payments to the retired employees are equally assured. The growth in pension fund assets, covered employees, and beneficiaries since 1940 is shown in Table 20. In 1950 the trusteed or noninsured plans had assets that were only slightly larger than those of insured plans, but by 1967 they were more than twice as large. The primary advantage of the noninsured plans has been their wider latitude in the selection of investment media. Until 1951 the life insurance companies generally could not invest in common stock; since then investment regulations have become somewhat more liberal.[7] By the end of World War II about 10 per cent of the assets of noninsured pension plans were invested in common stock, and that percentage has grown steadily. During the 1960s the proportion invested in common stocks exceeded 50 per cent. Relatively little is known of the portfolio details of the large noninsured corporate pension funds, but my own studies show that the percentage invested in common stock varies from 15 to 90 per cent.

One of the basic reasons for advance funding of pension benefits is to permit investment in income-earning assets, thereby reducing the cash outlay needed to meet the obligations of the plan. Higher expected rates of return on investment cut down the current obligations sharply. For example, let us assume that the annual current service costs of a plan are $1 million when 3.5 per cent return is assumed. An increase in the rate of return to 4 per cent will reduce the annual cost to $880,000, and an increase to 5 per cent will reduce the cost to $690,000 or by 31 per cent as compared with the 3.5 per cent assumption. In 1964 the actuarial assumption of well over half of the insured pension plans was 3.5 per cent or less.[8] The actuarial factor for interest is changed slowly because it is intended to represent average rates over periods of up to fifty years or more. Rates of return on noninsured corporate pension funds at levels of 5 to 7 per cent or more have been reported by leading actuarial firms.[9] The problems of accounting for pension fund income are complicated by the changes in the market value of common stock and are extremely subject to controversy, arising especially because of the differing views of public accountants, actuaries, the Internal Revenue Service, and corporate managers themselves.[10]

The funding of corporate pension plans has been an element in their rapid growth. The smaller annual outlays associated with the use of common stock (as contrasted with bonds) as an important investment vehicle have led to the rise of bank-administered corporate pension funds. What little is known about the size of common stock holdings or portfolio policies of the individual corporate funds will be brought together in the next section before discussion of specific problems concerning the size and portfolio concentration that the trust departments of the commercial banks themselves must face.

Individual Corporate Pension Funds

Almost all large corporations use the noninsured type of pension funds and have the assets administered by the trust departments of large commercial banks. In view of the fact that the market value of the common stock held by these funds is about as large as, and growing faster than, the amount held by rapidly growing investment companies, the paucity of information about their portfolios is surprising. The Welfare and Pension Plans Disclosure Act of 1958 has done nothing to provide the kind of information needed for the analysis of various aspects of investment and portfolio concentration. The objective of the legislation was to prevent the occasional—but sometimes large in terms of the amounts involved—abuses in collectively bargained and jointly administered employee benefit plans.[11]

Each retirement plan must report annually the information required under the Welfare and Pension Plans Disclosure Act, using Form D-2, January 1959, U.S. Department of Labor. The total assets and liabilities of each plan must be reported, but very little portfolio detail needs to be disclosed. Copies of these completed D-2 forms are available to the public in a reading room in Washington, D.C., and photographic copies may be obtained for a small fee. A very few large corporations, such as United States Steel and General Electric, do include a statement of the asset value of their pension funds in their annual reports.

A special sample tabulation of corporate noninsured pension funds for 1957 (Table 21) showed that only about 1.5 per cent of the funds had assets of $100 million or more, but these funds held slightly more than half of all the assets and common stock held by these funds. A corresponding study nine years later shows that the 16.8 per cent of the number of funds which held assets with a book value of $20 million or more owned 83.6 per cent of all pension fund assets. If the asset size of the individual pension funds is growing about 15 per cent per year, which is somewhat less than the average growth rate during the past decade, they would double every five years and quadruple every ten years. There are no strong indications that the asset distribution by size class has shifted.

Portfolio practices and rules

Some two hundred of the nation's largest corporations were approached in my effort to obtain information about various aspects of their pension funds.[12] About one hundred of these corporations provided the 1966 asset size of their pension funds. The total assets of forty-seven of the respondents with the largest pension funds amounted to about $13 billion, and total common stock about $7 billion; both figures represented about 20 per cent of the total amounts held by all such funds.[13] The number of respondents and the total asset values held by these respondents is large enough to assure that their responses were representative. The size distribution of the funds of the respondents is shown in Table 22.

Five responses to my pension fund survey came from funds that have more than $1 billion of assets, but only three funds had more than $500 million of common stock at book value. In 1967 twenty-three mutual funds had assets of that amount and more (see Table 8). Given the relatively small size of many individual pension funds, one can sympathize with the surprise of many pension fund administrators at being asked about the impact of the stock held by their fund on the concentration of control of voting stock. Many administrators had honestly not considered the question, and others were apparently offended by the questions themselves.

The proportion of corporate stock in the aggregate investment of the non-insured corporate pension funds has grown from less than 10 per cent (in terms of market value) at the end of World War II to about 55 per cent. This percentage varied widely between funds. The five respondents with $1 billion or more of assets were slightly conservative investors; the common stock percentage for these funds ranged from 37 to 50 per cent. One $300 million fund had only 14 per cent of its investment in stock, while a $125 million fund invested about 93 per cent of its assets in stock. Several respondents had more than 80 per cent of their assets invested in stock.

It is extremely unlikely that such large proportions of common stock investment would prevent a pension fund from meeting its obligations to its beneficiaries, because the cash inflows of these pension funds generally are three to four times as large as their outflows. No loans may be made by employees against their accounts. This situation differs from that of insurance companies, which may be called upon to make policy loans from time to time. Furthermore, if the cash-flow safeguards for the liquidity needs of a fund should be inadequate because of some most remarkable set of circumstances, a portion of debt or fixed income securities could be sold to meet immediate needs without panic or emergency selling of stock. The drive to increase the rate of return on pension funds and thereby decrease the cash outlay that shows as a cost in the statement of income and expense is so intense that some further general upward movement in the aggregate stock percentage would not be surprising.

Common stock portfolio diversification

In the absence of published and fully detailed information about the common stock owned by corporate pension funds, several alternative approaches to the problem were attempted. The number of common stocks in pension fund portfolios has been compared with the number in investment companies portfolios, and pension fund practices and rules about portfolio concentration have been summarized. Abstracts from the comments of these respondents are quoted here in an effort to present their viewpoints fairly and vigorously.

Corporate pension fund officials were asked how many different common stocks were included in the portfolios for which they were responsible. The average number of different stocks for the seven pension funds with common stock holdings of $250 million to $1 billion which responded to the survey was 185.1, slightly more than twice the number held by twenty-three investment companies in the same size range. Eight respondent pension funds with common stock holdings of $100 to $250 million held an average of 142.4 different stocks, compared with 75.3 for twenty-nine investment companies in the same size range. In the $50-$100 million size range the average was 102.6 for the pension funds, compared with 54.5 for the investment companies.[14] If wider diversification is a sign of more conservative investment policies, pension funds are generally quite conservative. Life insurance and property and casualty insurance companies are about equally conservative.[15]

The concentration aspects of a common stock portfolio may be analyzed also in terms of the investment concentration; that is, the proportion of the stock investment held in one security; and the portfolio concentration, that is, the proportion of the common stock of portfolio companies themselves that are held. These two categories may each be viewed in terms of pension fund practices and portfolio rules. Only forty-seven companies provided some useful information about either their practices or rules, or both of these. Most of these companies also stated the common stock and total asset size of their pension funds. As a matter of practice, about half of the pension funds responding to this question had maximum investment concentrations of 6 per cent or less in stock. Three investment concentration percentages were above 10 per cent, as shown in Table 23, even though the holdings of stock in their own company was specifically excluded. Eleven of fourteen respondents said that they held less than 2 per cent of the stock of any portfolio company as a maximum. Most of the respondents did not make such a calculation. One official of a $150 million fund wrote, "We have made no special study of this except to note that a holding as great as 1 per cent is a practical impossibility considering the size of our fund."

About half (24 out of 47) of the funds providing such information did not have any formal or informal rules for investment concentration or portfolio concentrations. As shown in Table 23 the percentage given most frequently for both of these rules was 5 per cent; but the average for the investment concentration rules was 5.6 per cent, and for portfolio concentration rules it was 3.4 per cent. The actual portfolio concentration percentage, which is of greater interest to this study, is close to 1 per cent and well below the maximum indicated in the few decision rules received.

Two of the $1 billion fund respondents did not provide any information about their practices or rules. One of the remaining three set both its investment concentration and portfolio concentration at 5 per cent, and a second one set both of these at 3 per cent. The fifth of the group set its investment concentration maximum at 3 per cent and its portfolio concentration maximum at 5 per cent.

Concentration problems seen by corporate pension fund officials

The pension fund questionnaire sent to the fund administrators asked for their rules and practices as discussed above and then asked:

What do you see as the three most serious questions or problems relating to such existing concentrations of ownership?

Forty-one unstructured responses to this question provide very considerable insight into fund management problems and into the attitudes of these officers, but they are extremely difficult to summarize briefly. Table 24 illustrates the diversity of views, and the accompanying discussion will be enlivened by the remarks of the officials themselves. The responses varied from a few lines up to as much as a full two-page letter.

Two officials took issue with what they perceived to be an assumption that concentrations of ownership existed. One of them wrote, "This question would indicate that you have arrived at a conclusion before receiving the facts." As some of the quotations will illustrate, it is difficult to decide in many instances whether the concern about portfolio concentration stems from its wider, long-run implications or from its more immediate bearing on price and performance risks. Parts of some of the respondents' answers were placed in the "no serious concern" section, and other parts in the "serious concern" section.

The comments of twenty-six respondents were interpreted as indicating that they believed no serious problems about the concentration of ownership existed. Some respondents dismissed the issue with a simple statement such as, "We can see no serious questions or problems relating to the existing concentration of ownership," but others gave one or more reasons for their opinion. The most frequently stated reason was that the firm's pension fund trustee was responsible for investments within the limitations of a prescribed general policy. An officer of one of the largest pension funds wrote:

> The pension trusts established by ____ ____ are invested by three bank-trustees. Each trustee has sole discretion as to the investments of such funds. The trustees advise us of investment actions, but do not consult us in the formulation of investment policy or the implementation of the policy by specific investment selections. Our interests lie entirely in the measurement of investment performance.

Another official wrote:

> If our trustees did not have sole investment responsibility and if our Company took an active part in directing which securities the trustee should purchase, one might hold that unfavorable elements of control could be introduced that would not be in the best interest of the pension fund beneficiaries or of the company being controlled.

Such statements are especially important when the responsibility and positions of power of the trustees are considered, as they will be later.

Several corporate pension fund officers are skeptical about the very existence of portfolio concentrations, and about their significance if they do exist.

> Much of the current literature raising the issue of concentration of ownership in funds management, has, in my opinion, lacked authority, documentation, and, therefore, conviction. While there have undoubtedly been shifts in ownership concentrations concomitant with the growth of funds of various types, it must be recognized that at least to some extent these funds and their managements are competitive and becoming increasingly performance minded. Under such conditions, they haven't the time or inclination to influence management; i.e., if they disapprove of management, they sell their stock.
>
> I see no reason for concern by anyone about any possible increase in concentration of holdings. Furthermore, even if we were to assume a contrary purpose, it is hard for me to see any problems to the corporation, its stockholders or the public at large from the transfer of some voting powers from many thousands of individual stockholders to some hundreds of institutions (who are represented by thousands of different individuals). This transfer is from a group which, necessarily, is somewhat less informed to another group which is more informed.

One of the two major banks responding to the question stated that it did not want to see the portfolio concentration percentage approach 10 per cent, and the other suggested a limit at 5 per cent for all employees' benefit funds administered by the bank. The administrator of one of the smaller pension funds made a statement that shows considerable vision:

> We could even speculate further by asking the question, is the time coming when the equity holdings of retirement funds will be so great that they will be in the position of exerting a real influence on corporate management? If this is so, the pension fund administrator will have fallen heir to a new responsibility, one that he may not even want or be qualified to handle.

Fourteen of the statements indicated a wide variety of reasons for serious concern with ownership concentration; some respondents gave more than one reason for their position. Such causes related to the influence of management, the influence on price and on the trustee, and to several miscellaneous and important items. Respondents differed about the way in which management of portfolio companies might be affected:

> Characteristically, shares are voted in favor of management. We go so far as to say that if a case arose where an open conflict with present management occurred, the trustee may have been derelict in not foreseeing the problem and disposing of the stock on a timely basis.
>
> It seems to me that insofar as the institutional holder is concerned he normally exercises "control" through buying or selling shares, not through voting. Institutional holders are much less active in voicing opinions directly than are many individual shareholders.
>
> The best method for dealing with these problems is self-regulation. A principled, ethical approach would avoid serious problems. Unfortunately, however, such an approach would not be very consistent from company to company or trustee to trustee. Consequently, there appears to be a certain element of inevitability of eventual governmental "influence" in private noninsured pension funds.

Some of the responses were concerned with both price changes and portfolio concentration. In a few cases the major concern seemed to be with concentration, but others might view the emphasis differently. One such statement is:

> The most serious question relating to concentrations in ownership in pension funds and other institutions, in our opinion, is that it tends to reduce the floating supply of stocks available, which, in turn, causes pressure on either the buy or sell side.

But others like the following indicate the primacy or priority of the price and performance question:

> ...the only serious problem that might arise from the concentration of ownership is the market behavior resulting from large blocks being bought or sold.

Another respondent made a similar point somewhat differently:

> ...the serious problems might include: a) Risk of a serious loss if a single large investment proved unprofitable....

The viewpoints expressed by responsible corporate officers have much to commend them. The individual pension funds are relatively small; only a few approach the size of the large mutual funds. The performance of a pension fund is uppermost in the thoughts of its immediate managers; their personal performance also is likely to be measured by the performance of the fund for which they have some responsibility. Whether the investment performance, degree of portfolio concentration, and the voting of the stock are responsibilities that are or should be passed onto the trustee could be argued. The fact of the matter, however, is that a few large commercial banks have become the focal point of enormous investment concentrations larger than those of the investment company groups. The very rapid growth of pension funds and their continued funneling of assets to the commercial banks show no signs of abating.

Commercial Banks as Trustees of Noninsured Corporate Pension Funds

The 1968 report of the Patman Committee has provided the most substantial information available about the absolute and relative size of the pension funds being administered by the commercial banks.[16] Some important data are provided on holdings of individual trust departments for portfolio concentrations that are greater than 5 per cent. As of November 1 to December 31, 1967, the employee benefit accounts administered by these trust departments had assets of $72.9 billion. The Morgan Guaranty Trust of New York City held $9.7 billion, or 13.34 per cent of this entire amount. The three banks with the largest such accounts held almost one third of all employee benefit account assets, and the ten largest held about 60.0 per cent as shown in Table 25. The employee benefit accounts amounted to 28.8 per cent of the $253.3 billion held in all these bank trust accounts at that date. The largest type of account, private trust accounts, had $126.2 billion; and the remainder, $54.2 billion, was in agency accounts.

Tables prepared by the Patman Committee staff from information requested from the banks show also the total amount of stocks, bonds, and other assets held in the trust accounts of each bank. The details for each of these broad groups of assets classified by type of account, such as employee benefit accounts, are not available. This lapse is unfortunate for the present purposes but is consistent with the committee's objective of obtaining heretofore secret information. The Patman Committee data show some $161.7 billion invested in stock in trust department assets as of April 1, 1968. The annual SEC study of corporate pension fund assets showed holdings of about $76 billion in market value as of 1967. Very roughly, about 55 per cent of trust account stock probably belongs to pension fund accounts. The total of $72.9 billion for employee benefit accounts at the end of 1967 as compared with the SEC total shows the amounts to be roughly comparable. The amount given in the Patman Committee report probably includes some funds for public as well as private retirement plans.

More than $1 billion of stock was held by each of 39 bank trust departments at the end of 1967; of these 13 held more than $2 billion and 10 had stock of $3 billion or more. The stock holdings of the trust departments that rank highest in terms of asset values are as large as or larger than those of the investment company complexes cited in Table 9. Furthermore, there are few limitations—other than those imposed by prudence—upon the investment and portfolio concentration percentages.[17] In the case of private trust accounts, such concentrations may properly be a matter of negotiation between the bank and the persons establishing the trust, but the question of public policy also may be raised.

The voting rights of some of the stock held in a trust department may be wholly in its own hands or retained elsewhere either wholly or in part. Detailed tables for almost 1,000 corporations, including the "Fortune 500" lists, provide information on the percentage of stock in each of these corporations held by each of the 49 largest trust departments. The details, however, are limited to those instances in which portfolio concentration is 5 per cent or more for the stock of that class. Scanning the detailed tables leads to two observations: first, in the largest corporations the voting rights are solely or very largely in the hands of the trustees; second, in the smaller corporations—which are still quite important to many people—the voting rights are more likely to be wholly or partly retained elsewhere. The percentage of voting control may be quite large in the latter cases, suggesting that they are related to private or agency accounts rather than to employee benefit accounts. Several interesting examples are set out in Table 26.

Only portfolio concentrations of 5 per cent or more were reported to the committee. A committee staff member told the author that this percentage was selected as a compromise; the staff wanted a lower cutoff percentage, but the banks argued that the amount of work required in furnishing the information on that basis would be too large. Only 49 banks were asked to provide even the detailed information agreed upon, but these banks held $135.2 or 54.0 per cent of all trust assets. Some 223 instances were counted in the Patman Report in which the portfolio concentrations were at the 5 per cent level or above, as reported in Table 27. About one fifth of these portfolio concentrations were at the 5.0-5.9 per cent level; the frequency of occurrence generally declines with the increase in the percentage size class.

Should more portfolio concentration data be provided?

If the minimum percentage reported were reduced to 4 per cent, 3 per cent, or even 2 per cent, the number of occurrences revealed in each rank would be expected to increase rather sharply. If the number of banks in the sample were expanded to include the one hundred holding the largest amount of trust assets, the occurrences or frequencies would also be very likely to increase somewhat further. According to indications in letters received from two major bank trustees and from several corporate officers responsible for pension fund administration, there is a widespread informal rule to keep portfolio concentration percentages at 5 per cent or less. Therefore, one would expect to find a large jump in the frequency of occurrence of concentrations just below the 5 per cent level.

The importance of data showing the contribution that portfolio concentrations at the 4 per cent, 3 per cent, or even 2 per cent level would make to overall concentration percentages hardly needs elaboration. Such information is essential to complete and accurate portfolio concentration studies. Table 43 will show that trust department portfolio concentrations contributed to twenty-seven of the fifty instances in which concentration levels of 20 per cent or more were accumulated.

Arguments can be made for and against requiring the trust departments of commercial banks to report such information and to report it on a regular basis. Most of the points against such a requirement have been made by the respondents to the author's survey:

1. Trust department concentrations are generally not large enough to be important.
2. Trust departments (and other institutional investors) are individualistic and do not cooperate in matters of voting.

3. The locations of bank concentrations are not known (or were not prior to the publication of the Patman study), so coordination of policy is not possible.
4. The primary interest of the bank trustee, the corporation, and the ultimate beneficiaries is in the performance of stocks and not in control of corporations.
5. Trustees do—or should—dispose of their shares if there is or may be an open disagreement on specific policies.
6. Providing concentration information would be a step toward breaking down the confidential nature of the trust relationship between the bank and its client.
7. The above step and others would reduce the freedom and flexibility of the investment policies.
8. Concentration of shares in the knowledgeable hands of bank trustees (and other institutional investors) is more desirable than leaving decisions to the generally poorly informed and less skilled individual investors.
9. The costs of providing concentration information are too great.
10. The potential adverse impact of concentration information on price and performance is the primary consideration.

Most of the arguments against providing data about portfolio concentration on a regular basis are so transparent, especially in the computer age, that the reader can very easily develop the counterarguments himself. The concern of informed citizens, the motivations of scholars, and the responsibility of Congress in seeking such information should be understood. Scholars, at least, are concerned about the trend toward the reconcentration of ownership in a limited number of owners. Study of these trends and their causes, study of the legitimacy of potential corporate control in the hands of the officials of financial intermediaries, and more discussion of the public policy questions that may be involved in the economic and political drift of the nation are the objectives for which such information is sought. Even furnishing concentration information once every two years with a lag would be satisfactory for discussion of the public policy; and the lag would overcome any resistance on the grounds that such information could be used to affect adversely a noninsured corporate pension fund's or bank trustee's interests in the price and performance of a given stock. Investment companies have learned how to cope with even more intense and immediate public scrutiny of their buying and selling activities. For the purpose of scholarly and public policy research, the names of the individual bank trustees need not be made public.

NONINSURED CORPORATE PENSION FUNDS

Other persons in public or private life could use such detailed information on concentration for purposes that some critics might deem to be unworthy. However, the genius of democracy and the continuing trend are running strongly toward making more information public. All arguments against making more information available on legitimate public policy issues have failed. What important adverse consequences would flow from making public the concentration ratios for widely held common stock held by trust departments?

The public concern with the importance of private pension funds has been pointed out. The circumstances that have given rise to these funds continue to propel their assets rapidly upward. The projections of the total amount of such funds in 1980 prepared by the National Bureau of Business and Economic Research is likely to be somewhat less than the actual amount by that date. The National Bureau projections are included in Table 20.

Most prior estimates have been low. In 1956 Mr. A. A. Berle, Jr., estimated that pension funds would have assets of around $80 billion in 1975. As a matter of fact, this amount in terms of book value was exceeded in 1969. In 1957 Mr. Vito Natrella, who was responsible for the SEC's surveys of pension funds for a number of years, projected the assets of noninsured private pension funds at $51.7 billion by the end of 1965. They actually reached this amount about a year sooner than he predicted.[18] Writing in about 1957 or 1958, Father Harbrecht projected that private noninsured pension funds would amount to $84 billion by the end of 1970 and that all pension funds could total about $125 billion by that date.[19] Father Harbrecht's estimate and that of Daniel Holland for the National Bureau of Business and Economic Research are very close to one another for the end of 1970, and both will be quite accurate projections for that year.

The estimates for 1980 are likely to fall considerably short of what occurs, however, if a prolonged and serious depression is avoided because of the higher rate of price increases, the pressure toward earlier retirement, and the demands for larger retirement benefits. Projections of the amount of common stock held by noninsured corporation pension funds and other institutional investors are set forth to the year 2000 in Chapter V.

NOTES

[1] Robert Tilove, *Pension Funds and Economic Freedom* (New York: Fund for the Republic, 1959), p. 9.

[2] Paul P. Harbrecht, S.J., *Pension Funds and Economic Power* (New York: Twentieth Century Fund, 1959), p. 6.

[3] For a more detailed statement of the changing provisions of the Internal Revenue Codes and the other factors that led to the rapid growth of pension funds see Dan M. McGill, *Fundamentals of Private Pensions* (Homewood, Ill.: Richard D. Irwin, Inc., 1964), pp. 16-31. This authoritative volume was published for the Pension Research Council.

[4] U.S., President's Committee on Corporate Pension Funds and Other Private Retirement and Welfare Programs, *Public Policy and Private Pension Programs,* a report to the President on private employee retirement plans (Washington, D.C.: Government Printing Office, 1965), p. 17 and Appendix A, Table 5. The members of the President's Committee were W. Willard Wirtz, Secretary of Labor; C. Douglas Dillon, Secretary of the Treasury; Anthony J. Celebrezze, Secretary of Health, Education and Welfare; Kermit Gordon, Director of the Bureau of the Budget; Walter W. Heller, Chairman of the Council of Economic Advisers; William McC. Martin, Jr., Chairman of the Board of Governors of the Federal Reserve System; and William L. Cary, Chairman of the Securities and Exchange Commission.

[5] *Ibid.,* pp. 18-19.

[6] Only about 500,000 of 25 million private-sector employees were in unfunded or pay-as-you-go plans in 1964. *Ibid.,* p. 6.

[7] See Chapter IV.

[8] Thomas A. Ganner and Walton W. Kingsery, "Determining the Cost of Pension Plans," *Financial Executive,* XXXIV (Aug., 1966), 16-26. This article also shows the cost effect of other actuarial assumptions such as labor turnover and retirement age. For example, if retirement age is sixty-five and the annual cost to provide a given level of benefits for the employees under the plan is $1 million, reducing the retirement age to sixty-two years will increase the annual costs by 21 per cent; and reducing the retirement age to sixty will increase the cost by 40 per cent as compared with retirement at age sixty-five.

[9] R. Norman Wood, "Analysis of Pension Trust Investment Performance" (speech given at the Conference of Actuaries in Public Practice, New Orleans, Oct. 4 and 5, 1965). See also Hewitt Associates, *1965 Report on the Investment Performance of Retirement Funds* (Libertyville, Ill.: Hewitt Assoc., 1966).

[10] For an excellent introduction into the problem of accounting for unrealized appreciation and other complex topics see Ernest L. Hicks, *Accounting for Cost of Pensions,* Accounting Research Study No. 8 (New York: American Institute of Certified Public Accountants, 1965). This official statement of one of the two leading accounting associations includes an extensive bibliography on the accounting aspects of the controversy.

[11] The investigations, which were conducted (in part) under the chairmanship of Senator Paul H. Douglas, uncovered "embezzlement, exorbitant commissions, improper service fees, and other irregular insurance practices, and collusion and complicity among insurance, union, and employer representatives." For a discussion of the legislation, its background, and its shortcomings, see Harbrecht, *Pension Funds and Economic Power,* pp. 257-66.

[12] This study was conducted in 1967. Only a part of the questions asked are relevant to this study.

[13] The $1,858 million of assets of Sears, Roebuck and Company's profit-sharing plan, which had stock equal to almost 45 per cent of the total value of all plans covered by the SEC data, was not included in these data.

[14] The number of different stocks held by investment companies by size class was obtained by counting their individual portfolios. These are public and easily obtainable. Portfolio distributions are discussed in Chapter V.

[15] See Chapter IV. Chapter V introduces some theoretical results about the optimum number of stocks needed to maximize investment performance.

[16] U.S., Congress, House, Committee on Banking and Currency, *Commercial Banks and Their Trust Activity, Emerging Influence on the American Economy,* Vol. I, Staff Report for the Subcommittee on Domestic Finance, 90th Cong., 2d sess., July 8, 1968 (Washington, D.C.: Government Printing Office, 1968).

[17] See Harbrecht, *Pension Funds and Economic Power,* pp. 156-59.

[18] These projections are reported in *ibid.,* pp. 238-40.

[19] *Ibid.,* p.245.

IV

INSURANCE COMPANIES AND STATE AND LOCAL PENSION FUNDS

The three major institutional holders of common stock that remain—life insurance companies, property and casualty insurance companies, and state and local pension funds—have been mentioned in various regards in earlier chapters but have not been discussed at any length. This chapter will present in separate sections the history, size, rate of growth, and concentration of the common stock holdings of each of these institutions. Various aspects of their regulation and the availability of information about them will also be discussed. A final section will deal with the assets of charitable foundations and college and university endowment funds.

Life insurance companies are treated separately from property and casualty insurance companies for five reasons. First, persons who are expert in one of these fields may not be expert in the other. Second, the companies themselves tend to be active either in one field or the other; only a few parent companies or holding companies participate in both. Third, although regulations for both types of companies are at the state level, the regulations for each group are separate and distinct. Fourth, the history and growth of life insurance companies follow a different pattern from that of the other types of insurance companies. Fifth, the history, regulation, and extent of stock holdings are quite distinct for these two groups.

Life Insurance Companies

At the end of 1968, life insurance companies as a group held $10.0 billion of common stock; their common stock holdings increased by almost two-thirds during 1967 and 1968. Their preferred stock holdings increased from $2.8 to $3.2 billion, or about 12 per cent. During these two years their total assets increased from $167.5 to $188.6 billion—an increase of about 12 per cent. The reasons for this relative spurt in common stock ownership will be explained as a part of the history of the regulation and the growth of stock ownership by life insurance companies.

Reliable information about the total assets of life insurance companies has been available since about 1890; data series start a full fifty years or more earlier than they do for some other financial institutions. The effects of the irregular growth of the economy and the changes in the regulations of investment in common stock can be observed easily in Table 28.

In the decade prior to 1905 a number of malpractices and fraudulent activities, especially as related to investments, were well publicized. The public furor that followed led in turn to the 1905 Armstrong investigations by the New York state legislature. The investigating committee is known by the name of its chairman, but Charles Evans Hughes, later Chief Justice of the Supreme Court, was appointed as its counsel and became its dominant figure. As a result of this investigation of life insurance company practices, very strict regulations were enacted in New York. The New York law had widespread effects for several reasons. First, at the time of the investigations almost 60 per cent of all life insurance company assets were held by companies domiciled in New York. Second, several other states revised their laws during the next decade or so and used the New York code as a model. Third, New York, in 1939, adopted the Appleton Rule, which required all "foreign" insurance companies doing business in New York to comply with the state's insurance code. Even though the assets of New York domiciled firms have now dropped to about one-third of the total for the whole industry, the companies licensed to do business in New York account for about four-fifths of the industry's assets.

The 1906 New York Life Insurance Code made it illegal for life insurance companies to own common, preferred, or guaranteed stock. Houghton Bell and Harold G. Fraine reviewed the causes and recommendations of the Armstrong investigations, and they commented that the recommendation about common stock "has cast a long shadow over the legislative policy of New York State and other states as well."[1] Investment in preferred and guaranteed stocks was not permitted under the New York code until 1928. The preferred stock owned by life insurance companies increased from $21.3 million in 1927 to $351.5 million by 1930.[2] During this same period there was only a $23 million increase in common stock owned.[3]

In 1951 the life insurance companies in New York proposed that they be permitted to invest up to 2 per cent of their assets in common stock, and their proposal was adopted by the legislature. This amendment to the New York Life Insurance Code also restrained them from owning more than 2 per cent of the outstanding common stock of the portfolio company, or more than one-tenth of 1 per cent of the assets of the life insurance company itself, whichever was less. In 1957 the law was further amended to permit investment in common stock up to 5 per cent of a life insurance company's assets.

Starting about the end of World War II, pension plans and their assets grew rapidly, as shown in Tables 18 and 19. The insurance companies were severely restricted in their efforts to compete for this business because of the limitations on the proportion of common stock they could hold.[4] In 1962 New York adopted another amendment to the Insurance Code which permitted separate pension fund accounts; these special accounts have no restrictions on the proportion of pension fund assets that may be invested in common stock.[5] Since the enactment of this legislation the pension reserves or assets and stock holdings of life insurance companies have risen more rapidly. From the end of 1960 to the end of 1968 these reserves have increased from $18.9 to $35.0 billion. No separate asset distributions are available for the various types of insured pension accounts, but Table 28 shows that the amount of stock held by life insurance companies almost tripled between 1960 and 1968.

The percentage of life insurance company assets held in the form of common stock is very likely to increase from its 6.9 per cent level at the end of 1968. Under present regulations a maximum of from 13 to 15 per cent of industry assets appears plausible. This range will be reached if pension funds are generally set up as special accounts, and if about 50 per cent of these special account assets are invested in common stock. The suggested range assumes also that about 5 per cent of the other assets are kept in common stock and that the special accounts grow to represent about 20 per cent of all life insurance company assets. If the 5 per cent limit is raised, the suggested 13-15 per cent range for common stock as a proportion of total industry assets will probably be exceeded.

Investment concentrations

Investment concentrations may be viewed in terms of the asset size structure of the companies in the industry and—for the purposes at hand—the size distribution of their common stock portfolios. The assets of the life insurance industry are highly concentrated in the hands of the largest companies. Forty-nine life insurance companies held 97.7 per cent of the industry's assets in 1906 and 96.1 per cent in 1916.[6] By 1958 that percentage had dropped to about 84.2[7] and was down to 80.3 per cent at the end of 1967, according to *Moody's*. The total assets and stock holdings of each of the fifteen largest companies in the industry for 1966 or 1967 are given in Table 29. The five largest companies now hold over one-third, and the ten largest companies hold about one-half of all the industry's assets. Industry sources themselves are more inclined to stress instead the fact that there are currently more than 1,700 life insurance companies in the country.

The five largest life insurance companies in 1966-67 held only about $2.5 billion of stock or less than 25 per cent of the industry total. Only Prudential reported more than $1 billion of stock, and no other company reported as much as $500 million. These stock portfolios are relatively small compared with those of investment companies and investment company groups. The Patman Report, cited in Chapter III, shows that the trust departments of thirty-nine commercial banks held $1 billion or more of stocks.

For stock portfolios in the same size class, life insurance companies appear to have a lower average investment in individual common stocks than investment companies, but a higher average investment than noninsured corporate pension funds. Prudential Insurance Company had just over $1 billion in stock, distributed among 178 different stocks.[8] None of the investment companies with $1 billion or more of assets held quite that many stocks, as is shown in Table 40. In the $250 million to $1 billion class, the average number of different shares for investment companies was 91.0; for pension funds it was 185.1; and for insurance companies it was 107. The estimated number of shares for insurance companies is probably somewhat more conservative than these numbers would indicate, because none of the companies in this size class had assets of $500 million or more.

Portfolio concentrations

Portfolio concentrations of insurance companies may be studied from the viewpoint of both the legal restraints and their contribution to the overall portfolio concentrations of the highly concentrated companies. About one-third of all life insurance company assets belong to companies domiciled in New York state, and under the Appleton Rule most companies abide by the New York code in order to do business in that state. Other states with large proportions of the industry's assets are New Jersey (15.5 per cent), Massachusetts (10.3 per cent), and Connecticut (10.1 per cent).[9] In Massachusetts and Connecticut, stock is evidently held under leeway provisions which permit life insurance companies to own some assets otherwise forbidden to them.[10]

In New York, limitations on purchases of common stock must result in considerable diversification, but the actual diversification practice seems to be much wider than is required. The New York Life Insurance Code limits total common stock investment to the smaller of 5 per cent of total assets or 50 per cent of policy holders' surplus in the case of mutual companies. For stock companies, the 50 per cent applies to capital stock and surplus. Investment concentrations are limited to one-eighth of 1 per cent of the insurance company's assets and the portfolio concentrations are limited to 2 per cent. In New Jersey the investment concentration limitation is 2 per cent of life insurance company assets and 5 per cent of the issuer's stock.

Life insurance companies generally must deposit detailed investment schedules, at least in the state in which they are domiciled. When I requested copies of investment schedules from the largest companies, almost all of them complied. All of them would have complied, I believe, if additional copies had been available, or if I had waited until the time of the next annual report. The United Statistical Associates of New York City annually collects the investment schedules of insurance companies and collates and publishes the holdings of bonds and stocks so that anyone with access to their reports can readily identify all of the holders of each corporate issue and the extent of their holdings.

Several of the largest insurance companies in states where many insurance firms are domiciled sent detailed information in answer to my request. For example, the Metropolitan Life Insurance Company of New York said that as of December 31, 1967, the market value of its common stock was $170,111,465.24 and that its cost was $144,583,484.48. They held 156 different issues, and the largest investment concentration—American Telephone and Telegraph—was 8.8 per cent. The next largest were General Motors (2.4 per cent) and Standard Oil of New Jersey (2.1 per cent). All of these represent miniscule portfolio concentrations.

The *Corporate Holdings of Insurance Companies, Volume 1, Common Stock* was used to check the extent of insurance company concentrations in the companies that might have seemed likely to have overall concentrations of 20 per cent or more. These overall results are reported in Table 43. Table 30 is based upon the holdings of both life insurance and property and casualty insurance companies. The portfolio concentrations for life insurance companies are generally modest at the present time. The state laws and the very conservative policies of these companies do not seem to make them important contributors to overall portfolio concentrations, at least now or throughout the 1970s. Even though none of the largest individual companies may ever have substantial portfolio concentrations—more, for instance, than 2 per cent that they do contribute to overall concentration ratios is shown in Table 30. As the life insurance companies individually and as a group increase their relative and absolute holdings of common stock, their portfolio concentrations will increasingly help to push the concentration percentages of individual portfolio companies past the 30 or 40 per cent levels; and before the end of the 1970s a few overall concentration ratios are likely to pass the 50 per cent level.

Property and Casualty Insurance Companies

At the end of 1968 property and casualty insurance companies held about $16.0 billion in stock; $12.6 billion of this amount was held in stocks listed on the New York Stock Exchange, according to NYSE estimates. This estimated $16.0 billion exceeds the $13.2 billion for life insurance companies; but the figure for the latter companies is growing somewhat faster and it is likely to overtake that of property insurance companies by the end of the 1970s. At the end of 1965 the assets of the property and casualty companies were estimated at $42.1 billion, as shown in Table 31, while at the same date life insurance companies had assets of $158.9 billion. For more than twenty years the stock owned by property and casualty insurance companies has fluctuated within a range of 25-30 per cent of industry's assets, but that percentage may increase slightly in the future. Over the decade 1955-65 the total assets of property and casualty insurance companies have grown at 6.8 per cent per year and those of life insurance companies at 5.8 per cent.

Regulation of the insurance business in the United States started in 1851 with the establishment of a board of insurance commissioners in New Hampshire.[11] As already mentioned, malpractices and unfair treatment of insured persons resulted in numerous legislative investigations, the most famous of these being the Armstrong investigations in 1905 in New York. Another New York legislative committee, the Merritt Committee, was formed in 1910 to look primarily into practices in the fire insurance industry. The committee was charged:

> To investigate as speedily as possible, all corruptions and corrupt practices shown to exist by the evidence of the recent investigation before the Senate of the State of New York; all matters indicating corrupt practices in connection with legislation which have developed in the recent investigation [of the life insurance industry]; the business methods, operation, management, supervision and control of all insurance companies other than those doing life insurance business, including fire exchanges. . . .

The Merritt Committee's investigations do not appear to have had any important effect on the stock investment aggregates of this group of companies; the proportion of stock in their portfolios was still at 20 per cent after these investigations and it has increased since then.

Investment concentrations

The property and casualty insurance industry covers a wide and diversified range of operations. In 1960 some $5.9 billion, or about 47 per cent of the industry total premiums written of $12.7 billion, were for automobile insurance. Fire and extended coverage accounted for about 19 per cent of the total; other important classes in descending order are workmen's compensation; multiple perils, including homeowner's and commercial package policies; inland marine; surety and fidelity; ocean marine; and others.[12] The diversity of these insurance activities, the variety of trade associations, and the post-World War II trend to multiple-line insurance companies all have increased the difficulty of gathering financial information.

Alfred M. Best Company, Incorporated, the principal publisher of this information, ranks the leading companies according to premiums written in the various fields, rather than in terms of asset size. The ten largest companies or consolidated companies have about 25-30 per cent of the total assets and stock of the entire industry. In 1959 an official source reported that there were some 3,300 different companies in the industry. Of these, the largest number (2,208) were mutual property companies, but the largest premium volume was attributed to 344 stock casualty companies.[13] The assets are not nearly so highly concentrated as they are in the life insurance industry, in which the ten largest companies own about 50 per cent of the entire industry's assets.

Fifteen of the largest property and casualty insurance companies are listed in Table 32. People who are knowledgeable about this industry have expressed surprise at these data, because they are not accustomed to approaching this subject from the viewpoint of capital market analysis. The largest of these insurance company complexes, Continental Insurance, has less than one-tenth the assets of Prudential Life or Metropolitan Life. A very surprising point is that Continental Insurance reports owning a larger amount of stock than even Prudential.

The Continental Insurance Company's investment portfolio listed 284 different issues of stocks, more than was held by any other insurance company, pension fund, or investment company for which information was obtained. Three other property and casualty insurance companies also had more than 200 different issues in their respective portfolios. Companies whose stock portfolios ranged from $250 million to $1 billion are about as conservative as the pension funds, but in the $100-$250 million range they are by far the most conservative, or diversified, stock investors observed among the financial institutions.

Portfolio concentrations

The various state regulations (where they exist) governing the investment and portfolio concentrations of property and casualty insurance companies are far more difficult to follow and to interpret than are those governing the life insurance companies. *Property and Casualty Insurance Companies: Their Role as Financial Intermediaries,* prepared by the industry, does not attempt a consideration of these rules. Connecticut has no legislation governing investment by property and casualty insurance companies. New York state sets the pattern for the industry because of the volume of business written there and because of the Appleton Rule. In New York a property and casualty insurance company may not lend more than 10 per cent of its admitted assets to one customer. Furthermore, not more than 2 per cent of the stock of one company or more than one-fifth of 1 per cent of its admitted assets may be invested in one company. In other words, investment concentration for stock is limited to less than 1 per cent and portfolio concentration to 2 per cent. The limitation on the proportion of a company's admitted assets that may be invested in stock is procedural, in the sense that it depends upon the size of required reserves, unearned premiums, loss reserves, and policy holders' surplus.[14] These legal requirements and differences in company policy lead to wide differences in the proportions of stock represented in the total assets of these companies as shown in Table 32. These percentages run from about 6 to 60 per cent for major corporations.

Under these circumstances, several illustrations of portfolio concentration may be helpful. The Great American Company held some 190 different stocks. The two largest holdings were Texaco, amounting to $13,289,960, and IBM, $13,158,849. Each of these constitutes about 3 per cent of the stock portfolio of the Great American Company but represents a very small fraction of the outstanding shares of these billion-dollar portfolio companies. Continental Insurance Companies, which is domiciled in New York, had almost $200 million at market value in IBM stock at the end of 1967. An amount that large is likely to be the result of an early advantageous purchase. Investment in several other stocks was in the $30-$50 million range according to this company's annual report. Correspondence with the State Farm Insurance Companies provided the information that their largest individual stock investment was 28,500 shares of Kentucky Fried Chicken at a cost of $1,836,375, but elicited no explanation of their very conservative stock investment policy.

The relatively small size of the stock portfolios of the property and casualty insurance companies—with the possible exception of Continental Insurance Companies—their extremely wide diversification policies, and their modest rates of growth make it very unlikely that this group of companies will contribute importantly to overall portfolio concentrations in the future. Nevertheless, such concentrations now and in the future will raise the portfolio concentrations from the level attributable to the more dynamically growing financial institutions. Existing portfolio concentrations, including those of life insurance companies, are summarized in Table 30.

State and Local Pension Funds

The same underlying forces that resulted in the rapid growth of corporate pension funds since World War II have been operating on the growth of state and local pension funds.[15] In the dramatic push for increased pension benefits the public sector has lagged behind the private sector, because a goodly part of the labor force in the former is more "genteel," less skilled, and less militant. The change in school teachers' attitudes during the latter part of the 1960s is one of the major elements of social unrest. In any case, the growth of a militant spirit, the spreading unionization among public employees, the high level of employment, and the example of private pension funds are among the major forces that are resulting in the rapid and continuing growth of public pension funds. Another factor is the relative growth of the public sector itself.

State and local pension fund data are, as Professor Victor L. Andrews has characterized them, a "patchwork."[16] The steady growth in assets of state and local pension funds is shown in Table 33, along with the asset projection to 1981 prepared by Professor Daniel M. Holland.[17] These assets have been growing at about 11.1 per cent annually during the 1960s, but Professor Holland's twenty-year projection from his base date of 1961 is at the annual rate of 9.1 per cent. For the decade 1971-81 alone he projects a lower growth rate of 8.4 per cent per year. The forces suggested above, along with a faster rate of price increase than existed generally in the United States up to about 1965, will result in a very substantial underestimation if one follows the technique used by Professor Holland.

Investment concentrations

In one sense the state and local pension funds in the country are very highly concentrated. In 1967 the five largest "systems," which include New York City, controlled 49.1 per cent, and the ten largest systems controlled 61.7 per cent of all assets of state and local pension funds. But in another sense the concentration is not nearly so high, because there are numerous "independent" systems within most of these states. In some cases a board of investment provides coordination, but anyone who has attempted to correspond with the officials of state and local pension fund systems knows that there are many degrees of variation between independence and coordination. New York City, for example, has five different systems: Employees, Teachers, Police, Firemen, and Board of Education. Information on the size and investment practices of the separate funds is hard to obtain. At the end of 1967 the New York State Employees Retirement System had assets of $2,929,686,675, including $120,956,675 in stock (at cost), or about 4.1 per cent. At the same date the New York State Teachers Retirement System had assets of $1,871,841,434, including $174,113,282, or about 9.3 per cent, in stock. These two independent systems within the state of New York are among the largest in the nation.[18]

Only two states reported stock holdings at the end of 1967 amounting to $200 million or more. For this reason no attempt was made to obtain these portfolios or to count the number of different stocks owned. Experience in this field and the public nature of the individual pension or retirement systems gives me very strong fundamental reasons to believe that any person could obtain at least an annual statement of the investment portfolios. Gathering the details of these portfolios, however, is likely to be frustrating and time consuming.

Portfolio size and concentrations

The investment size, investment concentrations, and portfolio concentrations which are the concern of this study are obviously interrelated. The major retirement funds of state and local governments are growing at an annual rate of 10 to 15 per cent. At the 10 per cent rate $1.00 will increase to $2.59 in ten years, to $6.73 in twenty years and to $17.45 in thirty years. At the 15 per cent rate $1.00 would increase to $4.04 in ten years, to $16.37 in twenty years and to $66.21 in thirty years. There seems little doubt that the retirement funds of several states will be larger than $10 billion by 1980 and that others will be approaching that level. Projections for more distant dates become increasingly hazardous, but there is every reason to believe that several individual retirement funds will have assets in the $50-$100 billion range by the year 2000. Even though the absolute amounts of stock held by individual state and local pension funds now appear to be small, the combination of their continued growth at a 10-15 per cent annual rate and the rapidly increasing proportion of common stock investment will result in explosive increases in their individual and aggregate common stock portfolios.

Changes in state regulations

During the biennium 1967-68, twelve state legislatures increased the proportion of common stock permitted in their state and local pensions. Such changes have been occurring rapidly in this field. Kansas, for example, first authorized purchases of common stock in 1961; at that time the proportion of stock was limited to 5 per cent. In the next legislative session, in 1963, the proportion allowed was increased to 15 per cent, and in 1968 to 25 per cent. In California, where the authorization of common stock required an amendment to the constitution, an attempt to amend the constitution failed in 1965 but passed in 1967. California's law, like several others, set limits on the rate at which stocks may be accumulated toward that maximum percentage: the maximum was 10 per cent up to October 8, 1969; 15 per cent up to October 8, 1970; and 25 per cent thereafter. Other states did not authorize such rapid accumulation of common stock. At the end of 1967, only nine states were known not to have authorized common stock for public pension funds. The largest of the funds involved are those in Pennsylvania, as shown in Table 34. Among states with the larger pension funds, Texas will permit up to 50 per cent in corporate stock, and Louisiana has no limitation at all. The frequency distribution of maximum permissible amounts of common stock is shown as Table 35.

Wisconsin is an especially interesting case, because variable annuities are authorized. Variable annuities, as they have developed, invest almost entirely in common stock, and the amount of the retirement benefits varies with the performance of the stocks. Provisions for the number or periods of payments are the same as for the familiar type of insurance annuity, but the annual amount of the payments is not fixed. In Wisconsin at the end of 1967, $102 million of the $175 million of common stock in the funds was managed by the Wisconsin Investment Board.

Reasons for investment in common stocks

After World War II corporate pension funds moved rapidly into common stocks, primarily to hold down their current charges against income for a given amount or package of retirement benefits. This motive only partly explains the drive toward the use of common stock in state and local pension funds, because in many of these the benefit schedules will increase if the fund earns a rate higher than that used in the actuarial assumptions. The administrators of leading state and local pension funds were asked to give the three or four most important reasons, in their opinions, why their state legislatures approved their present common stock ceiling. They were also asked to elaborate on the meaning of the first two reasons. The correspondent from the Department of Control, State of New York, listed the following three reasons:

1. To hold risk to a minimum
2. To provide diversity in the total portfolio
3. To provide a diversity of industries in the common stock portfolio

INSURANCE COMPANIES AND PENSION FUNDS

In explanation of his reasons he wrote:

> Although common stocks have proven to be a good investment over a long period of time, there can never be the assurance that is available in other types of investments, that you will receive a stated amount of money at a certain time.

This person seems conservative in his investment view as well as perhaps defensive toward a larger authorization of common stock. The California correspondent gave only one reason:

> The greater rate of return available over the long term on equities over fixed income investments. I can't recall any other reasons being considered—at least publicly.

In explanation of this reason he wrote:

> In anticipation of a higher rate of return on investment, the actuarial assumption rate can be increased to cover the funding of an automatic cost of living adjustment in retirement allowances.

At legislative hearings in California, investment experts introduced the Merrill Lynch-University of Chicago evidence of the rate of return on New York Stock Exchange stocks since 1928. There was no controversy about the recommended maximum percentage of common stock.

The reasons and explanations given by the State Teachers Retirement System of Ohio are very similar to those given above. A statement prepared by that organization for other purposes included the following two important observations about the recent increase in the limit from 10 to 25 per cent:

> Only the Executive Secretary of the Retirement Board and Mr. Charles Behrens, Vice President, Moody's Investment Service, appeared before the Senate and House Committees as proponents of this bill.

> The System is a buyer of yield. Maturities are of secondary importance. During the past 35 years and for the foreseeable future, it has never been and will not be necessary for the System to sell investments in order to meet its obligations. Fluctuations in the bond market do not affect bonds in the portfolio. . . .changes in the market prices will not be to the disadvantage of the System since income enables it to meet its obligations.

Several of the smaller state retirement systems used the word inflation as the major or sole reason for adding common stock to their system or for their states' having increased the authorized percentage. Many of these seem to be playing follow-the-leader with reference to both corporate and other state and local pension fund systems.

Investment and portfolio concentration rules

Most states that have authorized investment in common stock for public retirement systems have also established rules about investment concentration, portfolio concentrations, and matters concerning the quality of stock—such as corporate size, dividend and earnings records, markets where stocks are traded, and ratings by better-known rating agencies. All of the states which had common stock holdings of $100 million or more at the end of 1967 had investment and portfolio concentration rules.

The regulations in the state of New York are very conservative; they read:

> ...that no more than one-half of one per centum of the assets of any fund shall be invested in the equity securities of any one corporation and subsidiary or subsidiaries thereof; and not more than one per centum of the total issued and outstanding equity securities of any one corporation shall be owned by any fund.

For the authorized equity proportion of their portfolios under these rules, no more than 2 per cent of stock in one corporation can be owned by either the New York State Employees Retirement System, which had assets of $2,929,686,687 at the end of 1967 or the New York State Teachers Retirement System, which had assets of $1,871,841,434 at that time. The new California statute limits the investment concentration in one stock to 2 per cent of all assets owned but permits portfolio concentrations up to 3 per cent. California now has two funds with assets above $1 billion. In Texas the investment concentration is limited to 1 per cent, but portfolio concentrations of 5 per cent are permitted. Minnesota has a more circumspect rule which limits the portfolio of all public retirement funds in the state to 5 per cent of the voting stock of any corporation.

Although the common stock held by the pension funds in any one state is well under $500 million at present, the combination of the rapid growth of the public pension funds and the much more rapid growth—explosive is the term used earlier—of their common stock proportion will push the common stock holdings in some states, and perhaps individual funds as well, past the $1 billion mark by 1980. Several funds of this size with portfolio concentrations up toward or at the typical 5 per cent limit would contribute substantially to the continuing portfolio concentration that the nation is experiencing. At this point the reader may already have wondered about the propriety of allowing either public officials or those appointed by public officials to vote large and powerful blocks of corporate stock. Concentrations of corporate stock in the public retirement funds of one state or one geographic area could turn out to represent quite large percentages in sizable corporations. This possibility exists because in most states each fund may own up to the portfolio concentration limit, and because of the number of independent systems within the state or area.

Growth of stock holdings

In 1961 only three state pension fund systems had more then 10.0 per cent of their assets in common stock: Rhode Island (30.9 per cent), New Hampshire (14.4 per cent), and Wisconsin (14.4 per cent). By the end of 1967, some thirteen states and six cities held more than 10.0 per cent of their funds in stock. In fact, seven states—led by Idaho (34.1 per cent), Alaska (24.2 per cent), and New Hampshire (23.7 per cent)— were above the 20 per cent level. The percentage of assets held in common stock by most state pension funds since 1961 has been increasing rather steadily; such growth seems to be a matter of prudence or statute, or both of these. Again New York, which is dominated by a rural or conservative legislature, is among the most conservative states. The average new investment in stocks each year may not exceed 2 per cent of assets. At the very least, ten years would be required to build the common stock in the portfolios of the individual funds to the 20 per cent limit that is now permitted; the actual increase has been even less rapid. The stock percentage in the New York state funds increased from 1.0 per cent at the end of 1961 to 6.1 per cent at the end of 1967. Many states have built their common stock percentages faster than New York. Thus far, as states have approached the statuatory limitation on their common stock portfolios, the limit itself has been raised. If the pattern of corporate pension funds is followed, most states will continue to move the percentage up toward 50 per cent.

If the total assets of state and local pension funds continue to grow at their present rate, they will be in the neighborhood of $175 billion by 1981. If the average percentage invested in common stock rises to the 20-25 per cent range, the amount of common stock held by these funds will be about as large as that held by life insurance companies. By the year 2000 the stock holdings will far exceed those of life insurance companies. The portfolio concentrations of the individual funds will contribute substantially to the overall portfolio concentrations at the beginning of the twenty-first century.

Foundations and College Endowments

The foundations and the college endowment funds receive much publicity, but they are minor elements in overall concentration of stock ownership. At the end of 1967 the value of stocks held by foundations was estimated at $14.7 billion and of those held by college endowment funds at $8.1 billion. The aggregate stock holdings of foundations were somewhat larger than those of either the life insurance companies or the property and casualty insurance companies, and they were considerably larger than stock holdings of state and local pension funds at that date.

Foundations

The 1960 edition of *The Foundation Directory* reported that only four foundations had assets above $100 million, measured in book value. The list was dominated by the Ford Foundation, which had assets in excess of $3 billion.[19] No other foundation either in 1960 or in 1967 approached the size of the Ford Foundation as shown on Table 36.

The New York Stock Exchange studies of the value of listed stocks held by institutions show very rapid growth for foundations from the end of World War II until about 1960. According to these data their growth was 14.0 per cent per year from 1949 to 1960 and 11.1 per cent per year from 1960 to 1968. The SEC estimates that the market value of stock owned by foundations was $12.9 billion at the end of 1964 and that the amount grew to $15.8 billion by the end of 1968.[20] The period of very rapid growth may be over. The continuing interest of Congress in the operations and advantageous tax status of foundations makes any projections of their future growth unduly hazardous.

The stock ownership pattern of the largest foundations suggests that the stocks owned are frequently highly concentrated in one company. Families associated with the development and growth of leading companies have placed large amounts of their stock in their "own" companies' foundations primarily for philanthropic reasons and because of the income tax. The largest such case is the $1.4 billion in Ford Motor Company stock owned by the Ford Foundation as of 1967. The Duke Endowment held $533 million of Duke Power stock. Almost all of the Lilly Endowment is composed of Eli Lilly Company stock, and the Danforth Foundation owns about 20 per cent of Ralston Purina's stock, which makes up about 70 per cent of the foundation's total assets.

When these large holdings of foundations in their related companies are considered—and there are very likely others as well—the "outside" holdings of the foundations are reduced substantially. A surprising fact worth noting is that the Rockefeller Foundation's largest holding (1964), was $22,948,000 of Ford Motor Company stock; its holding of Standard Oil of New Jersey was only second with $22,256,000. The Carnegie Corporation's largest stock holding was $6,335,000 of General Motors.

The foundations' modest diversification of the "outside" stock holdings and the relative smallness of their remaining stock portfolios do not make them directly important as a factor in any study of overall concentration of ownership in corporations by financial institutions. The overlap of directors and senior officers between foundations, nonfinancial corporations, and banks merits careful additional study.[21]

University endowment funds

The value of stocks held by colleges and universities has been rising at an annual rate of almost 10 per cent for the past two decades. As Table 37 shows, however, only Harvard University held more than $500 million in stock at the end of 1967. As of June 30, 1968, Harvard's endowment fund had almost $700 million of stock at market value.[22] Even the amounts of stock held by the highly endowed universities are small compared with the multibillion dollar concentrations that exist in investment company groups and the trust departments of commercial banks. The combination of the relatively small holdings and the broad diversification of these portfolios makes them of minor importance in the study of the concentration of corporate control.

Two points should be noted, however. First, many financiers and other important persons are on the boards of colleges and universities or act as financial advisers to such endowment funds. Their influence on the voting of corporate shares might be investigated. For example, State Street Research and Management Corporation, which manages a $500 million open-end investment company, is associated in the management of Harvard's endowment funds.[23] Second, the question might be raised as to the legitimacy (or desire) of college and university trustees to vote corporate stock. Whether or not professional educators—other than professors of finance, of course—have the knowledge necessary to vote such shares wisely might also be asked.

The "favorite" stocks of the seventy-one leading college endowment funds as of June 30, 1968, have also been compiled by the Boston Fund. The largest total investment was $298 million in IBM stock. The next largest holdings were $205 million of Eastman Kodak held in thirty-four endowment funds, and $132 million of Xerox in nine funds. The other stocks in the favorite ten were Standard Oil of New Jersey, General Motors, Gulf Oil, Texaco, Coca-Cola, Ford, and Sears, Roebuck.[24]

NOTES

[1] Houghton Bell and Harold G. Fraine, "Legal Framework, Trends, and Developments in Investment Practices of Life Insurance Companies," *Law and Contemporary Problems,* XVII (Winter, 1952–"Institutional Investments"), 74-75.

[2] Alden C. Olson, *The Impact of Valuation Requirements on the Preferred Stock Investment Policies of Life Insurance Companies* (East Lansing, Mich.: Bureau of Business and Economic Research, Graduate School of Business Administration, Michigan State University, 1964), p. 4.

[3] Bell and Fraine, "Investment Practices of Life Insurance Companies," p. 55.

[4] See the section of Chap. III, "Funding and Investment Policy," for a discussion of the importance of the higher expected return on common stock in relation to the current cost of pension plans for business.

[5] John M. Hines, "The Insurance Company Breakthrough in Pension Funding" *Financial Executive,* XXXIII (Apr., 1965), 31-35. Several other changes were enacted at the same time to improve even further the competitive position of insurance companies in seeking the administration of pension funds.

[6] Bell and Fraine, "Investment Practices of Life Insurance Companies," p. 55. The data were from the Life Insurance Association of America and Institute of Life Insurance.

[7] The assets for forty-nine legal reserve life insurance companies for 1959 are given as $95.8 billion. Life Insurance Association of America, *Life Insurance Companies as Financial Institutions* (Englewood Cliffs, N.J.: Prentice-Hall, Inc., 1962), p. 264, a monograph prepared for the Commission on Money and Credit.

[8] The number of stocks in insurance company portfolios was counted either by the author directly, from copies of annual investment supplements furnished by each company upon request, or by the companies and then sent to the author.

[9] Life Insurance Association, *Life Insurance Companies as Financial Institutions,* p. 78.

[10] *Ibid.,* pp. 87-88 and 142-50. The nature of leeway provisions is discussed on pages 87-88, and the details by state are given in the tables on pages 142-50.

[11] The few facts related here rely heavily upon John H. Magee and Oscar N. Serbein, *Property and Liability Insurance* (4th ed.; Homewood, Ill.: Richard D. Irwin, Inc., 1967), chap. 3, "Governmental Supervision," pp. 853-77.

[12] American Mutual Insurance Alliance, Association of Casualty and Surety Companies, and National Board of Fire Underwriters, *Property and Casualty Insurance Companies: Their Role as Financial Intermediaries* (Englewood Cliffs, N.J.: Prentice-Hall, Inc., 1962), p. 10. This volume was prepared for the Commission on Money and Credit.

[13] *Ibid.,* p. 28.

[14] For an excellent, brief discussion of this topic, see Allan Comrie, "Construction and Composition of a Property and Casualty Securities Portfolio," *Financial Analysts Journal,* XXI (July-Aug., 1965), 95-97. Mr. Comrie is Vice-President and Secretary of the Great American Holding Corporation and its subsidiaries. This company is domiciled in New York.

[15] For a statement of these general forces, see the section in Chap. III, "Growth of Private Pension Funds."

[16] Victor L. Andrews, "Noninsured Corporate and State and Local Government Retirement Funds in the Financial Structure," in *Private Capital Markets,* ed. by Irwin Friend, Hyman P. Minsky, and Victor L. Andrews (Englewood Cliffs, N.J.: Prentice-Hall, Inc., 1964), p. 390.

[17] Daniel M. Holland, *Private Pension Funds: Projected Growth,* National Bureau of Business and Economic Research, Occasional Paper 97 (New York: Columbia University Press, 1966).

[18] Investment Bankers Association of America, *State and Local Pension Funds: 1968,* prepared by Thomas M. Adams (Washington, D.C.: Investment Bankers Assoc., 1968).

[19] Russell Sage Foundation, *The Foundation Directory* (New York: Russell Sage Foundation, 1960).

[20] U.S., Securities and Exchange Commission, *Statistical Series,* Release No. 2358, May 1, 1969, Table 3, p. 6.

[21] In 1960 the market value of the stock held in the individual companies by 51 large foundations exceeded $50 million in 14 cases and $100 million in 9 cases. In 7 cases the accumulations were owned by 1-4 foundations only; in another (Ford Motor Co.) the stock was held by 15 foundations; and in the 6 remaining cases the stock was held by 20-30 foundations. Ralph L. Nelson, *The Investment Policies of Foundations* (New York: Russell Sage Foundation, 1967), p. 70.

[22] Armon Glenn, "Class of '68; College Endowment Funds Continue to Like Blue Chips," *Barrons,* Apr. 14, 1969, pp. 9-10. This article reports a survey of 71 college endowment funds made by the Boston Fund.

[23] *Ibid.,* p. 10.

[24] *Ibid.,* p. 9.

V

GROWTH OF STOCK OWNERSHIP BY FINANCIAL INTERMEDIARIES TO THE YEAR 2000

The portfolio concentration ratios for the common stock of individual companies vary widely around the average, and such dispersion will continue to be an important characteristic. As the percentage of all marketable stock held by financial intermediaries moves upward from its present 20-25 per cent level to the 45-58 per cent range, the average of portfolio concentration ratios may double also. What are likely to be the characteristics of the corporations that will have about half or more of their voting shares held by financial intermediaries? A simple tabulation of a sample of such corporations, which relates size and concentration ratios, will be introduced first to help answer this question, and then the results of several multiple regression analyses will be reported. This statistical analysis is only modestly helpful, but it suggests both the complexity of existing financial and market relationships and the further work that needs to be done during the next decade or two.

Institutional and Aggregative Stock Market Values to the Year 2000

Economic and financial projections are inherently risky, and the individual or organization making them is open to widespread criticism. However, in a planning society, in a society in which the social-political institutions change slowly, and in a country in which the political process reacts to fundamental shifts in realities only after long lags and great personal travail, it is already somewhat late to review the changes that have taken place in the ownership of major corporations and to point out what is likely to happen in the future, including possible alternative developments. Nevertheless, such a review is essential.

The gross national product and aggregate market value of stock

The gross national product (GNP) was estimated by Willford I. King at $29.6 billion for 1909. Since then it has grown at a rate of 5.9 per cent to $865 billion for 1968; these numbers are not adjusted for price changes and do not represent changes in per capita income. The growth rate will vary somewhat, depending upon the base date that is used and whether or not adjustments are made for price changes. If the GNP of $103.1 billion in 1929 is used as a base, the growth rate to 1967 is 5.5 per cent. The GNP rate since 1950 has been 6.1 per cent. The continuing controversy concerning the sustainable real growth for the GNP will not be discussed in this study.

The GNP projections to the year 2000 to be used are those prepared by Resources for the Future, Incorporated, and the Hudson Institute. Resources for the Future used a 3.8 per cent real growth rate for the GNP and projected high, medium, and low levels for the year 2000. These levels are: high GNP, approximately $3,300 billion; medium GNP, approximately $2,200 billion; and low, approximately $1,600 billion.[1] Two major considerations in determination of the growth rate are the continuing increases in productivity and population.

Herman Kahn and Anthony J. Wiener estimated that the GNP in terms of 1965 prices would range from $2,177 to $3,628 billion by the year 2000 for their surprise-free "Standard [U.S.] Society."[2] They built their GNP projections on the basis of studies of population, productivity, and the labor force. Their GNP projections imply growth rates ranging from 3.4 to 4.9 per cent per year.[3] If adjustments for expected price increases are added to Kahn-Wiener projections, the resulting numbers are much higher. In a way these price-adjusted projections are more useful, however, because these GNP levels in current prices are the ones that are published and will be experienced. A reasonable range for the continuing rate of price increases, as measured by the Consumer Price Index or other less well-known measures such as the Gross National Product Implicit Price Deflator, is 2-4 per cent per year. Table 38 presents the Kahn-Wiener standard-society surprise-free projection to the year 2000 and the same projections after I have adjusted them for price increases.

The historical GNP growth rates, including price changes, have ranged from about 5.5 to 6.1 per cent. If the future growth rates from whatever combination of price, productivity, and population increases correspond to those of the earlier part of this century, the GNP will range from $4,800 to $5,700 billion by the year 2000. The projected GNP range generated by the 5.5-6.1 per cent growth rates is included in Figure 1. The purpose of this GNP projection is to provide both a framework and a parameter for the projection of the total market value of stock in the economy.

The total market value of stock has grown faster than GNP. From 1909 to 1963 the market value of stock traded on U.S. markets grew at 5.9 per cent when measured on the basis of Irwin Friend's series, as shown in Table 5. The aggregate long-run growth rate is very difficult to establish because there are no continuous series and because the series that go back to the beginning of the century are not of such high quality that they allow the annual growth rates to be confidently stated.

Perhaps the best and most consistent data are those prepared by the SEC for other purposes. As shown on Table 4, the growth rate was 8.6 per cent from 1940 to 1967 and 9.4 per cent from 1950 to 1968. The latter rate could be somewhat high compared to the very long-term trend because in 1950 stock prices were relatively low in terms of current and prospective earnings. The markets were still reflecting the depressions of the 1930s and World War II. The great bull market which emerged from the restoration of confidence in stocks started in 1951. A 9 per cent growth rate in the total market value of stock might be sustained for the next three decades, but that would appear to be the highest rate which one could reasonably expect. The growth rate for the total market value of stock has been higher than that for the GNP for reasons that will be stated below. Therefore, the minimum aggregate growth rate is set at 7 per cent. At this rate the aggregate market value is expected to increase from $761 billion at the end of 1968 to $1,755 billion by 1980 and to $6,792 billion for the year 2000.

The single most likely growth rate is set at 8 per cent; on this basis the total market value of stock will grow to $1,966 billion by 1980 and to $9,161 billion by 2000. This range is pictured in Figure 1, and the 8 per cent projection is included in Table 39. The reasonableness of the growth foreseen for the holdings of each of these intermediaries individually and as a group may be judged by comparing it with the total projected aggregate market value.

Two basic reasons why the growth rate for the aggregate value of stock has been greater than the growth rate for the GNP are suggested. First, the growth rate reflects an increase in market values when previously closed corporations "go public"; a most notable event of that kind was the first public offering in 1956 of Ford Motor Company stock, which added several billion dollars to the aggregate market values.

The second reason is that the market value of American corporations includes the value to the stock holders of these corporations' foreign investments. This consideration is likely to be the important one during the remaining part of the twentieth century. Published corporate income statements do very little toward providing information about foreign earnings in a way that is useful to security analysts. A third possible but controversial factor is the growth in the value of capital goods used relative to the GNP. The amount of capital funds would have to grow faster than the GNP in order to permit the acquisition of the capital goods if this relative increase took place.

Several other important considerations should be mentioned. These estimates assume not only that the surprise-free GNP will exist in the future but also that the relation of the per share income and dividends of corporations to their market prices will, on the average, be in about the same range as it has been during the 1960s. That assumption could be upset if the growth projected to the year 2000 is not expected to continue until well after that date. Expectations about the growth of income and dividends are built into the expected prices of shares. Furthermore, the relation between the yields on common stock and on bonds is expected to be more or less unchanged.[4] A decline in the added rate of return for accepting or undertaking the higher risk inherent in common stock could lower the proportion of these securities in portfolios, particularly those of pension funds. In the past, much attention has been given to bond-stock or leverage ratios of business corporations, but in the future the emphasis may be placed on relative rates of return or rates of cost.

The projected GNP for the years 1980 and 2000 forms the basis of the projected market value of stock that will be traded in United States markets in those years. Even if the GNP projection turns out to be quite close to what occurs, the expected market value of stock could be further from the mark because of changing relationships among dividends, earnings, and market prices. For example, the continuing rise in the institutional ownership of stocks could push up share prices, which is another way of saying that yields could be driven down. Some investment managers openly express this fear. Lower (relative) yields, at first glance, seem to lead to a higher market valuation for outstanding stock. That may be a correct anticipation, but the decrease in yields would also drive knowledgeable investors toward other investment media, such as corporate bonds and privately placed corporate notes whose yield and risk are both lower than those of common stock. Surely expected yields will continue to be rationally related to risk. The increased flow of funds to institutional investors from new monetary savings, or the transfer of funds from other investments, do not warrant the conclusion that market yields will be forced downward.

Almost all new monetary savings in the private sector of the economy are reflected in the prices and volume of corporate debt and corporate stock; but the monetary savings process is highly complex, and it changes over time. Furthermore, nothing has been said about the private demand for savings and for investment compared to the public demand. The identification and specification of the boundaries of "public" and "private" sectors of the economy are changing; the traditional definitions will be subject to more intense challenges in the final decades of this century. The flow of savings and investments in the economy, the general performance of the economy, and the growth of public and foreign investment form a part of the unseen background for the projections of GNP and the market value of stock.

The rate of inflation too must be close to what it has been since World War II if these aggregate projections are to be approximately realized. If a change in the method of taxing corporate income or an unexpectedly large decrease in the corporate income tax rate occurred, the aggregate amounts that develop could also be pushed further from the present projection. The Kahn-Wiener surprise-free projection precludes depressions much deeper than those experienced since World War II.

Projections for Stock Holdings of Financial Intermediaries

The stock holdings of investment companies, corporate pension funds, and state and local pension funds are increasing much faster than the aggregate market value of all stocks. The market value of stocks held by life insurance companies is increasing somewhat faster than the total market, and those held by property and casualty insurance companies are growing in value at about the market rate. Clearly the proportion of the marketable stocks held by financial intermediaries cannot exceed the market aggregate, and there appears to be virtually no chance during the next thirty to fifty years that the average percentage of institutional ownership will be moving anywhere close to 100 per cent.

However, the structure of security ownership has been changing and is continuing to change. Until at least World War I, over 60 per cent of corporate bonds were owned by private persons, but since 1950 this percentage has dropped to well under 10 per cent. An increasing proportion of the working population is gaining an interest in equities through pension plans, mutual funds, and life insurance. As personal financial security increases and as financial intermediaries' holdings of stocks grow in relative and absolute terms, large numbers of persons may also change their attitudes about the extent of personal savings that is appropriate to their salary, beyond the proportion required as a condition of employment. There may even be some further changes in the characteristics of the securities or other investment media in which individuals prefer to invest.

With these comments about historical developments in mind, those who have not considered the dramatic growth of stock holdings by the major financial intermediaries may find more plausibility in the conclusions reached about their probable relative and absolute holdings.

The market value of institutional holdings of NYSE shares has increased from 12.7 per cent in 1949 to 22.4 per cent at the end of 1968, as shown in Figure 2. The trend shows no signs of abating; the paramount question is the relative growth of these institutional holdings to 1980, 2000, and beyond. The hand-fitted trend lines suggest that the most likely limits of the reasonable range until the year 2000 is 46-58 per cent. This range will be used as a control or constraint upon the projections of total stock ownership by each of the major institutional investors.

In the consideration of the most probable growth of stock holdings for each institutional investor, the historical pattern of growth rates for each one will be examined. These patterns indicate that very high growth rates have not been sustained, and both experience and logic strongly indicate that during the rest of this century high rates will continue to decline toward the aggregate stock growth rate. As a matter of expediency, the projections will be made in two steps: (1) to the end of 1980; and (2) from 1980 to 2000. Less detailed projections for more distant points in time are in keeping with the general practice in business and economics.

Investment companies

The growth of investment companies and their stock holdings were discussed in Chapter II, and selected data were presented in Tables 2 and 3. Growth rates for their stock holdings and those of the other major institutional investors were shown in Table 4; investment company growth rates themselves were exhibited for eight different time periods.

Investment companies' stock holdings grew at 9.1 per cent per year from 1940 to 1950. This decade, which opened with the passage of the Investment Company Act of 1940, included World War II and ended before the great bull market of the 1950s began to overcome the reluctance of individuals and institutions to invest in common stock. Their growth rate for stock investments accelerated to 16.9 per cent in the 1950s and dropped back to 14.3 per cent for the period 1960-68. The growth rate in the 1960s through the period covered in this writing could be somewhat distorted because the period is shorter and rates will be more strongly influenced by the opening and closing prices of stocks.

The decline in the growth rate is expected to continue despite the efforts of investment companies to make their product extremely attractive. Numerous new features such as withdrawal plans and dual funds[5] have been developed, and new types of specialized arrangements may be expected to continue to appear. The efforts of the industry and the attractiveness of mutual funds, especially to small investors, is expected to keep the growth rate at 13 per cent for the period 1969-80. This rate is still well above the total market growth rate.

In the 1970s, and especially the two next decades, social security improvements and the continuing improvements in pension plans are likely to lessen the concern with individual accumulations of wealth for financing retirement. Changes in character structure and attitudes toward economic ideologies are continuing also. Chapter VI comments on these changes and how they will affect individuals' willingness to save as large a proportion of their income as they have done in the past and to invest it in stocks either directly or through investment companies. The rising commissions and other costs associated with small purchases and sales of stock also tend to discourage direct personal ownership. For these reasons the growth rate for stocks held by investment companies for 1980 through 2000 is set at 10 per cent, which is still above the expected average growth rate. The combination of the growth rate of 13 per cent until 1980 and 10 per cent from 1980 to 2000 makes the projected stock holdings at the final date $1,730 billion, as shown in Table 39. The projection implies an increase in investment company holdings of stocks from their 1968 share of 7.8 per cent of the total market to 18.9 per cent.

Corporate pension funds[6]

The major social, economic, and political factors have resulted in the very rapid growth of corporate pension funds since about the time of World War II, as shown in Table 18. Growth rates for the total assets and stock holdings were examined for five-year and ten-year intervals as far as the data exist; both book value and market value growth rates were computed and reviewed separately.

From 1950 to 1960 corporate pension fund assets grew at about 17.5 per cent per year in terms of book value and at about 19.8 per cent per year in terms of market value. Growth rates were considerably higher in the first half of that decade than in the second half, irrespective of the valuation method used. In 1951 stock held by corporate pension funds amounted to only 16.3 per cent of their assets measured in terms of book value, but increased to 41.9 per cent by the end of 1960. Stock increased at about 28 per cent per year, in book value terms, and about 35 per cent per year in market value terms. Such rates are clearly unsustainable; over a period of thirty years, an amount growing at even 28 per cent per year compounded annually increases 1,004.3 times. The astounding growth rates during the 1950s were the result of both the extremely rapid growth of corporate pension plans and the shift of assets toward investment in stock.

During the 1960s the growth of total assets, expressed in book value, has slowed to less than 12 per cent; but stock holdings have continued to grow faster—about 17 per cent—as the proportion of stock to total assets continued to rise to 52 per cent. The pattern of market value growth is similar, but in a sense it is less useful for projections because of the somewhat low prices of stock prevailing at the end of 1968.

The growth of corporate pension funds will continue strong during the 1970s because of such factors as inflation, improving relative benefit levels, and earlier retirement goals. The shift toward higher proportions of stock in pension funds may be expected to continue but not as rapidly as in the 1960s.[7] An examination of these factors led me to project a growth rate of 14.0 per cent per year for the stock owned by noninsured corporate pension funds through 1980, and 11.5 per cent from 1980 to 2000. Consequently, the stock holdings are projected at $269 billion for 1980 and at $2,362 billion for 2000 (see Table 39). The noninsured corporate pension funds held about 7.3 per cent of all marketable stocks at the end of 1968, and that figure is likely to grow to about 25.8 per cent by the end of the century. In dollar terms the corporate pension funds' stock holdings are projected to be about one-third larger than those of investment companies by the year 2000. These two financial intermediaries together will hold almost 44 per cent of all outstanding marketable stock by the turn of the century. The third largest class of stockholders is expected to be state and local pension funds.

State and local pension funds

On the basis of available data, state and local pension funds have been growing at an annual rate of slightly more than 11 per cent since 1960. This average growth rate seems very likely to be maintained to the 1980 bench mark because of the increasing proportion of employment in the public sector of the economy and the effort to improve retirement benefits of these employees in relation to their expected terminal salaries. During the 1960s large numbers of persons working for state and local governments found that their initial retirement benefits were only 10-20 per cent of their terminal salaries.[8]

Continued growth at the 11.0 per cent rate results in projected state and local pension fund assets of about $162 billion for 1980 and stock holdings of about $37 billion if the anticipated increases in the proportion of stock owned occur. The total market value of stocks held will have to grow at 17 per cent per year compounded through 1980 to reach this projected total. From 1980 to 2000 the total assets will grow at a somewhat slower rate, and the stock holdings are expected to continue to expand to about 35-40 per cent of the total assets. By the year 2000 the market value of their stocks will be around $357 billion, which is about 3.9 per cent of the expected total market value. In 1970 the stocks held by state and local pension funds approached the 1 per cent level of total market value of all stocks.

Life insurance companies

The growth rate of life insurance company assets has been dropping: from 1940 to 1950 the annual growth rate was 7.6 per cent, from 1950 to 1960 it was 6.5 per cent, and from 1960 to 1968, 5.9 per cent. The declining growth rate of assets is attributed to the growth of social insurance and group life insurance, and to the attractiveness of investment in stock—particularly through investment companies. Group life insurance is a form of low-cost term insurance and does not build up asset reserves to nearly the extent that ordinary level pay life insurance contracts do. The increase in personal financial assets in the generally very prosperous years since World War II, the low rates of return on the largely fixed-income assets (bonds and mortgages) held by life insurance companies, the higher rates of return that were expected in the stock market, the increasing acceptance, or even popularity, of stock investment, and the very convenient investment media like mutual funds for conservative investors have combined to slow the growth rate of insurance company assets.

The growth rate is most likely to continue to drop during the remainder of this century. The ultimate fate of the industry obviously will depend upon developments in the social insurance field; but a very long sustained growth rate that parallels that of national income appears to be reasonable. For the years until 1980 the assets are expected to grow at about a 5.4 per cent rate and for the remainder of the century the rate may average only about 4.5 per cent.

Stock ownership will grow faster than total assets because life insurance companies will probably continue to increase the proportions of common stock in their portfolios. The separate pension account device which was described in the life insurance section of Chapter IV will be especially important in this growth in stock holdings. If stocks reach 13 per cent of life insurance companies' total assets by 1980, the market value of their stock holdings will be about $46 billion. In order to reach this amount, an annual growth rate of 13.5 per cent is implied. During the 1950s the growth rate of their stock was only 9.1 per cent; it accelerated to 12.5 per cent during the first eight years of the 1960s. Stock ownership may continue to expand moderately to, perhaps, 20 per cent of assets by the year 2000. The combination of the total asset projection and this 20 per cent estimate gives a stock projection of $171 billion for life insurance companies at the terminal date of this study. A 6.8 per cent annual growth rate for stock holdings for the twenty years after 1980 will enable them to reach this target. The projected $171 billion will be less than 2 per cent of the projected $9,161 billion for total stock market values for the year 2000.

The projections are intended to apply to the range of services that life insurance companies have been providing since the beginning of this century. These strong organizations with excellent leadership cannot be expected to accept a declining role or a diminution of the scope of their activities without extending their present efforts in several directions. A principal goal of such efforts would be for these companies to maintain their asset growth rate and their dominance individually and collectively as financial organizations. Life insurance companies already are showing considerable interest in selling mutual funds. For all practical purposes, the entry of life insurance companies into the mutual fund industry began in 1966. By mid-1969 mutual funds were being offered by more than a hundred life insurance companies.[9] Their sales force and investment organizations may be thought of as having the excess capacity as well as the skills—or closely allied skills—needed to market and to manage mutual funds. Life insurance companies can move into investment company activities either by organizing their own mutual funds or by buying existing mutual fund organizations. After such changes become substantial, they may affect the visible growth rates of both investment company and life insurance company assets. Unless the consolidated balance sheet statements of life insurance companies in the future separate the totals for traditional life insurance company assets from those of assets derived from related activities, comparison of the projections made here with the assets of the life insurance industry at future dates will be misleading. If variable annuity contracts grow, separating the investment and life insurance aspects of their activities will not be feasible. Another possibility is the development of life insurance policies that have face-value or protection levels—at least above some minimum floor—designated or determined by the success of a company's investment policy. Such developments would be both a hedge against potential inflation and a way of participating in the real growth of the economy.

Property and casualty insurance companies

The asset growth rate for property and casualty insurance companies has generally declined since 1940 and now stands slightly under 7 per cent per year. If the proportion of common stock in their aggregate assets increases slightly from 30 to 35 per cent by 1980, the total value of the stocks they hold will increase from an estimated $14.7 billion at the end of 1968 to a projected $37 billion by the end of 1980; the implied growth rate is 8 per cent per year. From 1980 to 2000 the growth rate of the industry's assets is expected to drop back very close to that of the GNP. The nature of the insured risks in this industry is such that further growth in the proportion of assets invested in stocks seems unlikely. Therefore, both the total asset growth and that of their stock portfolio were projected at 6 per cent. These growth patterns result in a projection of $118 billion for the stock held by the industry in the year 2000, as shown in Table 39.

The asset growth rate may be affected by changes in the range of risks insured by the industry, by the development of social insurance in some of the areas of insurable risk covered by property and casualty insurance companies, or by movements into other related service areas. None of these changes seem likely to develop—or to be quantitatively large if they do occur. The industry is still in the process of completing its rationalization toward multiple-line companies.[10]

A movement in another direction among companies in this industry has become evident in the last year or two. Several leading companies have paid large dividends because they could not employ all their funds at an adequate rate of return. Some takeovers by conglomerate corporations also are occurring. These two changes reduce the confidence with which the projection is put forward.

Other financial intermediaries

Common trust funds and university endowment funds are projected to grow at rates close to those that they have experienced during the past two decades. The tax position of university endowment funds could become less favorable, and the general public attitude toward universities could become highly unfavorable over the next three decades. However, the role of universities and their central position as centers of research, as leaders in a very wide range of social developments, and as the growing focus of energy and excellence in both the performing and plastic arts seems to be enlarging rather than diminishing. The assets of foundations grew very rapidly in the 1950s, but their growth rate has fallen since then. Legislation that would reduce their tax advantages is being considered. Whether or not laws changing the income tax regulations will be passed by Congress soon, some such legislation appears to be likely. Therefore, the growth rate of foundation assets was projected to be below the expected growth rate for the total market value of stocks (see Table 39). Even a considerable error in these three "minor" projections will not have a large impact upon the general level of the expected institutional holdings of stock.

Projected total stock holdings of financial intermediaries

The institutional holdings of NYSE stocks have been projected by two independent systems. The first method, as pictured in Figure 2, extrapolated the actual rate of growth of these holdings of NYSE listed stocks by using semilogarithmic scale. An obvious question is whether the longer trend line starting with 1949 or the shorter trend line starting from about 1961 provides the better indication of future developments. There is no direct way of resolving this question. The range between the two extrapolations is taken to be the most likely area in which the holdings of financial intermediaries will move during the remainder of the century.

The SEC recently published other data about the total stock holdings of financial intermediaries.[11] After some adjustments to approximate the same group of financial intermediaries as the NYSE study covers, these data show the following growth pattern for financial intermediaries' stock holdings in relation to the market value of outstanding stock:

Year	Percentage of Total
1964	17.5
1965	18.9
1966	20.1
1967	21.2
1968	23.2

An extrapolation of the rate of growth implied in these SEC data would bring the financial intermediaries' stock holdings up to about 45 per cent of the total market value by 1980. Such rapid growth in the proportion of stock held by financial institutions hardly appears sustainable to 1980; and if it continued it would imply that all stock would be in the hands of the financial intermediaries before the year 2000, an outcome that is clearly nonsense.

The second independent system is the separate projection of the most likely growth rate, as it appears today, of the stock holdings in each of the financial institutions. These projections have been the burden of the discussion in the preceding pages. These independent projections placed the financial intermediaries' stock holdings as a percentage of the total market at 37.8 per cent for 1980 and at 55.2 per cent for 2000, as shown in Table 39. The detailed projection for 1980 is about 4 percentage points higher than the Figure 2 high aggregate projection of 33.5 per cent[12] and falls close to the middle of the 45-58 per cent range for the year 2000.

Stock holdings of individuals

Some observant readers may be uneasy about the projected shrinkage in the relative amount of stocks held by private individuals either directly or through the use of personal trust funds. Several reasons have been suggested for believing that less stress would be laid upon such personal direct investments in stock (as contrasted with indirect holdings managed by one or more intermediaries). The total amount of stock held directly is projected as growing very considerably. The estimates in Table 39 imply that individual holdings were approximately $584 billion at the end of 1968 and that they will grow to $1,223 billion by 1980 and to $3,106 billion by the year 2000. The growth rate implied from 1968 through 1980 is 6.4 per cent per year; from 1981 through 2000 it is 4.8 per cent.

The success of the foregoing discussion depends on readers' being convinced of its inherent reasonableness. Disagreement with parts of the individual projections for the various financial intermediaries is to be expected, and there also may be disagreement about the methods or results of the aggregate projections. The objective of this presentation will not fall either if the individual projections do not turn out quite close to those suggested. The individual projections could be relatively further from their projected levels than the aggregate ratio of the financial intermediaries' holdings. The object of this presentation is to emphasize the structural changes in the ownership of business units that are now proceeding rapidly.

Diversification Practices

The number of different issues held in a stock portfolio differs systematically both by financial intermediary and by the dollar value of the portfolio. Investment companies in the $1,000 million size class held an average of 120 different stocks, but the number decreased regularly to 64 in the $50-$100 million class. No individual corporate pension fund responding to my survey reported more than $1,000 million in its stock portfolio; one life insurance company and one property and casualty insurance company were in this size class. No inferences should be drawn from these two individual insurance company cases, but they do appear consistent with the data in the $250-$1,000 million class. The average number of stocks held in corporate pension funds declines as a function of size except in the smallest size class for which data were collected. The average number of stocks in life insurance and in property and casualty insurance companies follows the same pattern, with the exception of the $100-$250 million class. Closer examination indicates that each of the four life insurance companies in the $250-$1,000 million class had less than $500 million in its stock portfolio. This fact helps to explain the small difference in the number of stocks held by these two adjacent class sizes of insurance companies. The problem is not related to sampling procedures, because only one of the thirty-four largest insurance companies, measured in terms of asset size, did not provide the information requested.

Investment companies are more concerned with "performance" than are other stock-owning financial intermediaries. Even though the exact meaning and measurement of performance is not clear, the result of the investment policies of mutual funds and other investment companies is readily available to anyone who is interested.[13] Investment companies compete with one another in terms of performance, and the investment companies as a group or industry compete for part of individual savings. Little direct competition exists between the investment companies and the other three financial intermediaries for which data are presented in Table 40. Investment companies are considered to be the most aggressive stock investors among these financial intermediaries, and that popular belief is borne out if diversification is taken to be a proxy for aggressiveness when portfolios are matched for dollar-size class.[14] The investment companies in the ranges from $50 million to $1 billion in Table 40 have only about half the number of securities held by corporate pension funds. In the $50-$100 million and $100-$250 million classes, property and casualty insurance company portfolios show less aggressiveness than those of corporate pension funds. Life insurance company portfolios are well below those of investment companies in aggressiveness, but they show more aggressive portfolio policies than corporate pension funds. The reasons for these observed differences are not obvious and will require additional study.[15]

A popular expectation is that the number of stocks held would be a function of the dollar size of a portfolio. Managers of state and local pension funds as well as corporate pension fund managers with whom there has been correspondence have voiced their fear of having too much of a stock whose performance or expected performance turns sharply downward. The larger the fund, the greater the possible losses appear to be in absolute terms. For example, a $20 million investment in stock X amounts to only 2 per cent of a $1,000 million fund, but a drop in the market price of stock X to $12 million is a loss of $8 million. Such drops in price over a month or two are not rare in the stock market. Also, larger funds presumably spread their investment overhead costs more successfully than smaller funds.

Legal requirements

The number of securities held is hardly explained by administrative or legal requirements. Investment companies, as discussed in Chapter II, may not, by a combination of federal and state regulations, invest more than 5 per cent of their assets in the stock of one company; this rule leads to a minimum number of twenty stocks in a portfolio. The state laws governing life insurance companies are less clear. A life insurance company need not own any stock; but if a New York company has 5 per cent of its assets in stock, the minimum number of stocks it must hold would appear to be twenty-five.[16] The maximum percentage of stock relative to total assets that property and casualty insurance companies operating under New York law may hold is procedural, as explained in the section on property and casualty insurance companies in Chapter IV. Therefore, even though not more than one-fifth of 1 per cent of such an insurance company's assets may be invested in one asset—presumably including stock—little more can be said. If such a property and casualty insurance company holds 10 per cent of its assets in stock, it would appear to be necessary to hold a minimum of fifty different stocks. States' regulations in this field apparently vary widely, as implied by the data in Table 32.

The legislation governing state and local pension funds does not require as much diversification as in fact exists in these portfolios. In New York a public pension fund may place up to one-half of 1 per cent of its assets in a single equity. A minimum of forty stocks could amount to 20 per cent of the fund's total assets, which is the highest percentage of total assets permitted in equity securities. A reading of the California law indicates that ten stocks could comprise the entire allowable percentage of the total investment in stock in a pension fund in that state.

The diversification practices or policies of bank trustees who administer corporate pension funds are subject to agreement between the bank and the pension fund or to the prudent man rule. Textbooks on investments have very little to say about the implications of the prudent man rule for diversification. Discussion still rages over the proportion of common stock that may appropriately or prudently be held in a portfolio by a trustee. Mr. Joseph B. Breen argues for a 100 per cent common stock portfolio for reasons related to inflation.[17] Many trust officers apparently believe that you can't have too much of a good thing when it comes to diversification. Mr. Ward Randol, Jr., cites some evidence that trust department officers are beginning to reduce the number of stocks in personal trust accounts. One large bank is aiming to reduce the number of stocks in $2 million trust accounts from between 55 and 60 to about 40.[18] There have been very few court cases on the duty of a trustee to diversify, and no law review has published articles on the subject since 1963.[19]

Empirical studies of diversification and risk

Three very recent empirical studies bear upon the question of the minimum number of stocks required in a portfolio for sufficient diversification to reduce "risk" to about that existing in the entire stock market.[20] Each of these papers used a somewhat different approach to the problem, but the conclusions are strikingly similar. In one of their experiments, Evans and Archer picked portfolios each having from one through forty different stocks.[21] That is, one portfolio had one stock, a second portfolio had two stocks, a third portfolio had three stocks, and so on, up to forty portfolios and stocks. Stocks were picked at random from the 470 stocks in Standard and Poor's 500-stock index for which complete data were available. This process was repeated sixty times, so that 2,400 different portfolios in all were assembled. The performance of these simulated portfolios, which used semiannual data, was calculated by computer for the period from January, 1958 through July, 1967. The investigators determined by statistical tests that much of the variation in yield not related to general stock market movements was eliminated with a portfolio of eight securities. They could not achieve any further reduction of statistical significance in "unsystematic" risk by adding securities to these random portfolios after the number had reached twenty.[22]

Gaumnitz used monthly data and studied the performance of random and other portfolios for the period January, 1960 through December, 1965. He ran fewer simulations than Evans and Archer, but like them he reports finding stability of return and variance "somewhere around eighteen" securities.[23]

Jennings' study utilized the monetary performance of all common stocks listed on the NYSE during the period 1955-65 for holding periods of one to eleven years. The basic approach was to compare the changes in the probability of a portfolio loss and the probability of an exceptional portfolio gain as securities were added to the portfolio. Alternative definitions of loss and gain were used also. Jennings concluded that a portfolio of approximately twelve securities produced about an equal trade-off between protection against risk and opportunities for gain. The study also suggested that the "unsystematic" risk was virtually eliminated for portfolios of more than sixteen to eighteen securities.[24]

One possible implication of these three studies is that the number of securities in institutional stock portfolios is several times larger than necessary. The success of investment companies with many fewer securities than other financial intermediaries in the same size classes should raise some questions in the minds of portfolio administrators who are seeking to improve performance in terms of higher yield, stability of yield, or both. However, the three experiments reported do assume that the purchases, sales, or holdings of an investor will not affect the market price, yield, or stability of each stock itself. Administrators of very large stock portfolios are well aware that one or a few large funds with a considerable interest in a particular stock may both immediately and persistently influence its price and performance. Nevertheless, the questions about an optimum number of securities in relation to the objectives of a financial intermediary will be raised in the years ahead.[25]

This discussion of new empirical research on portfolio diversification should demonstrate that, with the possible exception of investment companies, financial intermediaries in each portfolio size class could hold fewer securities in their stock portfolios without increasing the risk of being affected by the fluctuations of particular stocks. Academic research into such topics as optimum diversification could exert a considerable influence, at least on some portfolios, after a cultural lag of some years. If legislative restrictions should stand in the way of rationalizing the degree of diversification, laws will tend in due time to be changed. Another factor that has been mentioned is that the conglomerate corporation itself may be less subject to income fluctuations because it represents greater diversification under one corporate skin. The potential impact of lessened diversification by financial intermediaries could be to increase the portfolio concentration percentages which are a primary concern of this entire study.

The next obvious question is whether or not the portfolios will actually become more concentrated. Even though many large individual portfolios decrease their diversification (increase their investment concentration), the overall portfolio concentration ratios could remain largely unchanged unless selection of stocks for portfolios becomes limited to a smaller number of attractive stocks. An important question is: What characteristics of individual stocks make them attractive to institutional investors? Unfortunately there is little systematic study of the factors that probably account for the differences in observed portfolio concentration ratios.

Portfolio Concentration Ratios

Popular, professional, and academic discussions all suggest that not only the size, earnings growth rate, and market or price stability, but also the expected changes in these characteristics are of primary importance when individual as well as institutional investors decide to buy, hold, and sell common stock. Data were collected for corporate size in terms of market value of common stock, earnings growth rates, and market price stability from *The Fortune Directory* and *Value Line Investment Survey*.[26] Comments and tables in Chapter II (see Tables 10 and 12) suggest that size is an important consideration in portfolio concentration ratios, and this suggestion is confirmed by the statistical tests reported below. First, however, a straightforward tabulation of company size, measured in terms of the market value of common stock, and of portfolio concentration percentages, helps one to visualize some of the characteristics of these distributions. Some 170 companies with the highest concentration ratios located were ranked by the market value of their common stock into ten size classes for statistical purposes. Later a sample of 200 additional companies was drawn by size class for some statistical experiments. This step provided a total of 370 companies which were later cross-classified by market value of equities and by portfolio concentration ratios, as shown in Table 41.

Although the table is not ideal it has several important aspects which merit comment. The number of corporations in a size class ranges only from 23 to 44, but the dollar-size interval of the classes differs greatly. For the four smallest dollar-size classes, the interval which provided the roughly equal number of companies was about $40-$60 million. Starting with the size class V, the class interval increases for each dollar-size class up to an interval of about $34 billion for the largest size class. Another way to look at the lopsidedness of the size distribution in the market is to observe that the total market value of all 28 corporations in class I is less than the minimum size of class X and the total market value of the 176 corporations in the five lowest sizes is about the same as that of the 30 corporations in class X. This skewness should be recalled when some statistical tests are discussed below.

A striking but not surprising feature of Table 41 is that only two corporations in the size class X have concentration ratios above 20 per cent. These corporations are Polaroid and Burroughs (see Table 43). The larger of the two, Polaroid, had an equity value, in market price, of $3,965 million, which is in the lower part of the range for size class X. The frequency of concentration ratios of 25 per cent or more is greatest in size classes V, VI, and VII, that is, in the range of about $190-$525 million.

The existence of fewer high concentration ratios for the larger and supersized corporations is explained by the very size of these corporations. As discussed in the section of Chapter II dealing with portfolio concentration, large numbers of financial intermediaries make very sizable investments in the supersized business corporations, but even such investments result in only modest portfolio concentration ratios.

One could conjecture that the small size of corporations in the first four size classes is frequently an adverse factor in terms of portfolio concentration. As shown in Table 43, only a few investment companies owning stock in these smaller corporations are needed to run the portfolio concentration ratio up rapidly. These intermediaries are very likely to be concerned with the market price stability of the portfolio company's stock under such circumstances. Buying, holding, or selling stock in quantities that are relatively large for this specific market or product is very likely to have an influence on the market price itself. Managers of institutional stock portfolios, like other persons, seem to be strongly averse to losses or "downside risk." Before purchasing a considerable proportion—1 to 5 per cent as a minimum—of a small company's stock, the investor would consider the special problems he might have to face if it became necessary or desirable to dispose of this stock quickly. A minimum-sized purchase or holding of a large financial intermediary, as pointed out several times, could be larger than even 5 per cent of the outstanding stock of an attractive smaller company. The market for specific stocks under such circumstances more nearly resembles the economist's model for oligopoly than his model for pure competition. The assumption is made that the higher or more exciting the possibilities for capital gains, the more likely they are to overcome the adverse consideration of size in relation to the market. Of course, fund managers are expected to act prudently, which is to say that there is some image in their minds of a reasonable degree of risk for an individual stock and for a portfolio of such stocks.

Statistical "explanations" of portfolio concentrations

Statistical methods were used to determine what proportion of the observed portfolio concentration ratios taken as the dependent variables could be "explained" by two or more independent variables. The results of this step will be utilized in considering what level and distribution of portfolio concentration ratios may be expected in the future as the financial intermediaries continue to enlarge their holdings of common stocks as a proportion of the entire stock market.

The first statistical tests used three independent variables: size in terms of the market value of each company's outstanding stock at the end of 1966, historical growth rates of earnings for the previous ten years, and *Value Line's* stability factor.[27] The stability factor did not turn out to be statistically significant in the initial experiments, and it was not used in later runs. The explanatory power of historical growth rates was significant but disappointingly low. Projected growth rates were substituted for historical growth rates, both because investors are believed to buy, sell, or hold stock on the basis of their expectations and because the historical growth rates reflect numerous real and random events and accounting practices which distort the results and make intercompany comparisons especially difficult.[28]

When expected growth rates of earnings were substituted for historical growth rates, the explanatory power of the growth factor increased sharply and was generally much greater than that of the size variable.[29] The logarithm, square roots, cube roots, fourth roots, and other transformations of the independent variables were tested in the search process.

The highest correlation coefficients were obtained when the five smallest dollar-size classes were omitted from the runs and the remaining observations were split into two populations at about the 10 per cent portfolio concentration ratio level. When this step was taken, the coefficient of multiple determination, R^2, was .445 for the companies whose portfolio concentration ratios were greater than 10 per cent. The growth variable was the most important explanatory factor, and the fourth root of size was next; the R^2 for these two variables only is given above. The other forms of the variables added very little additional explanatory power. The slope coefficient for the growth rate, 0.857, as shown in Table 42, indicates that one additional percentage point on the portfolio concentration percentage is associated on the average with each .857 per cent of the growth rate when size is held constant.

Some companies have had, and are expected to continue having, growth rates in the range of 15-20 per cent per year for some years. The size coefficient, -2.328, for the fourth root of size, is somewhat difficult to visualize. First, it shows that as size increases, the associated portfolio concentration ratio decreases. This expected result was generally found for the size variable in all of the runs that were made through the computer. The fourth root suggests that the association of size and portfolio concentration drops rapidly as size increases and then becomes nearly flat—but at a value close to zero—as size continues to increase. In terms of the largest five size classes used in this run, this result is sensible because the "density" of high portfolio concentration ratios is greatest among the smaller companies and decreases rapidly with increases in size, as one may observe in Table 41. In size class X, the class interval runs from $1.3 to $35.1 billion. According to the data, portfolio concentration ratios for companies above the $5 billion level fall off rapidly.

The R^2 for the 104 companies in size class VI and above which exhibited concentration ratios below 10 per cent was .345. This correlation is largely explained by the growth variable which had a coefficient of 0.480. The slope coefficient for size was again negative, but the square root of size was the most suitable form of the variable. All the statistical results, including the tests of significance, are reported in Table 42.

When the data for the entire group of 370 companies, selected as described above, were put through the same statistical process, the R^2 for the 200 companies with portfolio concentrations below the 10 per cent level was .108, and for the group above the 10 per cent concentration level it was .0879. The regression equations and related statistical tests are shown also in Table 42. The increase in R^2, achieved as successive dollar-size classes were removed from the experiments, is quite puzzling. After considerable discussion about this point with colleagues and students, I concluded that for smaller companies there are a number of factors, extremely subject to chance, that must help to explain the observed portfolio concentrations. As size increases, the factors that led to higher portfolio concentration ratios become more orderly.

Several other problems merit more comment and more careful attention than they have been given. First, there appear to be several distinct populations with different operational characteristics within the "stock market"—at least in relation to portfolio concentration. An attempt was made with all 370 companies to use a complex form of the dollar-size variable which permitted separate coefficients for companies above and below the $750 million level. The R^2 turned out to be .055 from this experiment, and growth was still the most important explanatory variable. In some of the initial, straightforward multiple correlation runs, even lower results were achieved. Successive deletion of dollar-size classes improved the explanatory power of the growth and dollar-size variables until .110 was reached, with the five classes representing the smallest market values omitted. The results of using the whole population and splitting the population of 370 companies at almost exactly the 10 per cent portfolio concentration ratio confirmed the fact that systematic explanations for portfolio concentration for the smaller half of the companies, measured in terms of market value of equity, is less likely to be found. More comments about company size and portfolio concentration above the 20 per cent level are included below.

Possible ways of improving statistical results. Despite the discouragingly low coefficients of multiple determination that resulted from fairly elaborate and sophisticated data processing and search methods, the results are not discouraging for several reasons. First, existing portfolio concentrations are continually in flux because of expected changes in size, growth rates, market prices, and other factors. If the direction and extent of changes in portfolio concentration ratios could be tabulated, a search could be made for the statistically significant causes of these changes. Third, a large number (perhaps hundreds) of high portfolio concentration ratios are understated or were not even included, primarily because although individual portfolio concentrations at the 4, 3, 2, and 1 per cent levels clearly exist in the hands of individual trust

94   INSTITUTIONAL HOLDINGS OF COMMON STOCK

departments of commercial banks they are not known to the public.[30] If and when more portfolio concentration data become available from these trust departments, the multiple correlations resulting from efforts such as those reported here may be much more rewarding.

High concentration ratios

The number of high concentration ratios (20 per cent or more) is growing, but evidence of this growth is limited to the investment company industry. Table 13 shows the growth of these portfolio concentrations from 1952 through 1966. The 20 per cent portfolio concentration level was exceeded by only one company in 1952, two in 1958, and 26 in 1966. Portfolio concentrations ranging from 10.0 to 19.9 per cent totaled 7 in 1952, 22 in 1958, and approximately 142 in 1966.

Public information about the portfolio concentrations of investment companies, insurance companies, and the trust departments of commercial banks is assembled in Table 43.[31] The known holdings of trust departments contribute substantially to both of the portfolio concentrations of 40 per cent or above and one of the eight portfolio concentrations between 30.0 and 39.9 per cent. How much higher would these concentration ratios be if complete data from trust departments were included? Another factor which merits separate consideration is the bunching of high portfolio concentrations in one industry. The common stock of four major airlines is found among the ten companies that had concentration ratios of 30.0 per cent or more at the end of 1966. Six of the forty companies with concentration ratios in the 20.0 to 29.9 per cent range also were airlines.

Two obvious characteristics of the companies high on the list of portfolio concentration ratios were their medium size—as size is counted at this date— and their excellent growth prospects. Among those over 30 per cent, there is no company whose common stock market value is close to $1,000 million; and there are two companies, Armstrong Rubber and Mid-America Pipeline, whose common stocks had a market value of less than $100 million each. As pointed out earlier in discussion of the inner structure of portfolio concentration ratios in Chapter II, Investors Diversified Services and Wellington Management complexes held 13.7 per cent and 7.7 per cent, respectively, of Armstrong Rubber's outstanding voting stock. An investment of $10 million in Armstrong would amount to about 13 per cent of its stock but would represent only 1 per cent of any $1,000 million fund. Wellington Management Company controlled about $2,000 million at that date, and the Investors Diversified Services complex controlled more than $5,000 million. There were at least ten—and perhaps one or two more—investment company complexes with assets above the $1,000 million level; 39 bank trust departments, one life insurance company, and one property and casualty insurance company also held $1,000 million or more in stocks in 1966 or 1967. Investments of $10 million or somewhat more by such large financial intermediaries are not imprudent. In fact, the minimum size of an investment—consistent with the optimum number or range of different securities—that should be held for adequate diversification in a normative sense will be one of the questions that comes to the fore in the future. A previous section described some of the empirical research about optimum investment diversification that has already been completed.

Seven of the corporations listed in Table 43 had common stock holdings with market values of less than $100 million; ten ranged from $100 to $200 million; seven from $200 to $300; and nine from $300 to $400 million; only four were in the range from $400 to $500 million. Thirteen of the entire fifty had common stock with market value of $500 million or more. The relative sizes of portfolio companies and financial intermediaries helps to explain why high portfolio concentration exists for some smaller- or medium-sized companies.[32] The structure in the "inner portfolio concentration ratios" has already been discussed for investment companies only in Chapter II. The importance of considering the holdings of insurance companies and banks' trust departments, in addition to those of investment companies, in constructing portfolio concentration ratios is developed in the next section.

The list of portfolio favorites ranked by the market value of investment in them is in sharp contrast with the list of companies subjected to high portfolio concentration ratio. As shown in Table 12, for 1964 the total market value of stock investment in the fifth most popular company was $307 million. By the end of 1968 the $300 million investment level was exceeded by fifteen companies in a full list of portfolio favorites. Virtually every company among the thirty favorites for 1964 listed in Table 12 by the end of 1966 had a market value of $1,000 million or very close to it. Only Burroughs Corporation and Polaroid Corporation appear among both the top thirty of the portfolio favorites and those with high portfolio concentrations. The fact that the largest corporations are less likely to appear among those with the highest portfolio concentration ratios is confirmed by the statistical tests that were reported.

The attraction of high rates of net earnings and dividend growth for both individual and institutional investors is well known. The dividend growth rate plus the dividend yield is widely accepted as a good indicator of the long-run rate of return.[33] The dividend yield usually is defined as the annual dividends per share divided by the market price. At least this relationship of growth rates and rates of return is expected to hold as long as the market price is roughly a constant multiple of either earnings or dividends. On the one hand, when a stock is becoming more popular, its price may increase faster than its earnings or dividends; and it may provide extremely large gains for its owners. On the other hand, even a modest decline in expected growth rates or loss of some popularity for other reasons could result in low returns or even losses. Such intermediate-term losses may occur despite the fact that the earnings growth rate is expected to stay above the average. Such considerations help to explain why growth is so important to large groups of investors and why it turns up as a highly significant factor in the multiple correlation studies that were done.

Airline industry

Most of the airline revenues in the United States are earned by ten domestic trunk lines and two overseas companies. The ten domestic trunk-line companies accounted for about 75 per cent of the domestic passenger miles flown in 1966. The five largest domestic carriers accounted for about 60 per cent of these totals. The rather surprising fact is that in 1966 the portfolio concentration ratios for ten airlines were above 20 per cent, as shown in Tables 43 and 44.

The concentrated common stock ownership is brought together in Table 44 for insurance companies and investment company complexes owning 1 per cent or more, and for some banks' trust departments owning 5 per cent or more of the shares of individual airlines. The Chase Manhattan Bank held an interest of 5 per cent or more in each of six different airlines, and in each case it was the largest holder identified. The Morgan Guaranty Trust held more than 5 per cent of the stock of two airlines. Its holdings of American Airlines stock made Morgan Guaranty the largest identified holder amongst the financial intermediaries; Prudential Life Insurance was second with 4.7 per cent. In the case of Trans World Airlines stock Morgan Guaranty's 6.1 per cent was second to Chase Manhattan's 7.4 per cent, but exceeded that of Waddell and Reed (United Funds), which amounted to 4.9 per cent. These three financial intermediaries alone held 18.4 per cent of the outstanding stock of Trans World Airlines. The bank holdings included are only shares for which the bank has the voting rights. Table 26 showed the distribution of the sole, partial, and nonvoting rights of the shares of Trans World Airlines and Northwest Airlines stock held by these two banks.

Most of the investment company groups held more than 1 per cent of the outstanding shares of several airlines; six of these groups held 1 per cent or more in five or more different airlines. There is substantial overlapping of mutual interests in the holdings of trust departments, investment companies, and the Prudential Life Insurance Company in several of the same airline companies (see Table 44).

Given the overlapping ownership and potential control, numerous and obvious questions come to mind for the present and future of the airline industry.[34] Many of the airlines that were presumably competing for business in 1966 and 1967 were owned by financial intermediaries, at least to the extent indicated. The approximate structure of these financial interests was presumably known to the intermediaries themselves and to a somewhat lesser extent, perhaps, to the financial managers of the airlines. These circumstances lead one to wonder whether they do not offer some possibility of outflanking the antitrust laws, which were hardly designed to deal with the legitimate development of interrelated ownership that has been described.

In a number of respects the airline industry is higher regulated. Entry into the business, prices for services, authorization of routes and flight schedules, and the safety of equipment and landing fields are all regulated. The increasingly complex problems associated with the physical management of commercial passenger airline service and the dangers of accidents are obvious to most people who use the service and to an even wider, informed public. Given the governmental controls over the price of services, the physical management problems of the airlines conceived as a total system, and the present—and probably increasing—portfolio concentration, it is clear that more and more questions about the organization—or reorganization—of air transport in the United States will be asked between now and the end of the century.

Table 43 does not indicate any other industry-wide problems among the companies whose portfolio concentration ratios were known to be 20 per cent or above. The airline industry is peculiarly subject to portfolio concentrations because of the relatively modest market values of the companies, their expected high growth rates of earnings, the limited number of companies, and the very limited entry of new companies into the industry. Similar problems may exist now or may develop in other industries, but until more complete data are available they must remain unknown. Meanwhile the financial intermediaries should not be viewed as seeking widespread and overlapping ownership or control in any given industry, and they may not be particularly pleased to discover—or to have the general public become aware of—the extent to which it exists.

Growth and Distribution of Portfolio Concentration Ratios

According to the projections of growth in the total market value of common stocks and the stock holdings of the financial intermediaries as a whole and individually that have been set forth in this chapter, financial intermediaries can be expected to hold about 52 or 55 per cent of all common stock by the year 2000; the most likely range within which the overall ownership would fall was set at 45-58 per cent. At the end of this century the noninsured corporate pension funds will be the largest stock-owning financial intermediaries; their common stock holdings will be about $2,300 billion and will comprise about 26 per cent of all stock market values at that time. The second largest of these financial intermediaries will be the investment companies with stock holdings of about $1,750 billion. The state and local pension funds will hold about $360 billion but will be far behind in third place.

The important point made earlier that the overall market concentration ratios and portfolio concentration ratios are constructed on different bases needs to be elaborated. The overall market concentration ratios simply divide the known estimated market value of institutional holdings of common stock by the total market values. The same total market value of institutional holdings may be consistent with quite different averages and distributions of portfolio concentration ratios because of the size distribution of companies. Table 45 provides a very simple illustration of the difference between these two concepts for a hypothetical market of ten stocks. In the demonstration case the overall market percentage of total investment is 17.6 per cent, and portfolio concentration pattern A has an average of 18.1 per cent, while portfolio concentration pattern B has an average of 30.2 per cent.

What are these two ratios at present? The NYSE 1968 overall market concentration estimate for NYSE listed stocks only was 22.4 per cent, and the comparable 1968 percentage computed by the author from SEC data for all stock was 23.2 per cent. The existing average of the portfolio concentration ratios is unknown, but on the evidence scattered through this study, it may be between 15 and 20 per cent. One might observe in Table 41, on the one hand, that the modal portfolio concentration reported there is 10.0 to 14.9 per cent, but the techniques used there do not fully represent the total population of companies with lower portfolio concentration ratios. The distribution of the portfolio concentration ratios will very likely turn out to be a more important statistic than some measure of central tendency alone.[35] On the other hand, the most important data omitted from that table are portfolio concentrations of 1-5 per cent held by the trust departments of those banks that reported in detail to the Patman Committee, and all bank portfolio concentration ratios for smaller banks.

This chapter has served to set the stage for some discussions of the probable future trends in portfolio concentration in the economy. The phase "portfolio concentration" may seem cold, austere, and abstract to many people, but the concern of individuals, various agencies and levels of government, and the variety of business institutions, including the financial sector which some may consider to be linked more directly to government, is vital, immediate, and concrete. The concern, basically, is with some of the directions and general policies of a very wide range of American business. The question at issue is who or what instrumentalities of society shall help to determine the variety, quality, and volume of the economy's output. This concern is broader than a mere tabulation of goods and services; this output influences the quality and complexity of our environment, and the form and structure of governmental response or leadership. These influences of the economy and government have direct and lasting impacts on our personal lives and the formation of our individual goals—the goals of the substructures of society and those of the society at large.

NOTES

[1] Hans H. Landsberg, *Natural Resources for U.S. Growth: A Look Ahead to the Year 2000* (Baltimore, Md.: Johns Hopkins Press, 1964), pp. 16-21. Resources for the Future is a nonprofit corporation that was established in 1952 with the cooperation of the Ford Foundation.

[2] Herman Kahn and Anthony J. Wiener, *The Year 2000—A Framework for Speculation on the Next Thirty-Three Years* (New York: Macmillan Co., 1967), pp. 167-84. In their terms, the "Standard Society" is distinguished from a "Leisure-Oriented Society." Both their Standard and Leisure-Oriented societies assume a population of 318 million and a work force of about 38 per cent or 122 million persons. However, it is assumed that in the Standard Society the hours of work per year will be 1,600, and in the Leisure-Oriented Society only 1,100 hours per year. The hours of work per year per employed person were about 2,000 in the year 1965. See Kahn and Wiener's recurring discussions on these topics, pp. 118-98.

[3] *Ibid.*, p. 167.

[4] For evidence on these past relationships and the possibility of some shifting in relative yields on securities, see Robert M. Soldofsky and Roger L. Miller, "Risk-Premium Curves for Different Classes of Long-Term Securities, 1950-1966," *Journal of Finance,* XXIV (June, 1969), 429-45. For a discussion of the history of debt-equity ratios, see A. W. Sametz, "Trends in the Volume and Composition of Equity Finance," *Journal of Finance,* XIX (Sept., 1964), 450-69.

[5] Richard Stevenson, "Dual Funds Discount: A New Technical Indicator," *Commercial and Financial Chronical,* Sept., 1969, pp. 12-13. Also see references cited in this article. If commercial banks, other financial institutions, and even primarily nonfinancial corporations successfully market mutual funds, identification of investment in mutual funds will be more difficult.

[6] Data are published by the SEC for both noninsured corporate pension funds and for other noninsured private pension funds; the latter include multi-employer funds, nonprofit organizations, and union-administered plans. The total of noninsured corporate pension funds and other noninsured private

pension funds is labeled private pension funds. Corporate pension funds constitute almost 90 per cent of all private funds.

[7] A study of 502 corporate pension funds showed that the modal range for common stock as a percentage of the total fund was 65-69 per cent; 83 funds were in this range. The mode increased from 50-54 per cent for 1964. Almost half of the respondents expected to increase the common stock proportion of their pension funds; the most frequently named percentage was 70-75 per cent in terms of market value. Chase Manhattan Bank, *Summary of the Findings from a Survey on Pension Fund Financing* (New York: Chase Manhattan Bank, 1969), Tables 17 and 18.

[8] However, a number of states base retirement benefits on a fixed percentage of average salary for the last five to ten years of employment times the number of years the person is covered within the retirement system. The percentage is frequently 1.50 or 1.67 per cent per year of employment. In most states in which such formula plans are used, the state's contribution is largely or entirely unfunded. If funding were started or the percentage of the obligations funded were increased, the assets of state and local pension funds would increase somewhat faster. For a summary of benefit formulas and other details relating to these plans, see William C. Greenough and Francis P. King, *Benefit Plans in American Colleges* (New York: Columbia University Press, 1969), pp. 20-73.

[9] Charles M. Linke, Associate Professor of Finance, University of Illinois, "Phase One of a Cost-Benefit Analysis of the Life Insurance-Mutual Fund Combination." (Unpublished speech.)

[10] Also see Stanford Research Institute, *The Future of Insurance Agents,* Vol. I of *Planning for the Future of the National Association of Insurance Agents* (Menlo Park, Calif.: Stanford Research Institute, 1967). This report was prepared for the National Association of Insurance Agents and was reprinted in *American Agency Bulletin,* Sept., 1967, pp. 13-67. This report projects the average annual growth rate of premium volume in the industry at 5.8 per cent to 1975. Industry trends are discussed against the changing economic, social, and technical environment.

[11] U.S., Securities and Exchange Commission, *Statistical Series,* Release No. 2358, May 1, 1969, table 3, p. 5.

[12] The NYSE has projected that the overall institutional ownership of common stock will reach 31 per cent in 1970 and 33 per cent in 1980. Growth rates are given for the stock ownership by major types of financial institutions; they are similar to those developed for this study before the NYSE projection. New York Stock Exchange, *Perspectives in Planning,* No. 5, Jan., 1970.

This NYSE bulletin is supported by a technical appendix, "The Demand for Corporate Equity: Projections to 1975 and 1980," by Professor Arnold E. Saffer, Roth School of Business, Long Island University.

[13] A recent summary of the literature and comparison of the performance measures published to date are included in Keith V. Smith and Dennis A. Tito, "Risk-Return Measures and Ex Post Portfolio Performance," *Journal of Financial and Quantitative Analysis,* IV (Dec., 1969), 449-71.

[14] Other possible measures of aggressiveness need to be studied. One such measure would be based upon studies of the percentage distributions of the dollar value in each stock held to the entire stock portfolio, taken as 100 per cent. Preliminary studies indicate very substantial skewness to these percentage distributions. The extent to which preferred stocks, convertible stocks, and—in the case of insurance companies—stocks of closely held companies are owned may also prove to be useful. Studies of investment companies especially have focused upon portfolio turnover because of its implications for stock market organization and because it may indicate malpractices or, at least, unethical practices.

[15] Anyone who thinks that he can rank the performance of these stock portfolios over this span of financial institutions may have an extremely difficult if not virtually impossible problem laid out for himself. Transactions of the insurance companies can be surmised but not dated, and virtually no information is public on pension portfolios or transactions. Furthermore, the computational methods for published yields are not sufficiently consistent to give any meaning to comparisons.

[16] Not more than one-fifth of 1 per cent of total assets may be invested in any one stock. However, see the additional considerations described in the section on life insurance in Chapter IV.

[17] From a speech by Joseph B. Breen before the Southern Trust Conference, *Trust Bulletin,* XLVII (May 23, 1968).

[18] Ward Randol, Jr., "Duty to Diversify," *Trusts and Estates,* Jan., 1969, p. 35.

[19] *Ibid.*

[20] John L. Evans and Stephen H. Archer, "Diversification and the Reduction of Dispersion: An Empirical Analysis," *Journal of Finance,* XXIII (Dec., 1968), 761-67; Jack E. Gaumnitz, "Maximal Gains from Diversification—An Examination of the Number of Securities in a Common Stock Portfolio," *Working Paper No. 10,* School of Business, University of Kansas, Lawrence, Kan., June, 1968; Edward Jennings, "An Empirical Examination and Analysis

of the Diversification Requirements of the Common Stock Investor" (unpublished Ph.D. dissertation, University of Michigan, Ann Arbor, Mich., 1969).

[21] Evans and Archer, "Diversification and the Reduction of Dispersion."

[22] Evans and Archer also report that they observed the same general results using annual data for the period 1936-53. *Ibid.,* fn. 14, p. 766.

[23] Gaumnitz, "Maximal Gains from Diversification."

[24] Jennings, "Diversification Requirements of the Common Stock Investor."

[25] The organization of the stock markets to cope with ever larger trades of securities will continue to change. The development of the "third market"—the direct trading of very large blocks of stocks listed on the exchanges such as the NYSE, through channels other than an exchange itself—reflects one such development.

[26] *The Fortune Directory,* which is published annually in *Fortune* magazine, included in addition to the list of 500 largest industrials lists of the 50 largest commercial banks, life insurance companies, merchandising firms, transportation companies, and utilities. A total of 750 large companies are ranked in this directory, but not all of these companies are widely held corporations. These rankings are in terms of sales and book value of assets.

At the end of 1966 *Value Line* rated approximately 1,100 different issues; these ratings covered almost all the widely held stocks listed in *The Fortune Directory.* The *Value Line Investment Survey* prepares both historical and expected growth rates and a stability index. The market value of the common stock of each company at the end of 1966 was prepared by my research assistants.

For a discussion of the exact content of these and other measures of expected quality of common stocks, see *Value Line Selection and Opinion,* which is published regularly.

[27] Several thousand man hours and about two hours of computer time were used in these multiple correlation experiments and in assembling data used in various parts of this study.

[28] There are numerous discussions in textbooks and articles on this subject. For example, see Douglas A. Hayes, "Accounting Principles and Investment Analysis," *Law and Contemporary Problems,* XXX (Autumn, 1965—"Uniformity in Financial Accounting"), 752-71.

[29] The *Value Line's* Cash Earnings Expected Growth Rates were used for the companies for which they were available. The author had to prepare a few projections himself. Different projections of growth rates obtained from other

sources may have given somewhat different results. For a pathbreaking article that discusses different forecasts for the same stock and evaluates their accuracy, see John G. Cragg and Burton G. Malkiel, "The Consensus and Accuracy of Some Predictions of the Growth of Corporate Earnings," *Journal of Finance,* XXIII (March, 1968), 67-84.

[30] The evidence and discussion of this point is found in the last section of Chapter III, "Commercial Banks as Trustees of Noninsured Corporate Pension Funds."

[31] Again the limitation of the portfolio concentration data from trust departments is stressed. In view of the projected growth of the accumulations that will be located in these banks, the absence of more detailed information can hardly be allowed to exist by responsible government at the state and federal levels.

[32] For a previous demonstration of these relationships see Table 10.

[33] The student of finance will recognize this formulation as the Gordon-Shapiro model, which has become popular, at least in academic circles, since the mid-1960s. For an introductory discussion of this model and some of its limitations and a presentation of other models, see Robert M. Soldofsky and Roger Biderman, "Yield-Risk Measurements of the Performance of Common Stocks," *Journal of Financial and Quantitative Analysis,* III (March, 1968), 59-74. See also Robert A. Levy, "Measurement of Investment Performance," *ibid.,* 35-57. Anyone interested in pursuing these topics further will find frequent articles and excellent bibliographies in the *Journal of Finance* and the *Journal of Business.*

[34] No attempt was made to discover the extent to which the commercial banks and insurance companies make loans to these same airline companies.

[35] The data examined thus far strongly suggest that the distribution is skewed. Therefore, the future studies are likely to find that measurements of the standard deviation, skewness, and kurtosis—that is measurements of the second, third, and fourth moments—of the portfolio distributions are essential to a more complete understanding.

VI

THE EXPECTED GROWTH OF PORTFOLIO CONCENTRATION RATIOS AND THE SOCIETAL RESPONSES

The very rapid and continuing growth of the ownership of voting stock in widely held corporations by financial intermediaries has created a major problem area for American society. The recognized disturbance to our value system from the separation of corporate ownership and control will probably turn out to be minor compared with the reconcentration of power in the hands of a limited number of financial intermediaries. Financial intermediaries are primarily represented by their employees. The role expectations of these persons may not yet have included—or adjusted to—the potential power within their grasp.

The first part of this chapter will consider the expected portfolio concentrations and possible changes in legislation concerning these concentrations. The second part will be concerned with a broader analysis, interpretation, and resolution of the related general problems.

The proportion of the market value of stock held by financial intermediaries (on the basis of NYSE data) has increased from about 13 per cent in 1950 to about 22 per cent by the end of 1968. Projections show a further increase to approximately 48 to 62 per cent within about thirty years. When the overall market value ratio for financial intermediaries reaches this level, undoubtedly 50, 60, or 70 per cent or even more of the voting stock of individual corporations is highly likely to be in the hands of financial intermediaries. A review of the causes of this broad trend does not expose any conscious or deliberate motivation to achieve the results or consequences that are identified by the term "reconcentration of ownership."

The exact distribution of the individual portfolio concentration ratios around their own mean is still uncertain. The first part of this chapter will point out some of the large areas of economic, financial, and political uncertainty that will determine the eventual outcome. The term "political uncertainty" is intended to cover the available options in state and federal laws that may affect the distribution of portfolio concentration ratios, including the "inner concentrations" and overlapping communities of interest. The "inner concentrations" and overlapping communities of financial interests will provide the basis for more and more outcries or outrage from the public about conflicts of interest.

The second part of the chapter will be concerned explicitly with the growing societal disturbance and its possible resolutions—adjustments toward new norms or equilibriums—as the end of the century approaches. The already recognized disturbance has been characterized by such terms as "power without property," "paraproprietal society," and "the silent partners." Rather than use the specialized, restricted, legalistic frameworks associated with these terms, an effort will be made to organize perceptions of the societal changes according to two broad frameworks for social analysis that have wide, scholarly acceptance. The first of these is the analysis of power, developed by political scientists and behavioral scientists chiefly since World War II.[1]

The second framework is that of sociological theory in the tradition of Max Weber and Emile Durkheim and developed by Talcott Parsons and his various coauthors.[2] The sociological analysis leads directly to the suggestion that there will be further structural differentiation in the voting control of business units. This likelihood of further differentiation or separation of the monetary rewards or returns from the ownership of stock and the "control" of large business units by new agencies in society is consistent with continuing social differentiation within our economic, political, and household subsystems. The changes that are going on simultaneously in our internalized value systems, the growth of output and leisure, and the exigencies of maintaining a viable environment for human life, reinforce the view that further differentiation and articulation will take place in the mechanisms for the general policy control or guidance of many major business organizations.

Expected Growth of Portfolio Concentration Ratios

The growth of portfolio concentration ratios, which is expected to continue, is the core of the intensifying disturbance to the institutional value system. The future distribution of voting power will depend in part on possible changes in laws limiting concentrations of wealth and power in the hands of individual funds or organizations such as investment company complexes or commercial banks. Alternative possible developments will be suggested. Unfortunately, the concentration patterns of the past two decades and the present patterns are only approximately known. Projections are essential to cope with the growing societal disturbance but are less precise than they could be because an essential part of the underlying data is not made public. Recommendations will be made in this chapter on this and other topics.

The increase in the ratio of the overall market value of stock which is held by financial intermediaries (Figure 2) and in the portfolio concentration ratios (Table 13) has been documented since the early 1950s. Although these two concepts and their respective ratios are different, both averages have been rising. Even though the data are incomplete, Figure 3 sketches the approximate frequency distribution of the number of stocks held in various portfolio concentration levels.[3]

The broad, straight-line segments on Figure 3 show the historical and projected ratios for overall market value ownership in the years 1966, 1980, and 2000. As these overall market value concentration ratios continue to grow, the portfolio concentration patterns will continue to shift outward and upward as suggested on the figure. The portfolio concentration ratios that develop will be above the average market value ratio for about fifty to one hundred different companies. The highest known individual portfolio concentration ratios are about twice as high as the market ownership average. By 1980 more than half the shares of a dozen corporations are likely to be in the hands of financial intermediaries. As the expected trends continue to 2000, more than half the stock of one hundred or more corporations, and more than one-third of the stock of a thousand corporations will be in the hands of these organizations. If financial intermediaries own half the stocks of fewer companies than suggested above, there will be that many more corporations with portfolio concentration ratios higher than 33 1/3 per cent.

As long as the overall average market ownership ratio is close to that anticipated, the portfolio concentration ratios must be close to those pictured on Figure 3. The portfolio concentration ratios for individual corporations may be compatible with alternative "inner concentration ratios" (see Tables 15 and 16) among individual financial intermediaries. More specifically, the question is what is most likely to happen to portfolio percentages in the hands of individual investment companies, investment company complexes, and trust departments of commercial banks?

Alternative futures for portfolio concentrations

During the 1940 congressional hearings on investment trusts and investment companies, Mr. Arthur Bunker and Mr. Hugh Bullock, investment bankers and leading representatives of the nascent investment company industry, characterized as "theoretical" the possibility that investment companies as a group would own enough stock in any portfolio company to control it. The empirical data of thirty years ago appeared to confirm their position.[4] However, by 1966 three cases were found in which a single mutual fund group owned 10-20 per cent of the outstanding shares of a portfolio company.

During the deliberations leading up to the passage of the Investment Company Act of 1940, there was discussion as to whether or not the maximum investment concentration and portfolio concentration ratios should apply to individual funds or to groups of funds (complexes). The act that was passed limits the investment concentration and portfolio concentration ratios of individual funds only; the latter ratio, which was fixed at 10 per cent, should be a matter of great concern.[5] In 1966, individual investment company complexes, such as the Fidelity Group, held more than 10 per cent of the stock of six different companies, and six more were close to the 10 per cent limit. As individual investment companies and investment company complexes continue to grow, in relation to the size of most of their present and potential portfolio companies, the 10 per cent ownership level will be exceeded more frequently.

No legislative limit exists on the portfolio concentration percentage for investment company complexes. The existence of three of four large investment companies within one complex makes the ownership of 30-40 per cent of the voting stock of one portfolio corporation quite possible.[6] Even though it is doubtful whether any one management group would hold such a large proportion of the voting stock of any one corporation, the potential for portfolio control by two or three investment company complexes is quite clear. In 1966 some 21 per cent of Armstrong Rubber Company's common stock was owned by two investment company complexes.[7] As Table 15 shows, in eight instances, excluding Unilever's American deposit receipts, four fund complexes owned more than 20 per cent of the stock of individual portfolio companies.

During the hearings prior to the passage of the Investment Company Act, Mr. Merrill Griswold, chairman of the Massachusetts Investors Trust, indicated his willingness to accept a limitation on the portfolio concentrations of a fund complex.[8] Just where Mr. Griswold would have recommended setting that percentage for an investment complex is not known, but elsewhere in his testimony he indicated that 10 per cent was an ample portfolio concentration ratio and that even 5 per cent might be acceptable because of the widespread fear that mutual funds might acquire control of business units.[9] The success of mutual funds does not depend on a high level of portfolio concentration in any one company.

My recommendation would be that the Investment Company Act be amended to extend the present 10 per cent portfolio concentration limitation to investment company complexes. In those instances in which the concentration ratio is above 10 per cent, some period such as ten years might be provided to reduce the level to 10 per cent. Such a step would prevent two or three complexes from owning 50 per cent or more of the stock of individual companies but might only have a minor effect on the long-run concentration ratio for the four to eight largest fund complexes or individual funds. As these very large financial intermediaries grow in relative and absolute size, will a few of them grow to have the dominant if not controlling interests in numerous important businesses?

Another possibility is to set the maximum portfolio concentration ratio at 7.5 per cent or even at 5.0 per cent and require such "rollback" as is necessary over a period of years. However, the shares that are sold under any rollback might well be acquired in large part by other financial intermediaries. Expected growth rates and corporate size, which were identified as major determinants of portfolio concentration ratios in Chapter V, would still be operating factors. The "inner" concentration ratios for the two to four largest holders would be reduced, but that of the eight to twelve largest might be much the same. In fact, the breadth of the market and absence of overwhelming threats to the market price associated with very large individual concentration ratios could induce greater ownership by institutional investors.

The growth of corporate pension plans and the funneling of their funds into the trust departments of commercial banks has been discussed in Chapters III and IV. By the year 2000, which is only some thirty years ahead, corporate pension funds may grow to more than $4,000 billion with some $2,350 billion in common stock, which will be about 26 per cent of the market value of all corporate stocks. If the existing distribution of these funds among banks is maintained, the ten largest banks will hold about $1,600 billion in common stock for their corporate pension fund clients.

The limited study of commercial bank holdings of common stock showed that in 60 instances there were concentrations at the 10 per cent level or above; in another 163 instances there were portfolio concentrations between 5 and 10 per cent.[10] If complete data had been available, the frequency of 5-10 per cent portfolio concentrations would have been much greater—perhaps twice the extent reported. Data on portfolio concentration ratios below 5 per cent were not collected by the congressional study.

Several of the largest banks stated that they have internal rules limiting their ownership to 5 per cent of the outstanding shares of portfolio companies. Just below the 5 per cent level there may be a thousand or more instances of portfolio concentrations. The exact distribution of these percentages and the companies involved is not known. But if all bank holdings above the 1 per cent level were known and included, the level of portfolio concentrations would surely be significantly higher than reported here.

The author strongly urges the adoption of any necessary legislation to implement his earlier recommendation that all portfolio concentrations in the hands of commercial banks be reported to the Comptroller of the Currency, who is charged with the administration of the national banks, or to the Securities and Exchange Commission. Public discussion of the policy issues involved and the rapid development of such legislation and any necessary institutional innovations require that information be available about existing portfolio concentration ratios and their growth patterns. Such concentration data could lag a year or more and should not identify the individual banks. These two safeguards should be an assurance to banks operating as trustees and their clients that the market prices of shares held will not be affected by the delayed publication of the required information.

Individual pension funds may negotiate guidelines for general investment policy with the one or more commercial bank trust departments which safeguard and invest their funds. There do not seem to be investment or portfolio concentration guidelines or restrictions in these agreements. Even if there were restrictions in individual agreements, these limitations would hardly apply to the total holdings of each stock in the trust department's control. The trust department of each major commercial bank administers hundreds of individual corporate pension funds.

Limitations on investment and portfolio concentration are imposed on the common stock held by all other major financial intermediaries. Investment companies' portfolios are restricted by both federal and state laws; the insurance codes of the various states impose limitations even though they vary widely from state to state; and the state and local pension funds are regulated directly by state legislation. The most liberal of these regulations, the Investment Company Act, permits portfolio concentrations up to 10 per cent for each regulated, diversified investment company. The recommendation that the 10 per cent limitation be imposed upon investment company complexes has been made. In view of this historically acceptable pattern, the recommendation is made that appropriate federal and state legislation be enacted to place a limit of 10 per cent on portfolio concentrations for the pension funds administered by each bank.

This 10 per cent portfolio concentration ratio for bank holdings of stock for corporate pension funds may be exceeded only in a few instances now. In these cases the same rollback mechanism recommended for investment companies should be enacted in the suggested legislation. The expected growth of employee benefit accounts and their concentration pattern in individual banks make such legislation essential. For the three banks holding the largest dollar amounts of employee benefit accounts, the average amount held was over 10 per cent of all such assets as shown in Table 25. Thus in 1980 when a projection of $269 billion of stock in corporation pension funds is made, each of these three trust departments is likely to hold $25-$35 billion in stocks. Twenty years later in the year 2000, several trust departments may each administer more than $200 billion of stock. Corporate pension funds, which will continue to grow at well over 10 per cent per year, are funneling their explosively rising assets—measured in terms of dollars—into corporate trust funds.

Effect of declining diversification

These considerations alone make it urgent to enact laws limiting portfolio concentration by commercial banks. In addition, as Chapter V suggests, portfolio practices may move toward greater investment concentration in response to academic research into the effect of diversification on the yield-risk performance of stock portfolios. Large corporate pension funds had about twice as many stocks as investment company portfolios of the same dollar-size class, as reported in Table 40. A shift toward less diversification would surely increase portfolio concentration ratios in individual banks. Whether or not the possible future decrease in diversification would result in a higher or lower average for concentration ratios generally is a moot question. What is important is that many portfolio concentration ratios for attractive stocks would increase, though how much, given existing legislation, is difficult to foresee. Unless there are legal changes, by 1980 or before an increasing number of companies will come under the control of four to eight financial intermediaries; by "control" is meant that 50 per cent or more of their voting stock will be held by four to eight individual organizations. By the year 2000, under present legislation, almost half or more than half the voting stock of hundreds of corporations will be held by ten or fewer organizations.

Rollbacks on portfolio concentration ratios

If the prospects of effective voting control of many businesses by five to ten financial intermediaries is astonishing, repugnant, or frightening to the reader, one possible alternative would seem to be the placing of a ceiling of 40 or 50 per cent on the proportion of a company's voting stock that may be owned by all financial intermediaries as a group. But how could such a law be administered? How would it be known when the limit was exceeded? If several insurance companies, investment companies, or bank trustees wanted to increase their holdings in company X, who would decide which organization should have priority in making such a purchase? If the potential buyer had no holdings or relatively small holdings of company X stock, could the institution with the largest holdings be forced to sell? Should a "two-tier" price system be worked out—if the ceiling ownership in terms of shares could be known and kept current by computers—so that a premium price above the market could be offered to other institutions only? Such a system appears to be arbitrary and untenable.

Another possible alternative would be setting (or rolling back) the allowable portfolio concentration ratios to 7.5 per cent or even to 5 per cent. If such portfolio concentration ceilings were set, what would the consequences be? As the rollback took place, institutions would probably use the released funds for similar investments that were attractive to them. During the rollback period, which might last from five to fifteen years, the overall market concentration ratio in the hands of the financial intermediaries would be climbing.

If the ceiling were set at 7.5 per cent, seven individual organizations—whether they were investment company complexes, individual investment companies, or bank trust departments—could have control of a portfolio company. If the 5 per cent limit were established, the same process would push more companies' stocks to the new, lower portfolio concentration ceiling. Absolute voting control, i.e., ownership of more than 50 per cent of the outstanding voting shares, might be found in fifteen or so institutional owners rather than in seven to ten at the 7.5 per cent ceiling.

In fact, the chances of establishing a 10 per cent limit for individual financial intermediaries seem slim over the next few years and a limit at lower levels utopian. By the time the 10 per cent legislation would be enacted, even that upper constraint would require a substantial rollback.

The First Two Separations of Ownership and Property

During the coming decades, voting control of a rapidly increasing number of corporations will come into the hands of a limited number—perhaps five to fifteen—of individual financial intermediaries. The concentration of such power and its legitimacy will be called into question from many directions, some of which cannot yet be foreseen. The fundamental situation which validated the seemingly inevitable and natural connection between risk and reward in the ownership of property on the one hand, and the right to control the uses of that property, however tenuous that control might be, is being so stretched by circumstances that the basis of the relationship is being exposed and will be reconsidered.

Some persons might find justification for the close connection between risk and reward on the one hand and the control of property on the other hand on the basis of natural law. Others would see its origin in the common law. Still others find the justification of property rights in the puritan ethic which connects work, frugality, and the accumulation of goods with righteousness, morality, and even a sign of election to heaven. The puritan ethic has been credited with speeding the growth of capitalism in the seventeeth, eighteenth, and nineteenth centuries. In both modern and ancient times the rights and responsibilities of owners of property and the enforcement of contracts have also been concerns of the state. The exact meaning and content of the rights to acquire, use, and dispose of property are continuing to change. The theories of property are discussed further below in the subsection, "Legitimacy of power."

The close connection between ownership and control is exemplified by the fact that proxies for absentee shareholders are not permitted in common law. The historical development of the separation of immediate, direct control of a stock of goods or business property into physical control on the one hand and the rights of ownership as embodied in a stock certificate on the other hand are sketched also in the subsection on the legitimacy of power. When this first separation of functions took place in England in the seventeenth and eighteenth centuries, the people who managed the stocks of goods were almost always the ones who possessed stock certificates.

The first two-thirds of this century has seen rapid and fundamental changes in the private control of business corporations. As the century opened, the great businesses were identified with one person, family, or small group of wealthy and powerful persons. By the early 1930s, the separation of ownership and control of the large businesses, the second separation, had become so well accepted that Adolf A. Berle, writing in 1959, was surprised at the attention attracted by the book, *The Modern Corporation and Private Property*, which he and Gardiner C. Means had published in 1932. Since then the concentration of wealth in the hands of a limited number of corporate businesses has continued to be an important, well-documented feature of economic organization. Along with the growth of the size, productivity, and technical competence among business units, there has been a corresponding growth in the number of government agencies that control, coordinate, and even foster the growth of specific industries. New forms of technical and financial controls have been worked out in the interests of the general public and the business units themselves.

Neither of these two great functional separations of ownership and control has yet strongly eroded the public faith or the belief that stockholders have a legitimate right to elect directors of the corporations whose voting shares they own and that the directors so elected have the right to determine general corporate policies. In colonial America of the early eighteenth century and later in the nineteenth century the right of stockholders to vote their shares seems only to have been questioned if one person would come to dominate the corporation.[11] However, with few exceptions corporations were "closed" or closely held as the term is understood today.

There are only a few very large closely held corporations remaining in the United States. The three largest closely held corporations have annual sales estimated at more than $1 billion; another six have estimated sales of $500 million to $1 billion and seventeen have estimated annual sales of $250 million to $500 million.[12]

Voting by Proxy

Under English common law, proxy votes at corporate meetings were not permitted. The English law developed around municipal and other nonprofit corporations. In the colonial period, proxy votes were authorized in a very few cases. In 1812 a Massachusetts court upheld the use of proxies, but as late as 1834 the New Jersey Supreme Court ruled that they were invalid. When corporations were generally very small and personal organizations, some stockholders apparently took a dim view of absenteeism at such meetings. Voting on business matters required considerable personal judgment and could no more be passed on to an agent than a person's right to vote in a political election.[13]

As more corporations became widely held, the proxy vote grew in importance. Some of the early twentieth century abuses of the proxy were brought to public attention by such works as William Z. Ripley's, *Main Street and Wall Street*.[14] The efforts of Professors Ripley, Hadley, Berle, and others bore fruit in the passage of the Securities Act of 1933, called the "Truth-in-Securities" law,[15] and the Securities Exchange Act of 1934.

Power of Financial Intermediaries and Legitimacy of Their Voting of Stocks

What approaches to the analysis of the rapidly changing conditions that are centralizing or reconcentrating so much corporate ownership and control in the hands of financial intermediaries are most likely to bear results? One traditional (political) approach is to analyze the actual and potential power that financial intermediaries and the persons who vote corporate stock in these organizations are accumulating. The question of the legitimacy and other dimensions of the power that is flowing to these persons and organizations will be discussed here. As problems and conflicts occur such questions call forth more public attention.

A second basic (sociological) approach to the analysis of tensions and social change is to observe how such disturbances lead to structural differentiation and development. Some structural or organizational developments arise from problems that were originally unrelated or only tenuously related to other structures on which they later impinge. The developments related to the provision of information are especially useful and interesting as a background for understanding some of the major themes summarized by Berle and Means in their book, *The Modern Corporation and Private Property*.

The rapid growth of stock ownership in general and portfolio concentration in particular is very likely to upset the widely accepted equilibrium in the area of corporate control. The number of stocks listed on the NYSE grew from 377 in 1900 to 1,293 by 1930 and to 1,767 in 1968. American Telephone and Telegraph had 10,000 stockholders in 1901; 586,000 in 1930; and 3,142,100 in 1968. The voting of stock by owners is widely recognized as being a ritual that has no function as far as the vast majority of stockholders are concerned. The reasons for this belief are illustrated in the typical "stockholder pyramid" for two major corporations, as shown in Table 46. The control of voting by second parties so distantly related to the original savers or investors may initiate a fundamental rethinking of the relationship between the risk and reward from ownership of corporate stock and the control of these business units. The study, analysis, or even projection of the processes of continuing structural differentiation and the achievement of a new equilibrium will utilize conceptual developments in that part of sociology known as the theory of social action.

The conceptual and analytical frameworks of Talcott Parsons and Neil J. Smelser in *Economy and Society* will be utilized[16] to discuss prospective institutional developments. First, however, the present and prospective financial, political, and institutional situation of the stockholders, financial intermediaries, and corporations will be discussed in terms of power relationships. Frameworks for the "analysis of power" have developed rapidly since about 1950, with the work of political scientists like Robert A. Dahl and Behavioral scientists like Dorwin Cartwright and Herbert A. Simon.[17]

In 1959 Adolf A. Berle wrote of power: "It has had comparatively little philosophical analysis. There is (so far as the writer is aware) no presently accepted theory of power."[18] Berle does not define power directly but recognizes that it implies relationships that are observable between individuals, groups, or sociopolitical structures;[19] he contented himself with pointing out some direct and indirect effects of power in action, the limitation and control of economic power, the legitimacy of economic power, and the relation between economic and political power.[20] The earlier well-known book by Berle and Means, *The Modern Corporation and Private Property,* includes no explicit discussion of power.[21] Only a small portion of this book is concerned directly with economic concentration; its chief concern is with the legal rights of the stockholders and the imperative need to provide more financial information for prospective and existing stockholders.[22] The other major theme in this book, the relative power of the sovereign state and business corporations, recurs in Berle's later works.

When Professors Berle and Means published *The Modern Corporation and Private Property* in 1932, life insurance companies did not own common stock; the diversified investment companies were in a struggling, embryonic state; and only a few, small corporate pension funds existed. Some of the implications of the growth of regulated investment companies and corporate pension funds were apparent to A. A. Berle, Father Paul Harbrecht, Robert Tilove, and others by the end of the 1950s. The very title of Adolf A. Berle's 1959 book, *Power Without Property,* distills the following message which is repeated in numerous ways in this series of essays:

> We have noted that the financial power to determine who shall manage a corporation and, within limits, to influence the policy of such management rests with the holders of the common stock. We have seen that the holdings of common stock are gradually—or perhaps rather rapidly—beginning to be concentrated in the professional managers of the pension trust funds and mutual funds... .Power over management is power over the accumulation and handling of risk capital. We thus dimly discern the outlines of a permanently concentrated group of officials holding a paramount and virtually unchallenged power position in the American industrial economy.[23]

Paul P. Harbrecht, S.J., stresses his belief that power inevitably follows property. He goes over the same ground as Berle but adds that in our "paraproprietal society" the authority or power of pensioners over the managers is very little. The pensioner must look to union and government officials to protect his rights.[24] Another 1959 report, *Pension Funds and Economic Freedom* by Robert Tilove, stressed the sensational growth of private pension funds and raised two questions about their potential impact on economic freedom. The first is concerned with their impact on labor mobility, and the second with the concentration of economic power in the hands of the pension funds.[25]

The actual and potential power that the owners of voting stock—whether trustees or not—can exercise over business units is not to be doubted. The recent extent and expected increases of general and "inner" portfolio concentration ratios have been developed. The magnitude of the power of these concentrated stock holdings over the affairs of corporations will be increasing but may carry with it the germ of its own creative destruction.

Power relationships and applications

Before developing some of the characteristics and dimensions of power relationships and their potential importance, a working definition of power is needed. Cartwright quotes seven definitions of power, two of which seem especially useful to this analysis.

> Power may be defined as the capacity of an individual or group of individuals, to modify the conduct of other individuals or groups in the manner which he desires. [Tawney]

> Power may be defined as the realistic capacity of a system-unit to actualize its "interests" (attain goals, prevent undesired interference, command respect, control possessions, etc.) within the context of system-interaction and in this sense to exert influences on processes in the system. [Parsons][26]

Robert Dahl has stressed such dimensions of power as its magnitude, distribution, scope, domain, resources, skill, motivation, and costs.[27] Cartwright constructs a working set of power relations from an examination of the "primitives" that make up his system. In this way he avoids defining power in terms of itself.[28]

A description and analysis of some of the power relationships (or potential relationships) between the financial intermediaries and their portfolio corporations is useful to an understnading of problems that exist now or that may develop or become more important during the remainder of the twentieth century. Those relationships or problems that may lead to further structural or institutional differentiation will be stressed.

One of the essential features of power analysis is the repertory of potential acts. Two fundamental acts of the financial intermediary are: (1) to buy, sell, or hold the shares of its portfolio companies, and (2) to vote these shares. The major questions on which stockholders vote are: the annual elections of members of boards of directors, and mergers.[29]

The purchase, holding, or sale of shares and the resulting effect on immediate price fluctuations are likely to be of minor concern to corporate financial managers unless some event such as a merger is a near-term prospect. Investment companies report being consulted by their portfolio companies on such matters as merger proposals, selection of officers and directors, and even dividend policy and financing.[30] The secular growth of portfolio concentration is increasing the magnitude of the power of financial intermediaries in general. The actual and future potential power of mutual fund complexes and of the trust departments of commercial banks—because of the absence of any operational constraints on the extent of their portfolio concentration ratios—is unbounded.

The stockholders' second fundamental act is to vote their shares. Proxies have almost always been voted for management but occasionally they are voted against management on such proposals as stock options for management or preemptive rights on new stock offers.[31] In proxy fights for corporate control, antimanagement groups solicit the proxies of investment companies, and occasionally concerted action with other stockholders is undertaken.[32] The extent to which such proxies have been solicited and the positions taken by officers in financial intermediaries is not known. However, as the power of the financial intermediaries grows, such solicitations may be expected to increase in frequency and intensity.

Several of the other service functions of financial intermediaries are interrelated to the repertory of potential acts. The diversified investment companies are the most limited in this regard; they sell their investment services to the public and invest their funds primarily in common stock and securities convertible into such stock. The life insurance companies' and property and casualty insurance companies' major concern is protection against insurable risks. About 6 per cent of their assets are invested in corporate stock and about 36 per cent in corporate bonds and notes. The question may be raised as to whether or not investment in a corporation's stock influences the extent of its investment in its bonds or notes or vice versa. In the case of marketable corporate bonds, resale of the securities in the secondary markets does not affect the financial resources of the corporation itself. Privately placed notes are also occasionally traded. Neither as an insurer nor as the owner of these corporate securities is an insurance company likely to obtain any special financial information.

A commercial bank has many and complex relationships with its corporate customers; it provides checking accounts, savings accounts, short-term loans, credit information, foreign banking, trust services, and many other services. The credit relationship with customers is especially important because by this means bank officials become privy to corporate plans and usually receive regular reports that may not be available to holders of the public issues of the corporation's securities. The position taken by some banking officers that ownership of a corporation's stock and a credit relationship with the corporation—the extension, increase, decrease, or cancellation of loans—are unrelated operations is difficult to accept. The senior officers in charge of a bank's trust department are well acquainted with the officers of the industrial loan departments and meet both formally and informally.[33] Whether or not commercial banks will be able to continue to keep their decisions in lending absolutely separate from their trust operations is an open question. Various political and behavioral theorists have asserted that there is a tendency for power to spread over the range of potential acts. This double relationship sharply magnifies the "resources" that increase the ability of the bank, or its officers, to influence or affect corporate policies. The importance of short-term loans to business corporations is often so crucial that the bank gains prestige and potential power in all of its different roles or relationships with the borrower. At critical junctures such as a "credit crunch" or business reversal the borrower's alternative sources of funds may be greatly restricted.

The magnitude of the power or influence of investment companies and commercial banks over portfolio corporations is greater than that strictly indicated by the proportion of common stock which they own. They may be able to name one or more of the candidates for the board of directors and may even be consulted about appointments of senior officers. In those corporations in which cumulative voting is used, voting blocks of about 10 per cent or more are assured of placing one or more directors on the board.[34] As the portfolio concentrations increase—and especially holdings of the four to twelve organizations with the greatest holdings—these financial intermediaries will come to wield greater actual and potential influence whether or not that is their objective.

The boards of directors set the general policies of corporations in such matters as research and development, mergers, rate of growth and methods of financing expansion, development of international business, plant location, advertising, relations with unions, attitudes and practices towards minority groups, and outlays for protection of the physical environment.

The power of a corporate board of directors is very great; the larger the business, the more widespread its implications may be. However, the power of a corporation and that of its directors is limited by the pattern of market competition it faces, by federal, state, and local laws, and especially by the sanction or efficiency indicator of net income or—more popularly—profits. Some social and political commentators are overly impressed by a corporation's arbitrary power to set prices and establish the quality of its product, as well as by the quantity and variety of its output. They neglect the fact that an adequate rate of return consistent with the firm's risk class is essential for continued, efficient operation. The range of corporate power is constrained also by the widely accepted and rational goal of maximizing net present worth or wealth. When such maximizing is sought within recognized social, political, and legal environments, it can be strongly argued that firms are striving to reach efficiency in an economic sense.[35] Since about 1950 the technique of financial management known as capital budgeting in private enterprise—and as cost-benefit analysis in public enterprise—has improved vastly and has become widely accepted by major business corporations. Capital budgeting, which is designed to improve investment decisions within given environmental and policy constraints is designed to maximize simultaneously the value of a firm's stock and its economic efficiency.[36] One reason that such techniques are adopted is that they are consistent with the goals of the firm and the achievement of efficiency-oriented internalized value systems of corporate officers and other decision-making employees.

There are two additional questions concerning the distribution and legitimacy of the power—authority, influence, or persuasion—which the financial intermediaries have over their portfolio companies because of their stock holdings; this power is reinforced by other role relationships. The first concerns the operational meaning or importance of the redistribution of power from individual stockholders to financial intermediaries. Although the ritual elections have served to legitimize the position and actions of corporate directors, persons in such corporate roles and their critics have expressed uneasiness about it. Other ways of legitimizing the roles of directors, for instance comparing them with trustees, have been suggested.

Corporate directors presumably either do or should reflect the views of those who elect them in much the same way that elected public officials reflect the will of their electors. Both public officials and corporate directors have to run for reelection, but the voting records and general policy orientation of the latter group are seldom available to their "constituents."

A second question which may appropriately be asked is whether or not those employees of the financial intermediaries who vote for corporate directors and on other policy matters vote as the ultimate stockholders would have voted. How would the ultimate stockholder, whose voting power is displaced, vote on such matters as stock options? Pension plans for officers? Or mergers? What would the displaced stockholder say about preemptive rights? Whom would he recommend for a seat on the board of directors? The answers to such questions are not apparent, but owners of investment company shares and more especially participants in corporate pension plans are very probably members of lower socioeconomic groups than those who are actively voting their shares; and substantial differences in voting and policy recommendations would be expected.

Of course, the votes on corporate stock could be passed through the financial intermediaries to the "ultimate owners," but the administrative problems, the costs involved, and the burden on the ultimate stockholder seem to make such a solution impractical. These problems are too obvious to require much expansion. Consider how many people participate in a pension plan, own shares in one or more open-end investment companies, and have insurance policies with two or more different companies. Each person would be called upon to vote the proxies for several hundred different companies each year. Reading the proxy materials, doing the research required to make informed choices, and voting would be close to a full-time occupation in itself.[37] The developing distribution of power is clearly different from that pictured earlier in this century about the separation of ownership and control. The skill of the financial institutions and their officers generally is believed to be greater than that of the voter whom they have displaced. This skill element adds to the resources—as this term is used in the analysis of power—by which the financial intermediaries influence their portfolio companies.

Legitimacy of power

Professor Berle raises the pervasive question of the legitimacy of power and especially that of concentrated economic power. He applies this concept at two levels: (1) the use or exercise of power by any individual or institution; and (2) "...the legitimacy of the existence and use of the power itself."[38] The right of the political state or—roughly—polity, as Talcott Parsons uses the term, to impose its will on business units is not questioned. The fact that business units themselves need power in order to bring resources together, organize their efficient use, and sell the product is not questioned. Such uses of power are accepted as legitimate.

However, the changing locus of stock ownership and other developments in the economy and the society do call into question the legitimacy—the fitness or the appropriateness—of the influence and voting power of financial intermediaries over portfolio companies. One point to recall from earlier chapters is that the representatives of investment companies, pension funds, and commercial banks uniformly disavowed any interest in taking over or managing companies when stock was acquired for investment purposes. One of my correspondents went so far as to suggest that "the pension fund administrator will have fallen heir to a new responsibility, one that he may not want or be qualified to handle."[39] Their only interest is the income from the ownership of common stock, which is needed to fulfill the various responsibilities of the different types of financial intermediaries.

In general, establishment and maintenance of legitimate power are based on cultural values; on social or organizational sturctures, especially those involving a hierarchy of authority; and on designation by a legitimizing agent or procedure. That a person may obtain the ownership of property, including the rights to its use, disposal, and fruits, has long been established in western society and can be traced back towards the dawn of civilization. Only a very few points need be made here that relate to the origins of the modern corporation and the rights of shareholders.

In his *Wealth of Nations,* which was first published in 1776, Adam Smith discussed both the "sacred rights of private property" and the developments in the forms of business organization. He wrote, "The property which every man has in his own labour, as it is the original foundation of all other property, so it is the most sacred and inviolable."[40] In a later section of that work Adam Smith described and evaluated three of the legal forms of business organization of his time: regulated companies, private copartneries, and joint stock companies. Each of these organizational forms represents a step toward the modern corporation as it has been developed in the United States.

The companies (associations or groups in today's terms) of merchants who traded upon their own stocks of merchandise at their own risk, but agreed to submit to the regulations of the company, were called regulated companies. Smith discusses the history of each of the five regulated companies in foreign trade that existed then. "When they traded upon joint stocks [of goods] and each member sharing in the common profit or loss in proportion to his share of stock, they are called joint stock companies."[41] The liability or potential loss was limited to the stock used in the enterprise. In a copartnery, each partner was bound by the debts of the whole; but he could, after proper warning, demand payment for his share of the common stock (of goods). In the joint stock company, a person could trade his share to another person without the consent of the other members. "The value of a share in a joint stock company is always the price it will bring in the market."[42]

The joint stock companies were managed by a court of directors. In a copartnery each partner had an equal voice or vote. This practice initially was carried over into the joint stock company but was changed to voting by number of shares or "interests," in the terminology of the day, owned in the joint stock company; this latter practice was followed in the East India Company.[43] The practice of one vote per share was adopted in special corporate-enabling legislation authorized in North Carolina and Massachusetts before 1800 and in the first general corporate-enabling legislation adopted in the state of New York in 1822.

In legal theory, a corporation is a person or entity in its own right. The stockholder owns shares in the corporation, and the corporation owns and operates property. This earlier structural differentiation may be viewed as the separation of the direct and indirect control of property. The separation of ownership and control, as characterized by Berle and Means, was the next great step in structural differentiation. Is there any reason to believe that structural evolution in this area is now complete?

The right to the rewards from the use of property, the risk of loss, and the right to a voice in the management of that property have been built into our forms of business organization through their historical developments.

Private property and its owner's control of it have been justified on the grounds that it is indispensable to increasing production and for providing a personal economic security for the aged and widowed.[44] Lutheranism, Calvinism, and other religious doctrines tied earthly prosperity and heavenly election together. Work, prosperity, and property were legitimized by religious sanction.[45]

The philosophic and legal history of property is traced from the Greeks and the Romans by the preeminent legal scholar, Roscoe Pound.[46] The six theories that he identifies as the bases men have constructed to account for the social and legal institution of private property are: (1) natural-law theories, (2) metaphysical theories, (3) historical theories, (4) positive theories, (5) psychological theories, and (6) sociological theories.[47] In sociological theories property "is a social institution based upon an economic need in a society organized through a division of labor."[48] In a social-utilitarian view, property is justified insofar as it maximizes the satisfaction of human rights and interests; property in this sense is based on sound and wise social engineering and is, according to Pound, justified by its results. He sees it as an institution that is still unfolding and believes that human wants will continue to be best served by its maintenance. In the future theories of private property may combine social-utilitarian and modified economic-functional beliefs.

Private property and the rights of individuals to control and use it have been legitimized by the authority of philosophic arguments, political states, and religious and legal systems. Private property, including the right to vote corporate stock and to receive the rewards from the ownership of that property, is imbedded very deeply in our social structure and cultural values. However, the institution of private property is continuing to change. Private property will be increasingly justified or legitimized on the basis of its ability to satisfy the wants of individuals and the society of which they are a part.

The immediate relationship between labor and private property in productive or capital goods such as that found in early nineteenth century factories has been dwindling in relative importance. In the United States by the turn of this century, the stock of most large corporations was held primarily by their founding families or business groups. The legitimacy of the relation between the ownership and control of property through corporate stock on one hand and the right to receive the rewards and to sustain the risk on the other hand was still largely unchallenged. By the fourth decade of the century stock ownership had become so widely diffused that the relation between the ownership of stock and the right to vote for the corporate directors could be characterized as a ritual. The overwhelming majority of stockholders understood the essential nature of the ritual vote, but their concern was with the expected return—both in dividends and through capital appreciation—from the ownership of those shares.

As the open-end investment companies started to grow spectacularly in the 1940s and the corporate pension funds a few years later, an essentially new element appeared in the structure of property ownership. Shares accumulated in the hands of financial intermediaries[49] are held for the millions of persons who purchase investment company shares or are members of pension plans. The concern of these millions or tens of millions of persons is with their expected returns or benefits from the ownership of shares.[50]

If one listens to the officials of these organizations, their concern is also primarily with the returns on the shares and not with voting control and influence on policies. The ancient and legitimizing connection between control of property and the risk and reward from such ownership has been distorted and weakened, if not actually broken. As the proportion of the total market value of the stock owned by financial intermediaries increases and as portfolio concentration ratios continue to grow, the distortion and weakening of the voting ritual which legitimizes the power of corporate managers will become clearer. It is difficult to say at what point the tensions in the structure of ownership will break the function of control of property away from the return on property. Some events that the recognition of that rupture may cause can be suggested. Many of these events, tensions, or problems are already present.

Voting Control of Property and Return on Property

Many aspects of the actual and potential control that comprise the magnitude, range, scope, and resources of the power or influence of investment companies and bank trust departments over their portfolio companies have been developed. Before considering some tensions in these relationships, the interesting and symptomatic problems emerging for state and local pension funds will be considered.

State and local pension funds

Evidence in Table 39 showed that the stock held by state and local pension funds is expected to increase to about $37 billion by 1980 and to $357 billion by the year 2000. The stock held by this group of institutions is growing faster than that held by any other group. By 2000 they will be third in terms of the total market value of stock owned. There are safeguards to keep portfolio concentration ratios at very modest levels for each individual fund.

Who will determine how the shares owned by state and local pension funds will be voted? What position should the state-appointed investment board take on an increase in stock options for management? Or when a dissident group of stockholders tries to gain their support to win the control of a company? Or if one company makes a tender offer for the stock of another? These boards usually include some members of the legislature itself.

The problems will be more complex if one of the companies has important operations within the state where a pension fund owns 1 to 2 per cent of its stock. The combined holdings in the company of several public pension funds in the state could be considerably higher. Extreme tensions could also develop if two firms within a state are involved in a merger and if any state funds own stock in one or both companies involved. The personal holdings of some members of the investment board and the business connections of legislators may compound an already complex situation. In such a case the number or percentage of shares held might be less important than the positions and influence of some of the persons involved.

Such complex relationships are not purely imaginary. The Iowa Public Employees Retirement System (I.P.E.R.S.) owned 3,500 shares of Iowa Power and Light Company of Des Moines.[51] That company and Iowa-Illinois Gas and Electric Company, which has its headquarters in Davenport, Iowa, were in the process of merging. The details of the proposed merger had been discussed in the *Des Moines Register* for more than a year. The *Register* reported interviews with three members of the I.P.E.R.S. Advisory Investment Board:

> The I.P.E.R.S. board executive secretary, William F. Poorman of Des Moines, said he was not enthusiastic about the merger. . . .Iowa Power has its financing very well taken care of for the next several years. . .while Iowa-Illinois still has a lot of financing to do. . . ."If I had a block of Iowa-Illinois stock, I would have less trouble making up my mind." Mr. Poorman, who is the chairman of the board of a large life insurance company in Des Moines, had served on the I.P.E.R.S. board for many years without salary. State Senator James W. Griffen of Council Bluffs said "the merger is definitely to their [Iowa-Illinois'] advantage."

The fact that the treasurer of Iowa-Illinois, whose wife is a state representative from Davenport, had recently been appointed to the powerful State Board of Regents presents another complication in the case.

How many times will such incidents with their intense personal and political conflicts multiply in the years to come? If alleged conflicts of interest of persons in public life continue to become the subject of increasingly intense scrutiny, how will these conflicts be reduced or resolved? In fact, many persons may come to object to having public officials, whether elected or appointed, vote on matters that are in the realm of private business policy.

Several states, for instance Hawaii, use bank trust departments as investment advisers. Legislation which would impower such trust departments to vote the shares held by state and local pension funds might improve the local political situation but could increase the bank's potential or actual influence over portfolio companies. The voting record of the banks in these cases and its general record in voting stock could move into the domain of public information.

The returns from share ownership are needed to reduce the cost of providing future benefits. The problems related to voting shares of pension funds are not only the costs that are involved. Even in the best of circumstances they will turn out to be increasingly a source of embarrassment to state and local governments. In the worst of circumstances, the voting and control aspect of the ownership of shares could be a source of scandal and a target for confrontation by a variety of dissident citizens.

1970 project on corporate responsibility

Several related points are illustrated by "Campaign GM," launched by consumer protectionist Ralph Nader and his associates. They proposed that General Motors add three public members to its board of directors and establish a shareholders' committee on corporate responsibility. They then went out to try to get the votes for their proposal. They obtained a 7 per cent vote for their proposals. Geoffrey Cowan, one of the organizers, said at the General Motors annual stockholders' meeting, "Campaign GM has been designed to test the ability of large corporate and financial institutions in their increasingly monopolistic and bureaucratic forms to respond to the needs of the public and the wishes of shareholders."[52] In a sense General Motors was a poor target for their campaign because institutional investors probably own only a small percentage of the outstanding shares, and there are no very large concentrations.

The political and public policy issues made evident by Campaign GM are pertinent. Mayor Lindsay of New York City said that GM stock held by New York City pension funds would be voted for the Nader proposals. The officials of the Iowa Public Employees Retirement System were interviewed and announced that they would also vote for the consumer protection proposals. However, when the issue was brought before the Iowa Board of Regents they refused to order the University of Iowa and Iowa State University to vote for the Nader proposals.

A student referendum at the University of Pennsylvania was favorable to the consumer protection proposals and the University's investment committee ordered its stock to be voted for the proposal. Ralph Nader and two General Motors executives campaigned on the campus of M.I.T. for the votes on that university's 295,000-share block of stock; M.I.T.'s holdings of GM stock were reported to be the largest of any university. The regents of the University of Michigan, the University of California, and the University of Texas are all reported to have considered the Nader proposals and come out against them. A number of other universities, for example, Harvard, Yale, and Brown, also considered how to vote for the addition of three public members to the GM board of directors. The Rockefeller Foundation decided to vote its 100,000 shares of GM stock for management after an intense debate, according to Jay Rockefeller, a descendant of the founders of Standard Oil, a member of the Foundation's Board, and Secretary of State of West Virginia.[53]

Investment companies

The power or influence of investment company complexes seems to be based primarily upon the magnitude of their individual and collective portfolio concentrations. The skill of the individual investment company's analysts and officers is another power resource.

The very existence of investment company voting power in concentrated blocks of 7 to 15 per cent, as shown in Tables 13 through 17, prevents them from being neutral on many policy issues that concern their portfolio companies or those who would take over these companies.

The *Study of Mutual Funds* reports that one-fourth of the open-end companies responding to the SEC survey stated that they always returned their proxies to the management. Other companies study proposals from minority stockholders carefully but rarely vote for them.[54] A large investment company explained its policy of supporting the management of portfolio companies:

> The basic reason for this policy is that the corporation is engaged in investing and not in the management of companies or the reorganization or

revamping of businesses or corporate managements. . . .Without reasonable confidence in a management, no investment will be made. Action in supporting that management at annual meetings is. . .normal and natural.[55]

However, the range of power extends far beyond the ritual act of voting. As noted in the earlier section on power relationships, portfolio companies sometimes consult with open-end investment companies on such matters as dividend policy, financing, mergers, and the selection of officers and directors. The reason for naming these four specific areas of influence is that they are the areas included in the questionnaire sent to investment companies.[56] Other matters on which discussions may have taken place, such as new products, plant expansion, international business, closing plants, employment practices, and environmental control, are not mentioned. This study referred to events prior to June 30, 1958. How have the volume and range of these consultations changed since that date? At what rate will they grow in the future?

Starting about 1965 the great movement toward mergers and conglomeration has forced itself into public consciousness by the extent to which it has reorganized the familiar corporate scene. The role that investment companies have played in these massive adjustments is not known, but they must certainly have been consulted by the different parties involved in the mergers. Groups of open-end companies prior to 1958 occasionally discussed problems of their portfolio companies and even took some concerted action.[57] How frequent have such consultations and concerted actions become since 1958? The effectiveness of such actions will clearly increase as the total and inner portfolio concentration ratios increase. Concerted actions reported were by investment companies but included "other large stockholders." As shown in Tables 43 and 44 the power of the holdings of a few commercial bank trust departments when combined with a few investment companies would be extremely influential. For an increasing number of portfolio companies such informal groups would clearly have working control and as we approach the year 2000 numerous instances of absolute majority control will develop.

Commercial banks

The range of power of state and local pension funds and open-end investment companies is slight when compared to that of commercial banks as described in the section on power relationships. The traditional and basic element in the power of banks is their ability to extend or reject short-term loans. The skill of the bank's officers in transferring funds at home and overseas, in gathering credit information, and in evaluating potential merger partners all contribute to the bank's power base. The respect that bankers have among their customers, their moral standing, and their well-being contribute to their influences. The funneling of corporate pension funds to bank trust departments has added to this power or influence base.

The influence of the trust department and other bank officers on such basic matters of corporate policy as dividends, timing of financing, mergers, and selection of officers and directors has not, to the author's knowledge, been documented. The extent of bankers' influence on these and other matters may be brought to light by some state or federal investigation. Meanwhile, as their pension fund trusts expand, so does that part of their power which relates to voting the stock of their portfolio companies. By the year 2000 these stock holdings for pension funds will amount to more than $2 trillion. Unless state and federal regulations are changed the details of these vast holdings will remain secret!

The approaching separation of voting control and return on property

The responses by bankers to the author's survey indicated some awareness of the problem of portfolio concentration, but they were much more concerned with diversification of share ownership in order to minimize the income and price risk. Voting power may be neither needed nor wanted, but they possess it. Investment companies also emphasized the importance of income from the ownership of stocks and disavowed any interest in control, yet they have power and influence over portfolio companies. This power is exercised individually and at times jointly. State and local pension funds also want the higher income from owning shares but will increasingly find their voting power and influence a disadvantage and source of embarrassment for numerous reasons, including that of government ownership of business.

If these powerful financial intermediaries owning 20, 30, 40 per cent or even more of the stock of hundreds of companies do not want that power, what can be done about it? On what basis can the legitimacy of the control of these great business organizations be justified? The ownership of property has traditionally involved both the control of that property and the right to receive the income thereof. Now as the control of medium-sized, rapidly growing businesses falls increasingly into the hands of those who want the income but either do not want or disavow the increasing power, these two functions may be on the verge of splitting or coming to reside in different institutions.

The financial intermediaries want the income but not the voting control. If these institutions did not vote their shares, progressively smaller holdings of stocks outside of these institutions could control these large corporations. Such a solution—especially if and when control fell into the hands of financial buccaneers—would not be an acceptable one either to the financial intermediaries or the remaining small, independent stockholders.

If the portfolio concentrations grow as projected, the emptiness of the ritual that is intended to legitimize the economic power of corporations will be obvious. The connections between work, property, control, and reward no longer exist in many kinds of modern business activity. Once the holy bond is broken what can replace it? In other terms, the changes in cultural values and social structure, as well as the impending breakdown of the ritual that legitimizes corporate power, increase the tensions in the existing institutional structures.

New Structures to Legitimize the Voting-Reward Separation

Structural differentiation

As the productivity of our economy has increased, there has been a corresponding growth in the size and complexity of business units and in the associated public and private infrastructure. The legal and internal organization of business units has been changing rapidly, although maintaining a shifting equilibrium. Neither business nor social disorganization has developed in countries such as the United States because of stability associated with their underlying or fundamental beliefs. These fundamental beliefs, which include private ownership of property and purposeful human activity, change more slowly than particular institutions or the immediate goals of the economy or polity. The economy, including its business units, adapts to such pressures as the growth of labor unions, the relative decline of agriculture, the pervasive changes that follow scientific developments, and the growth in the relative size of business units. In response to these changes there has been structural differentiation both in business and in government or, in other terms, in private and public institutions. There is a continuous process of rationalization and structural differentiation.

In their discussion of the problems of growth and institutional change, Parsons and Smelser say: "We would like to reformulate the process of rationalization as the tendency of social systems to develop progressively higher levels of structural differentiation under the pressure of adaptive experiences."[58] The process of structural differentiation occurs over protracted periods of time such as decades or centuries. The Great Depression of the early 1930s, for example, gave rise to a number of new structures that are still developing. The need for old-age pensions and other forms of social insurance had been discussed for at least three decades in the United States and initial measures had already been adopted in other countries before the Social Security Act was passed in 1935.[59] Over the next thirty years, the range of employment covered under the act was progressively increased, but not until 1965 were medical benefits for the aged adopted by means of the Medicare and Medicaid programs.[60]

In the process of structural differentiation, one organization or institutionalized procedure splits into two parts. Parsons and Smelser illustrate this process with the differentiated functions of "ownership" and "control" in American big business.[61] The "functions" of voting control and monetary reward are both still tied to the ownership of corporate stock, but for most widely held corporations control through voting has become ritualized. The political basis of corporate control remains an essential consideration, and the legitimizing theories received from the eighteenth and nineteenth centuries have been maintained.

Stockholders, government, and critics all insisted that the stockholders be given adequate financial information and clear proxies so that they could maintain at least the fiction of control. Most shareholders applauded the 1933 "Truth-in-Securities Act" because they believed that it would help them to determine when to buy, hold, or sell shares, rather than because it would help them to vote intelligently on the issues covered by proxies. The fiction of the legitimacy of corporate power was bolstered, but there was also a new structural differentiation in the polity, namely the Securities and Exchange Commission (SEC). Ownership carries with it the reality of monetary risk and reward and the fiction of management control. The underlying disturbances that led to the establishment of the SEC were the widening of share ownership during the preceding thirty years, the malpractices or the high-handed practices of large numbers of corporations in disregard of their small or minority owners, the need for greatly improved financial statements, and the belief that economic units are and should be subject to the general control of the political state. The social crisis of the Great Depression and the advent of a new administration in 1933 were the immediate events that led to the establishment of the SEC. Since then its own actions to gain greater control over financial practices and its responses to dynamic developments in both corporate enterprise and the financial markets have led to its continued growth.

The developments behind the present stage and continuing growth of portfolio concentration in the hands of financial intermediaries may precipitate a more profound crisis than the separation of ownership and control. The two functions of ownership most likely to split are the power of revitalized voting control and the monetary risk and rewards of ownership. Some possible immediate causes that may lead to differentiation of these two functions will be suggested below. The underlying disturbances responsible for the growth of the different financial intermediaries and of portfolio concentration ratios have been discussed in detail; some of the reasons why the legitimacy of voting power of these financial intermediaries may now be open to question have been suggested also. Other fundamental causes of the impending differentiation are the changes in the value systems of Americans and the realities of poverty, pollution, and technological change. How these changes, experiences, and the related tensions develop will help to determine the specific form that the probable separation of the rights of control and reward inherent in the ownership of voting stock will take.

Initial steps toward separation

The separation of the income from stock ownership and the right to elect directors and to vote on such matters as new issues of stock, stock options, hiring of public accountants, and mergers may occur first in state and local pension funds, in investment companies, or in trust departments of large banks. Perhaps this first landmark in differentiation will occur because of overall high portfolio concentrations or because of technological problems in a particular industry, such as air transport.

A very modest amount of a specific stock held by a state or local pension fund may create a problem if an appointed member of the investment board has personal holdings of the same stock. Some vote on a merger may enhance his private wealth. There may be a conflict of opinion between legislators and investment board members about the appropriate vote on a specific merger or candidate for a directorship. Some outside financial group might influence the vote of an investment board member, and the fact might become public. A state employee who is a member of the pension system could raise a question about a particular vote. As in the Iowa case cited, competing business interests within the state might believe the vote on a specific issue by the investment board to be to their advantage or disadvantage. Other persons could raise the question of the appropriateness or even the constitutionality of permitting a unit of government to hold substantial amounts of voting stock. By 1980, the funds of several states will own (or hold as trustee) portfolios of more than $1 billion in stock. Such vast sums are sure to attract the attention of politicians.

Whatever the immediate cause, an attempt will be made to isolate the voting of the shares from political pressure, conflicts of interest, or other forms of influence. Initial attempts may be made to pass the unwanted voting rights into the hands of a third party, such as an actuarial firm, a firm of public accountants or lawyers, a nationally known investment house, or some other professional organization. The first case may be worked out on an *ad hoc* basis, and later such arrangements may become permanent.

Even when such steps are taken, legislators may still inquire into how the stock was voted, probably creating conflict that would reach the public awareness through newspapers, radio, and television. Hiring a third party costs money which must be deducted from the income of the state pension fund. Eventually a separate voting commission which includes members of the pension fund, legislators, and persons appointed by the governor may be authorized. Later still such a commission might develop its own professional staff.

In the case of the investment companies the separation of voting and income could come for different reasons. The voting stock of a large, widely held investment company could fall into the hands of a person or group of persons who could use the voting power for personal—and probably illegal—purposes and from such a power base sway the vote of other investment companies. A careful journalist in the future might bring several such cases to light. An SEC investigation might show how widespread questionable practices and influence over the management of portfolio companies had become.

Congressional approval or authorization

Existing law covering regulated investment companies sets the effective limit at 10 per cent of a portfolio company's stock, but this is for each investment company. Some investment company complexes owned more than 10 per cent of a portfolio company's stock by 1966 as shown in Table 17. When Congress becomes concerned about the high concentration ratios now existing and the still higher future ratios, they may order a rollback to the 10 or 15 per cent level for an investment company complex as previously suggested in this text for both bank trust departments and investment company complexes. They could also encourage or require investment company complexes to place the voting rights on all stock holdings above the authorized concentration ratio level in an independent, impartial agency with authorization to vote the shares.[62]

The extent of concentration ratios in the hands of investment companies, investment company complexes, and bank trust departments may come to public attention when a proxy fight develops for voting control of some well-known company. The impact of several such cases could move Congress to investigate the basis of these and future mergers or proxy fights involving financial intermediaries. Under such circumstances investment companies and trust departments might be very pleased to turn over part or even all of their voting rights on specific stocks to an independent, impartial agency. The financial intermediaries would be left with what they want: namely, the rewards—the income and capital gains from share ownership—and they would dispose of part (or all) of what they do not want—the voting rights.

The level of portfolio concentration ratios for trust department ownership (trusteeship) is only vaguely known. The investigations of Patman's Subcommittee on Domestic Finance gave the public its only glimpse of these ratios. The case that regular, detailed information should be available on trust departments' holdings of corporate stock for corporate pension funds was made in the last section of Chapter III. No investigations comparable to the 1958-62 *Study of Mutual Funds* have yet been made of how banks vote their stock. The desire of banks to avoid having such studies of their conduct is understandable.

Banks have such wide ranges and resources of power over the general policies and even specific decisions of business units that a separation of voting rights from the income of their stock holdings would not affect the historical bases of their power.

There are various bases for determining the maximum concentration level after which voting rights are separated from the monetary rewards of owning shares. So far the only basis which has been suggested is the portfolio concentration ratio for individual investment company complexes and individual banks. The separation of voting rights could come into force only when the aggregate, known portfolio concentration passed some predetermined level, such as 30 or 35 per cent.[63] Alternatively, the cut-off point could be established in terms of the absolute purchase price or market value of stock held by an intermediary in one portfolio company. A reasonable separation point on this basis might be in the neighborhood of $100 million. Separation of voting rights might also become effective at lower aggregate concentration ratios if and when several major companies in that industry reached a predetermined level. The separation of voting rights might be activated when the 10 per cent level was reached, for example, for any one financial intermediary. When that occurs, the voting rights for all financial intermediaries holding perhaps 5 per cent of that portfolio company's stock would pass to the Stockholders' Voting Council.

A possible organization for the impartial board will be suggested later. It is both appropriate and reasonable that the financial intermediaries should be concerned about the method and substance of such votes by the impartial board. By some mechanism, financial intermediaries that are passing on their voting rights should be able to elect a substantial proportion of the members of that board or council—which would be primarily private, rather than government—and which might be called by some name such as Stockholders' Voting Council.

Stockholders' Voting Council

The process of the structural differentiation and separation of some voting from the return on corporate shares parallels that of the initial separation of ownership and control. The total vote and total income from owning the shares is not reduced. Taken together, the same functions are performed; but part of the essential voting ritual would be carried on by the Stockholders' Voting Council. The voting on issues and other policy questions that come before the Council would be studied carefully in their own right before an action is taken or a recommendation is made. Most institutional investors that experienced directly the separation of the undesired voting rights from the desired rewards of ownership would applaud the law creating the Council. The fiction of the legitimacy of corporate power might be bolstered by the existence of the impartial Stockholders' Voting Council when its full membership and the method of electing members were developed. The Council would constitute a further *differentiation in the private section of the economy*.

The underlying disturbances that will lead to this Council include the growing portfolio concentrations, recognized as early as 1950, in the hands of financial intermediaries. There may be a span of thirty years or more from the recognition of the problem to the tension-reducing structural differentiation. The malpractices or high-handed practices of some financial intermediaries, public awareness of the problems involved, and the belief that such enormous amounts of economic power should not be concentrated in a small number of financial intermediaries and their officials will contribute to a crisis situation. The understanding that the power base of these financial intermediaries is several steps removed form the ancient and sacred bond of property, risk, reward, and control that existed when the nation was founded will heighten the traditional American fear of such concentrated economic and financial power. Some social crisis related to depression, poverty, pollution of the environment, technological change, or some other factor will develop, and a new administration will be elected. Such a combination is likely to form the immediate context for the establishment of the Stockholders' Voting Council.[64]

The differentiation of voting and reward will come about fairly slowly after the first flurry of activity. One must remember that the separation of ownership and control in Berle's sense had not yet taken place for many major corporations in the 1930s. Even in the 1950s the voting control of many large and medium-sized but widely held corporations was still in the hands of one family or closely knit group. Many important corporations are still entirely closely held.[65]

Voting-reward separation and underlying value system

The initial separation of the voting from the monetary reward of stock ownership will not gain acceptance unless it is consistent with the underlying value systems that individuals form through their families and educational experiences. Some of these basic, internalized values are themselves in the process of change. The adaptive process also will have to be compatible with other growing economic and related problems. The integration of the Stockholders' Voting Council, efforts to preserve the physical environment, and other measures related to technological problems should reduce the tensions or disturbances that have become of great public concern. As the Stockholders' Voting Council gains acceptance the revised meaning and structure which legitimizes corporate power will move toward a new equilibrium.

Some of the most fundamental value patterns that our culture has internalized and seeks to maintain in individuals and in institutions are expressed in the belief in private ownership of property, purposeful human activity, and economic efficiency and economic progress, as well as a faith that making information public will contribute to the solution of problems, and a distrust of big business and of the concentration of economic and financial power in the hands of an unresponsive elite. Our belief in economic and political egalitarianism remains firm, and the government and public opinion alike seek to eradicate poverty on the one hand, and to reduce the extremes of high income and wealth on the other.

Within this fundamental structure of beliefs, some values seem to be rising and others declining. Some basic values such as the belief in purposeful activity are changing radically, as a much wider range of activities are becoming accepted than the accumulation of wealth or the dedication to religiously sanctioned activities. The signs of a more intense, variegated individuality as characterized by the "beatniks" of the early 1950s has been noted. The growing national affluence will be able to support and to encourage the continuing emergence of new groups of this sort.[66] More information is being brought into the public domain. This change applies to the private lives of ordinary citizens; it applies more searchingly to those who are or would become public servants; and it applies to the transactions of units of business and government.[67] The immediacy and intensity of television helps to personalize what is reported on it. There seems to be a continuing increase in the idealistic standards of morality demanded of those who would provide leadership in public or private offices. Technology is seen to hold both great promises and great threats for the American citizens and all peoples of the world. Technocratic planning—that is, the long-lead time planning to achieve a union of technological and economic efficiency—is gaining acceptance.[68]

Some very strongly held opinions have been receding because of the passage of time. Demonstrations in the United States and elsewhere show that some of these beliefs were untenable or irrational, and others were irrelevant to the new problems that emerged. One such pressing problem is the pollution of our air, water, and soil. Recognition of the need to maintain our physical environment has burst into public awareness during the 1960s. Some of its first manifestations were the smog that killed twenty people in Donora, Pennsylvania, in 1948,[69] the Los Angeles smog, and the fouling of Lakes Erie and Michigan. New methods and coordination of public and private efforts are essential to maintain an even tolerable environment. New and daring massive measures will probably be required well before the year 2000. The need to coordinate our efforts to maintain our physical environment, the development of financial techniques to monitor the returns to corporations and to investors, and also the technical feasibility of a systems approach to such pervading problems as urban renewal and transportation are among the factors that have contributed and will continue to contribute to the rapidly growing disillusion with *laissez faire* as a viable economic policy for the United States as the twenty-first century approaches.

Legitimacy and private property. The proposed Stockholders' Voting Council will be consistent with these basic and changing value structures. In fact, several unexpected, desirable results will emerge that will help maintain the legitimacy, efficiency, and primacy of private industry, facilitate the introduction and coordination of measures to maintain the physical environment, and improve the social and human environments. All of these adaptive possibilities will help to reduce past tensions and to further the continuation of a viable society.

The increasing portfolio concentrations held by the financial intermediaries and the very magnitude of the wealth involved will contribute to the breakdown of what legitimacy remains in the ritual voting for corporate directors and control over corporate policies. The legitimacy of private property was sanctioned by and consistent with political, legal, and religious value systems. Until fairly recent times, such individualistic control contributed positively to our economic growth and development. Third-party voting of corporate stocks—that is, voting by bankers, investment company officers, and state and local pension fund officials—breaks the "sacred" bond and concentrates power in persons and organizations that have no inherent claim to it. So far as these persons (or committees) and organizations are concerned, the voting rights are almost incidental to the monetary return needed to discharge their duties as "trustees." The great size and unresponsiveness of these public or private organizations help to undermine their acceptability and are likely to make them increasingly the targets of cults of intense individuality.

A majority of the proposed Stockholders' Voting Council would be elected directly by the individuals who are members of pension fund systems or who own investment company shares. These individuals, who are the ultimate owners of pension fund or investment company assets, would be entitled to elect the Council members when the voting rights on a stock were passed to the Stockholders' Voting Council. The Council would consider on its merits each issue on which a vote was required and each policy or appointment on which it had some contact with a portfolio corporation. The long-run interests of the ultimate stockholders would be the primary consideration. The Council would in time develop its own staff and work out methods of determining the wishes of the ultimate beneficiaries of the stock; it would be sensitive to their best interests and to their wishes.

A new political alternative

The transfer of voting power to the Stockholders' Voting Council when the portfolio concentration ratios exceeded the cut-off criteria would have five very positive and salutary results. First, the legitimacy of the power of corporate business units—or at least those affected by this process—would be restored to the hands of the ultimate owners. The voting control and policy-influencing function of the shares would be exercised in the interests of these ultimate owners. The expert staff would represent the owners well and could follow up and even initiate questions on policy matters with the consistency, energy, and skill not available to busy persons. Other groups represented on the Council would include the financial intermediaries and the federal government. The roles and concerns of these groups will be suggested later.

Second, that part of the control passed on to the Council would remain in the realm of private ownership as contrasted with government ownership. Two important consequences flow from the maintenance of private property. The first consequence is that decisions concerning such vital matters as financing, investment, innovation, employment, and the products to be manufactured would remain in the private realm. Flexibility in the use and control of productive property would not be reduced by the deadening hand of primarily governmental control. The productivity of property is, in my opinion, enhanced by a system of private property. This opinion about the social utility of private property is confirmed by the experiences of other nations that have moved away from private ownership. However, the operational meaning of "private" has been steadily changing and will continue to change. Roscoe Pound suggested the possibility of combining a social-utilitarian and economic-functional argument for private property. Such a socially engineered system based on private property would bring greater satisfactions at less sacrifice than any other system we are likely to devise.[70]

The other consequence is that the fear of socialism would be dissipated. This ideological fear now blocks many needed actions and reforms, but in the next stage of our social and industrial evolution it could be cut away if the control of productive property was not shifting toward direct government ownership. Economic necessity is forcing a shift from ideological intensity toward pragmatic needs and is leading to a wider conception of individuality and personal development. In a wealthy society, less time needs to be devoted to work, and more time and goods are available to support other activities. Work need no longer be the primary mode of self-identification.

The third result is a tendency towards restoring the legitimacy of the relationship between ownership and control. Such power as is eventually placed in the Stockholders' Voting Council flows from the votes of individuals who are the ultimate owners of the property and recipients of the benefits from its productive use. Individuals could also under particular circumstances voluntarily pass their voting rights to the Council.

A fourth result will be that the actions and recommendations of the Council will be open to the public and reported back to the individual beneficiaries. The Council itself may be expected to seek more information about corporate operations, to have a more effective voice than scattered individual owners, and to make even more information available about corporate operations and policies than is now in the public domain.

Another result would be that such power as does develop would move away from the financial intermediaries, which are seen as "big business" and largely unresponsive to the wishes of those whom they should represent, to a more responsive, personal organization. Thus some potential influence and control would be moved away from a power elite. All of these results are consistent with the basic and changing underlying value systems.

Transfer of votes to the Council

The Stockholders' Voting Council also could vote shares voluntarily transferred to it under specified conditions by state and local pension funds, insurance companies, foundations, college endowment funds, churches, and other organizations. Individual stockholders too may wish to pass on voting rights on shares they own.

Some financial intermediaries such as state and local pension funds may decide that transferring voting rights to the Stockholders' Voting Council is highly advantageous in avoiding entanglements over conflicts of interests and questions of the constitutionality or appropriateness of government ownership of any fraction of a private business. They might also find that they would be better able to avoid pressures to vote shares in a particular way on a controversial topic. Churches, college endowment funds, and other organizations are likely to welcome the opportunity to pass their voting rights on to others more competent than they to vote for corporate directors or on other matters of business policy. Certainly the main function of churches and many other organizations is not to help establish business policies.

These various financial intermediaries clearly would still have a very large stake in the continued profitability and growth of those corporations for which they passed through their voting rights. That concern is directly related to the expected dividends and market prices of the shares of these portfolio companies. These financial intermediaries and other organizations should have the right to elect one or more members to the Stockholders' Voting Council. Probably there should be one—or perhaps more—council member representing the profit-seeking financial intermediaries and another representing governmental bodies such as state and local pension funds[71] and nonprofit organizations. Private citizens also may wish to transfer some of their stock voting rights. The typical stockholder pyramid displayed in Table 46 indicates the ineffectuality of the votes of those who own one hundred or even one thousand shares in a major company. Careful and prudent voting of these shares is time consuming, even for those who have the requisite skills to understand the often very complex materials received and the policy questions involved. The opportunity costs for a person who owns only a very few shares are probably greater than the dividends he can expect to receive.

Possible minimum controls on the acceptance of voluntarily transferred voting rights, the cost of performing the voting function, and the total membership of the Council itself remain to be considered. A legally established cut-off criterion for separating votes and rewards in existing portfolio concentrations would determine the number of the stocks for which voting rights would be received by the Stockholders' Voting Council. Voluntary transfers would be accepted from any corporation for which voting rights are received by this process, but in all other cases no transfers should be accepted until the transfers tendered totaled at least 1 per cent—and perhaps higher—of the voting stock of a corporation. To accept transfers of voting rights at any lower level would be to invite operating inefficiencies and increase the average cost to the Council per portfolio voting company.

Financing Council operations

The costs of operating the Stockholders' Voting Council would come primarily from fees paid by the financial intermediaries and other organizations. Such fees could include a base amount per corporate stock of which voting rights were transferred, plus something like one-fiftieth of 1 per cent of the dividends paid on the shares. In many cases, such fees would be less than the cost of performing even a rudimentary analysis of the issues and voting the shares.

The printing, mailing, return, and tabulations of proxies has a cost. Some corporations send follow-up materials to nonrespondents. The cost per proxy could be estimated. When voting rights are voluntarily transferred to the Council by the thousands of a corporation's small stockholders, the corporation would experience a substantial saving, which should be shared with the Council. The Stockholders' Voting Council might be adequately financed by such private sources of income.

The physical process of transferring shares after a purchase or sale has been a bottleneck for several years. Improved electronic, computerized transfer systems may be confidently anticipated. Such systems will be in operation before the voting-reward separation becomes a widespread reality. The accounting mechanics of voting-reward separation will be another among many details handled by such an electronic system.

Council membership

The terms of the Council members should be at least four years, perhaps as long as ten, and should be staggered. The members, ideally, should sever all business connections and place shares of corporate stock which they own in a trust account during their term of office without knowing what stock transactions are made in their behalf. Similar safeguards should be taken to avoid any suspicion of conflict of interests for *all* employees of the Council.

The roles of all Council members except the government appointees have been described. The government appointees, among other things, would be concerned with the representation and implementation of environmental controls, with programs to foster civil rights, and with the elimination of poverty. They would be concerned also with such matters as encouraging policies on investment, wages, prices, and similar matters consistent with the general public interest. Perhaps each appointee would have some specific responsibilities.

The Council itself might consist of at least thirteen members, with the representation distributed as suggested:

Private Individuals

Owners of investment company shares and members of pension plans	5	
Individuals who transfer votes voluntarily	1	6

Financial Intermediaries (except state and local pension funds)

Investment companies	1	
Trust departments of commercial banks	1	
Insurance companies and other profit-seeking organizations	1	3

Nonprofit Organizations

State and local pension funds, foundations, etc.		1

Government (federal)

	3
	13

The membership suggested for the Stockholders' Voting Council does have a powerful precedent in the nine-member board of directors that was established by law for each of the twelve Federal Reserve Banks.[72] Each Federal Reserve Bank has three Class A, three Class B, and three Class C directors. Class A and Class B directors are elected by the member banks, which own all of the stock of the Federal Reserve Bank in their district. One director for each of these two classes is elected by the small banks, another by medium-sized banks, and the third by the large banks. The Class A directors may be bankers, but the Class B directors must not have any banking affiliation as officer, employee, or director and must be actively engaged in other businesses or agriculture in the district. The Class C directors, who also cannot have any affiliation with banking, are appointed by the Board of Governors of the Federal Reserve System. The latter has seven members who are appointed for fourteen-year terms by the President of the United States and confirmed by

Congress. The members of the Board of Governors devote full time to their positions with the Federal Reserve System.

The recommendation that three members of the Stockholders' Voting Council be appointed by whatever procedure is established probably needs little more defense than already given. The Council's stature would be enhanced if the federal appointments were made by the President and confirmed by Congress.

The development of private and public boards and agencies has undoubtedly proliferated within the memory of the reader. The growth and stature of professional accrediting and coordinating agencies in private, semiprivate (quasi-public), and mixed private-public areas is well known. The means of controlling and coordinating business have grown more complex. The special case of the airline industry was described in Chapter V because of high portfolio concentrations noted for almost all major companies. Determination of the cost of money-capital since the Hope Natural Gas case of 1944 has been the primary method or basis for evaluating the charges or prices of firms regulated as public utilities. The Securities and Exchange Commission and the Federal Trade Commission are both working toward corporate financial reporting for major product lines. Additional instances in which the independence or scope of business activity has been circumscribed by regulatory bodies could be multiplied, and the reader may add other instances out of his own knowledge.

Corporate enterprises are certainly not sovereign or independent of the polity. Higher or more complex organizations for control and coordination will continue to emerge in response to tensions and disturbances in innumerable fields. The maintenance—or improvement—of the quality of our water, air, and soil will need increasing attention and outlay. The appointment of public members to the Stockholders' Voting Council is viewed as one among many possible devices that will contribute to the continued viability of American society.

Summary

The rapid growth of portfolio concentration ratios in the hands of financial intermediaries is assured and may average about 35 per cent by 1980 and 55 per cent by 2000. Portfolio concentrations will be much higher than the average for many medium-sized rapidly growing businesses. The inner portfolio concentration ratios will grow higher whether or not the suggested reforms are enacted to limit the extent of the ownership of investment company complexes and bank trust departments.

These growing concentration ratios will increase the power of the financial intermediaries. The very extent of that power, which is no longer based upon the earlier bonds of direct ownership and control of real property, will result in challenges to the already ritualized relation between ownership and control. The banks exert more power or influence over business than the other financial intermediaries. The range and resources of banking power are augmented strongly by their growing trust business in pension funds. Such growing and concentrated financial power is inconsistent with our very deeply rooted value system. Banks aggravate this problem by their secretiveness about the extent of their stock holdings.

A separation of the voting function from monetary rewards in those instances in which the portfolio concentration ratios in individual organizations exceed a predetermined level—such as 10 per cent—will help to reduce tension and to establish a new concept of what is being balanced in equilibrium. The separated voting function would be institutionalized in an independent organization that might be called the Stockholders' Voting Council. The very existence of the Council would tend to restore the legitimacy and improve the efficiency of stockholders' control of broad corporate policies. The ultimate beneficiaries of the corporate stocks would elect almost half of the Council members. Private ownership and control of productive property—as contrasted with government ownership—with its inherent advantages for society would be assured during the next stage in the evolution of American society. The separation of functions and the increasing complexity of social organizations is consistent with what is known about the growth and development of society. The functional separation of voting and monetary rewards will be an outgrowth of many forces whose origins have been traced clearly back to the 1930s and then more faintly into earlier economic and financial developments. The exact organizational form that the voting-reward separation will take is difficult to foretell, but the structure suggested is consistent with our underlying value systems and the changes that can be foreseen. The suggested structure also considers the changing environmental needs, our increasing gross national product, and the adaptive responses of the economy to these changes. More basically, the Stockholders' Voting Council will contribute to the integration of changes in the economy and polity with the underlying and slowly changing value system.

NOTES

[1] For a most admirable summary of many of these developments and an excellent bibliography, see Robert A. Dahl, "Power," *International Encyclopedia of Social Science,* IV, 405-15.

[2] Talcott Parsons and Neil J. Smelser, *Economy and Society: A Study in the Integration of Economic and Social Theory* (New York: Free Press, 1956). The "Sociology Bibliography" at the end of this book lists other major works of Professor Parsons and his various co-authors as well as other selected references, pp. 315-18.

[3] This sketch is based upon the data in Table 13. The number of common stocks at each concentration level is understated most for 1952, 1958, and 1966a on Figure 3 because only portfolio concentrations of investment companies are included. The incomplete distribution, 1966b, includes data for insurance company holdings of 1 per cent or more, and data for some trust departments of commercial banks are discussed in Chapter III.

[4] See the discussion in Chapter II.

[5] When these investigations were held at the end of the 1930s the possibility that other stock-owning financial intermediaries would evolve and grow rapidly was not considered. There is no reason to believe that such developments could have been foreseen. The present and future portfolio concentrations in the hands of financial intermediaries other than investment companies should now be considered in establishing limits on portfolio concentration ratios. Other possibilities, such as encouraging the development of alternative organizational structures, will be considered later.

[6] See Table 8 for a detailed statement of the growth and size of investment complexes and their individual component funds.

[7] Chapter II.

[8] *Ibid.*

[9] *Ibid.*

[10] See Table 27.

[11] There were numerous cases in early nineteenth-century Massachusetts, involving bridge, canal, banking, insurance, and other corporations in which one person could not vote more than ten shares of stock. Later the limit was frequently set at fifty shares. Edwin Merrick Dodd, *American Business Corporations until 1860* (Cambridge, Mass.: Harvard University Press, 1954).

[12] The three largest closely held corporations and their estimated sales are Cargill, Inc. ($2 billion), Bechtel Corp. ($1,500 million) and Continental Grain Merchants ($1,500 million). *Forbes,* May 15, 1969.

[13] See Dodd, *American Business Corporations;* and Frank D. Emerson and Franklin C. Latcham, *Shareholder Democracy* (Cleveland, Ohio: Western Reserve University, 1954), pp. 3-6.

[14] William Z. Ripley, *Main Street and Wall Street* (New York: Little, Brown and Co., 1927).

[15] The first state Blue Sky law intended to help protect investors from fraudulent promotions was passed by Kansas in 1911. The federal Postal Fraud Laws of 1909 made it illegal to use the mails for the fraudulent sale of securities or even to distribute misleading information about securities, but the administration of these sections of the law was ineffective. Merwin H. Waterman, Wilford J. Eiteman, *et al., Essays on Business Finance* (3d ed.; Ann Arbor, Mich.: Masterco Press, 1957), pp. 143-44.

[16] Parsons and Smelser, *Economy and Society.* This framework for analysis is very widely accepted by sociologists. This book, which is dedicated to the memory of Alfred Marshall and Max Weber, extends and develops the theories of the latter and those of Emile Durkheim, the French sociologist. Political scientists and sociologists have been fascinated by the ownership and control separation thesis as articulated by Berle and Means. Parsons and Smelser devote one section to this topic and illuminate its societal importance by means of their own analytical framework. The topic is utilized at several places by Parsons and Smelser.

Other conceptual and analytical frameworks, such as that developed by Kenneth Boulding in *Conflict and Defense: A General Theory* (New York: Harper & Row, 1963) might have been used. However, that of Parsons and Smelser seemed more appropriate for the way I wanted to develop the projections of economic and financial institutions.

[17] See footnote 1.

[18] Adolf A. Berle, Jr., *Power without Property* (New York: Harcourt, Brace & World, Inc., 1959), p. 77.

[19] *Ibid.*, p. 79.

[20] *Ibid.*, chap. iii, "The Philosophy of Economic Power," pp. 77-111.

[21] Adolf A. Berle, Jr., and Gardiner C. Means (New York: Commercial Clearing House, 1932).

[22] The preface of this joint work was written by Berle. He especially acknowledges his indebtedness to William Z. Ripley for his pioneering work. Professor Ripley of Harvard University was active for over twenty years in the research and publication that helped in the eventual establishment of the SEC. Professor Ripley's best remembered book is *Main Street and Wall Street.* This preface also states that the data describing the concentration of economic power had already been published by Means in both the *American Economic Review* and the *Quarterly Journal of Economics.*

[23] Berle, *Power without Property*, p. 52.

[24] Paul P. Harbrecht, S.J., *Pension Funds and Economic Power* (New York: Twentieth Century Fund, 1959). In the preface, Father Harbrecht states that the "inspiration and orientation toward this study. . .came originally from Professor Adolf A. Berle, Jr." At the time the work was published, Adolf A. Berle was chairman of the Board of Trustees of the Twentieth Century Fund, and Father Harbrecht was Dean of the Law School, Detroit University.

[25] Robert Tilove, *Pension Funds and Economic Power* (New York: Fund for the Republic, 1959). Professor Berle was the consultant of the Fund for the Republic especially responsible for this report.

[26] Dorwin Cartwright, "A Field Theory Conception of Power," in *Studies in Social Power*, ed. by Dorwin Cartwright (Ann Arbor, Mich.: Research Center for Group Dynamics, Institute for Social Research, University of Michigan, 1959), p. 156. Other definitions of power are quoted from the writings of Bertrand Russel, Laswell and Kaplan, R. Bierstedt, Herbert Simon, and Robert Dahl.

[27] Dahl, "Power," pp. 407-9.

[28] Cartwright, "A Field Theory Conception of Power," pp. 187-210. He uses "sanctions" as an alternative term, but a term consistent with the system of relationships he draws.

[29] The 1967 and 1968 annual report of the SEC lists the following occasions, in addition to the voting for directors, on which reported stockholder votes were held:

	1967	1968
Mergers, acquisitions, consolidations, etc.	427	634
Authorizations of new or additional securities, recapitalizations, etc.	819	1,420
Employee pension and retirement plans	81	75
Bonus and profit-sharing plans, etc.	106	n.a.
Stock option plans	523	687
Selection of independent auditor	1,608	1,666

Stockholders also submitted 192 proposals covering such topics as amendments to charters and bylaws, cumulative voting for directors, pre-emptive rights, stock options, charitable contributions, and other matters. U.S., Securities and Exchange Commission, *33rd Annual Report* and *34th Annual Report* (Washington, D.C.: Government Printing Office, 1968 and 1969 respectively), pp. 39-40 and 41-42 respectively.

[30] U.S., Congress, House, Committee on Interstate and Foreign Commerce, *A Study of Mutual Funds,* Report of the Committee on Interstate and Foreign Commerce, House, 89th Cong., Dec. 2, 1962 (prepared for the SEC by the Wharton School of Finance and Commerce and called the "Wharton Report"), pp. 417-28. The data in this section of the questionnaire were limited to events up to June 30, 1958. The material cited appears in the section, "Open-End Company Behavior as Stockholder." The author knows of no comparable study of banks as stockholders. Some very general statements of the voting policies of foundations have been reported in Ralph L. Nelson, *The Investment Policies of Foundations* (New York: Russell Sage Foundation, 1967), pp. 114-18.

[31] U.S., Congress, House, *A Study of Mutual Funds,* pp. 418-28. The organization of several large open-end funds to facilitate the voting of proxies is described.

[32] *Ibid.,* pp. 420, 427, and 428.

[33] One of the provisions of the Banking Act of June, 1933, was the separation of commercial and investment banking. This divorce was the result of a Senate investigation which revealed "the rather nauseating practices of banks and their affiliated investment houses." Ray B. Westerfield, *Money, Credit and Banking* (New York: Ronald Press Co., 1938), pp. 1076-78.

[34] Cumulative voting for directors is comparable to proportional representation in political elections.

[35] Ezra Solomon, *Theory of Financial Management* (New York: Columbia University Press, 1963), pp. 17-25.

[36] For excellent discussions of capital budgeting, see J. Fred Weston and Eugene F. Brigham, *Managerial Finance* (3d ed.; New York: Holt, Rinehart & Winston, Inc., 1969), pp. 169-277. In its applications to public expenditures the technique is called "cost-benefit analysis."

[37] For a statement about the awkward position that the Savings and Profit-Sharing Pension Fund of Sears, Roebuck and Company reached when it owned 26 per cent of Sears stock, see Tilove, *Pension Funds and Economic Freedom*, pp. 60-66. In this case there was an effort to "pass through" the voting rights on the stock to the individual members of the pension fund.

[38] Berle, *Power without Property*, pp. 98-116. The development of this topic herein will differ from that of Berle, but his discussion is strongly recommended to the interested reader.

[39] Chapter III.

[40] Adam Smith, *Wealth of Nations* (Modern Library ed.; New York: Random House, Inc., 1937), pp. 121-22. The phrase, "sacred rights of private property," is used on p. 170.

[41] *Ibid.*, pp. 691-92.

[42] *Ibid.*, p. 699.

[43] Samuel Williston, "A History of the Law of Business Corporations before 1800," *Harvard Law Review*, II (Nov., 1888).

[44] R. H. Tawney, *The Acquisitive Society* (New York: Harcourt, Brace & World, Inc., 1948), chap. v, "Property and Creative Work," pp. 52-83. These arguments and other justifications of private property are found in that chapter.

[45] Erich Fromm, *Escape from Freedom* (New York: Avon Books, 1965), pp. 130-34.

[46] Roscoe Pound, *An Introduction to the Philosophy of Law* (rev. ed.; New Haven, Conn.: Yale University Press, 1954), chap. v, "Property."

[47] *Ibid.*, p. 114.

[48] *Ibid.*, pp. 130-31.

[49] As documented in earlier chapters there had been some ownership of stock by financial intermediaries for decades. The magnitude of the growth of

[50] The term "benefits" includes the use of the original investment itself.

[51] The details that follow appear in the *Des Moines Register,* Oct. 17, 1964, p. 4, under the by-line of Jerry Szumski, "I.P.E.R.S. Board Neutral on Power Firm's Merger."

[52] *Des Moines Register,* May 18, 21, and 25, 1970.

[53] *New York Times,* Apr. 7, 10, 14, and 28, 1970; and *Des Moines Register,* May 14, 1970.

[54] U.S., Congress, House, *A Study of Mutual Funds,* p. 419.

[55] *Ibid.,* pp. 418-19.

[56] *Ibid.,* p. 578 reproduces this part of the questionnaire.

[57] *Ibid.,* pp. 427-28. For additional discussion on this topic see Arlene Hershman, "Will the Funds Run Companies?" *Dun's Review,* July, 1968, and Arthur M. Louis, "Mutual Funds Have the Votes," *Fortune,* May, 1967.

[58] Parsons and Smelser, *Economy and Society,* p. 292.

[59] In 1907 the first bill to provide for old-age pensions was introduced into Congress. By 1910 Civil War veterans had been granted pensions by all but six states. A 1914 Arizona law providing for old-age pensions was declared unconstitutional, and so were those passed in other states in the 1920s. California adopted a law in 1929 that required contributions from the state and county governments. Laws similar to that of California were adopted in seven other states prior to 1935. Paul A. Brinker, *Economic Insecurity and Social Security* (New York: Appleton-Century-Crofts, 1968), pp. 51-53.

[60] The Kerr-Mills Act of 1960 had provided some medical care for the aged whether they were receiving welfare payments or not; this assistance was on a federal-state matching basis. In 1950 the Social Security Act was amended to allow medical payments to be made for welfare recipients. *Ibid.,* pp. 231-34.

[61] Parsons and Smelser, *Economy and Society,* p. 256. This entire final section of Chapter VI utilizes and adapts the analytical frameworks of the structure of social action and institutional change to what I believe to be the problems inherent in the growth of the portfolio concentration in the hands of financial intermediaries and concurrent social changes. Parsons and Smelser say (pp. 305-6) that, "Economic theory as such has been unable...to cope with the problems of long-term institutional change." And "...Economic

history...has tended toward theoretical nihilism." They believe that their analytical system will help to overcome the false dilemma between economic theory and institutional change.

[62] The reason for the concern involves price risk or price manipulation, but the more important question is corporate control by the use of other people's money. Such practices were made public by the 1905 Armstrong Investigations of the life insurance industry (see Chapter IV) and the 1940 SEC investigation of investment companies and investment trusts (Chapter II). The author knows of no comparable study of the practices of commercial bank trust departments.

[63] Both the Federal Trade Commission and the Department of Justice published guidelines in 1968 about the levels of industrial concentration that would be acceptable under federal law and Supreme Court interpretations. The Department of Justice has set out guidelines for horizontal, vertical, and conglomerate mergers. For example, in the case that the four leading companies in an industry control 75 per cent or less of the output, an acquiring firm that accounts for 5 per cent of the output may not acquire another firm that accounts for more than 5 per cent of the output in that same market. The details of these guidelines are summarized conveniently in Betty Bock, *Mergers and Markets: 7,* Studies in Business Economics, No. 105 (New York: National Industrial Conference Board, Inc., 1969), pp. 91-108.

The analogy between concentration in product markets, which has a long and stormy history, and concentration of stock ownership by financial intermediaries, which is a relatively new phenomenon, cannot be pushed very far. The point is that detailed guidelines have been prepared in a related and very complex policy field. There would seem to be no administrative reason that reasonable statutes, court interpretations, and guidelines should not be expected in this new area of public concern as well.

[64] The reader may wish to compare the structure of this exposition with the four-step statement of the process of structural differentiation in Parsons and Smelser, pp. 255-56, or their seven-step summary of their model for institutional change.

[65] See footnote 12.

[66] Herman Kahn and Anthony J. Wiener, *The Year 2000—A Framework for Speculation on the Next Thirty-Three Years* (New York: Macmillan Co., 1967), pp. 193-220.

[67] Harry Kalven, Jr., "The Problems of Privacy in the Year 2000," *Daedalus,* XCVI (Summer, 1967—"Toward the Year 2000: Work in Progress"), 876-82.

[68] For example, John Kenneth Galbraith's *The New Industrial State* (Boston: Houghton Mifflin Co., 1967) is accepted by many as a realistic picture of present and near-term industrial organization.

[69] Some 43 per cent of Donora's 14,000 population are reported to have become ill during the several days that the smog lasted. Donora, which is in the steep-walled valley of the Monongahela River, produces steel, zinc, and sulfuric acid. In 1930 about 60 people died of a similar disaster in the Meuse Valley, Belgium; and in 1950 about 22 died in Poza Rica, Mexico. The great London fog in December, 1952, lasted at least four days. Some 3,000 to 4,000 deaths were attributed to the fog which contained sulfur dioxide and coal smoke. *Collier's Encyclopedia*, I, 371-78.

[70] Pound, *An Introduction to the Philosophy of Law*, p. 132.

[71] The Tennessee Valley Authority, Federal Reserve Board, and other "federal level" organizations also hold common stock in their pension funds.

[72] The boards of directors of the Federal National Mortgage Association (1954), Federal Home Loan Bank System (1955), and the Communications Satellite Corporation (1962) also have various combinations of stockholder elected and government appointed members. The Federal National Mortgage Association (Fannie Mae) was organized to provide a secondary market for Veterans Administration mortgages, Federal Housing Administration mortgages, and Farmers Home Administration mortgages; the latter are guaranteed by the Department of Agriculture. Organizations selling mortgages to Fannie Mae must make capital contributions equal to 1 per cent of the principal of mortgages sold; and those borrowing from it must subscribe up to one-half of 1 per cent of the amounts borrowed. Under Title III of the 1968 Housing and Urban Development Act there are to be 15 directors, 10 of whom will be elected by the stockholders and 5 of whom are appointed by the President. Of those appointed, one is to represent the home building industry, a second the mortgage lenders, and a third the real estate industry. *Wall Street Journal*, Aug. 2, 1968.

The Federal Home Loan Bank Board (FHLBB) is similar in structure to the Federal Reserve Board. The FHLBB supervises the Federal Home Loan Bank System, the Federal Savings and Loan System, and the Federal Savings and Loan Insurance Corporation. The FHLBB has three directors appointed by the President for a four-year term; no more than two may be from the same political party. The FHLBB appoints four members to the board of each of the twelve regional banks of the Federal Home Loan Bank System. The remaining members of the regional banks are elected by the individual savings and loan banks in each region.

The Communications Satellite Corporation was established by a 1962 act of Congress. Three of its 15-member Board of Directors are appointed by the President with the advice and consent of the Senate. The common stock is divided into two series: Series I may be purchased by the general public, and Series II was reserved for communications carriers such as American Telephone and Telegraph and International Telephone and Telegraph. The Series I stockholders elect eight members to the Board of Directors, and the Series II stockholders elect the remaining four directors.

TABLE 1

Number of Portfolio Companies
in Which Investment Companies Held an
Influential Interest, by Industry Groups, 1935*

Percentage of Voting Stock Held	Industry					
	Finance	Manufacturing	Transportation	Utilities	Others	Total
10 per cent or less	14	31	11	12	13	81
10-50 per cent	18	29	3	10	8	68
Over 50 per cent	26	5	3	....	4	38
Total	58	65	17	22	25	187

*Data from U.S., Congress, Senate, *Investment Trusts and Investment Companies, Hearings,* before a Subcommittee on Banking and Currency, Senate, 76th Cong., 3d sess. (Washington, D.C.: Government Printing Office, 1940), Part 4, Table 2, p. 9.

TABLE 2

Total Assets and Stock Held by Investment Companies
(Dollar Amounts in Millions)

Year	Total Assets	Stocks	Percentage of Stocks to Total Assets	Mutual Fund's NYSE Listed Shares as a Percentage of All NYSE Listed Shares
*All types of investment companies**				
1940	$ 2.1	$ 1.8	85.7	...
1950	5.3	4.3	81.1	...
1955	13.77	12.1	88.3	...
1960	23.6	20.5	86.7	...
1965	47.3	41.1	86.9	...
Mutual funds only†				
1945	1.3	....	....	1.7
1955	7.8	6.4	82.1	3.8
1960	17.0	14.1	82.8	5.5
1965	35.2	30.3	85.9	6.6
1966	34.8	28.4	82.7	7.2
1967	44.7	38.4	86.0	7.4
1968	52.7	44.4	84.3	7.6

*Data from Raymond W. Goldsmith, Robert E. Lipsey, and Morris Mendelson, *Studies in the National Balance Sheet of the United States,* Vol. II (Princeton, N.J.: Princeton University Press, 1963), pp. 168-71.

†Data from Investment Company Institute, *Mutual Fund Fact Book, 1969* (New York: Investment Company Institute, 1969), pp. 30 and 32.

TABLE 3

Two Estimates of Investment Company Assets, 1929-68*
(In Millions)

End of Year	Closed-end Companies	Open-end Companies	Total	SEC†
1929	$2.6	$ .1	$ 2.7	$....
1930	1.8	.1	1.9	....
1935	1.0	.4	1.4	....
1940	0.6	.5	1.1	....
1945	1.0	1.3	2.3	3.2
1950	0.9	2.5	3.4	4.7
1955	1.2	7.8	9.0	12.0
1960	1.8	17.0	18.8	23.5
1965	2.5	35.2	37.7	41.3
1966	2.4	34.8	37.2	45.8
1967	2.8	44.7	47.5	53.2
1968	2.9	52.7	55.6	63.5

*Data from *Management Investment Companies,* a monograph prepared for the Commission on Money and Credit (Englewood Cliffs, N.J.: Prentice-Hall, Inc., 1962), p. 96; Investment Company Institute, *Mutual Fund Fact Book, 1969* (New York: Investment Company Institute, 1969), p. 7; annual reports of the Securities and Exchange Commission, various years.

†The values are reported as of June 30 each year. Those shown are for active companies. Assets of unit investment trusts, which invest in the securities of other registered investment companies, were first reported in 1965.

TABLE 4

Rates of Growth of Stock: Total Market Values and Amount Held by Selected Institutional Investors*

Investor	1929 to 1958	1929 to 1967	1940 to 1950	1940 to 1960	1940 to 1967	1950 to 1960	1950 to 1968	1960 to 1968
Investment companies	....	....	9.1	10.9	13.3†	16.9	15.7	14.3
Mutual funds only	....	....	....	....	....	24.3	20.0	16.1‡
Noninsured corporate pension funds	....	....	27.0	29.0	24.0	35.0	27.3	18.3
Life insurance companies§	8.2	8.9	13.3	11.1	11.3	9.1	10.6	12.5
Property and casualty insurance companies§	....	....	9.9∥	9.2∥	8.1	7.6#	8.1	8.8
State and local pension funds**	....	....	....	....	....	n.a.	n.a.	29.7
All marketable stocks	3.7††	....	6.9‡‡	8.8‡‡	8.6‡‡	10.8‡‡	9.4‡‡	7.7‡‡
New York Stock Exchange listed stocks only	5.1	8.3	8.4	10.5	10.4	12.6	11.7	10.7
Institutional holdings of NYSE, listed stocks—total	....	....	....	....	....	17.1§§	15.7§§	13.9
Mutual funds only	....	....	....	....	....	21.8§§	18.8§§	14.6

Noninsured corporate pension funds	....	31.4§§	27.3§§	17.5
State and local pension funds	....	n.a.	n.a.	34.5
Life insurance companies	....	10.2§§	12.0§§	14.4
Nonlife insurance companies	....	12.2§§	11.1§§	9.7
Foundations	....	15.4§§	13.5§§	11.1
College and university endowments	....	9.2§§	10.1§§	11.2

*Growth rates for many periods are not calculated because consistent data are not readily available.
†To 1965 only.
‡From 1955.
§See Table 31.
‖From data in U.S., Congress, House, Committee on Interstate and Foreign Commerce, *Report of the Securities and Exchange Commission on Public Policy Implications of Investment Company Growth*, H.R. 2337, 89th Cong., 2d sess., Dec. 2, 1966 (Washington, D.C.: Government Printing Office, 1966), p. 276.
#From data in Investment Company Institute, *Mutual Fund Fact Book, 1969* (New York: Investment Company Institute, 1969).
**1961 data from Investment Bankers Association of America, *State and Local Pension Funds: 1968*, prepared by Thomas M. Adams (Washington, D.C.: Investment Bankers Assoc., 1968).
††Based on Friend series. See Table 5.
‡‡Based on SEC special net estimates series.
§§From 1949 base date.

TABLE 5

Estimates of Market Value of Corporate Stock by Series, 1900-68
(In Billions)

Year	Goldsmith*	Friend†	S.E.C. Net Estimates‡	NYSE Only §	All Exchange Markets‖
1900	$ 13.9	$ 11.1	....	....	....
1912	38.0	....	....	....	....
1922	76.1	....	....	....	....
1924	....	....	....	$ 27.1	....
1925	....	....	....	34.5	....
1926	....	....	....	38.4	....
1927	....	....	....	49.7	....
1928	....	....	....	67.5	....
1929	186.7	144.4	....	64.7	....
1930	....	....	....	49.0	....
1931	....	....	....	26.7	....
1932	....	....	....	22.8	....
1933	101.7	....	....	33.1	....
1934	....	....	....	33.9	....
1935	....	....	....	46.9	....
1936	....	....	....	59.9	$ 74.7
1937	....	....	....	38.9	49.1
1938	....	....	....	47.5	58.3
1939	100.1	....	....	46.5	56.6
1940	....	....	$ 77.3	41.9	50.5
1941	....	....	....	35.8	43.2
1942	....	....	....	38.8	46.6

Year				
1943	....	....	....	57.5
1944	....	....	....	66.7
1945	135.9	122.0	....	88.2
1946	121.8	....	....	81.8
1947	119.2	....	....	80.4
1948	119.6	....	....	81.9
1949	134.8	....	....	91.6
1950	166.5	....	150.6	111.0
1951	190.8	....	....	129.2
1952	206.8	....	....	140.5
1953	204.9	....	....	135.4
1954	286.7	....	247.4	194.8
1955	353.7	....	309.5	238.8
1956	370.8	....	....	254.0
1957	335.5	....	....	224.2
1958	455.1	394.8	....	312.7
1959	....	....	....	338.4
1960	....	....	421.2	426.2
1961	....	....	513.2	426.2
1962	....	....	....	374.2
1963	....	411.0	....	441.7
1964	....	....	619.2	506.8
1965	....	....	674.7	573.1
1966	....	....	587.3	514.4
1967	....	....	707.8	652.7
1968	....	....	761.3	759.5
1969	....	....	....	....

(Continued)

TABLE 5 (*Continued*)

*Data from Raymond W. Goldsmith, Robert E. Lipsey, and Morris Mendelson, *Studies in the National Balance Sheet of the United States*, Vol. II (Princeton, N.J.: Princeton University Press, 1963), pp. 316-19.

†Data from Irwin Friend, *Investment Banking and the New Issues Market—Summary Volume* (Philadelphia: University of Pennsylvania, 1965), p. 113; amounts exclude holdings by nonfinancial corporations and include foreign issues and securities offered by financial intermediaries.

‡Data from U.S., Congress, House, Committee on Interstate and Foreign Commerce, *Report of the Securities and Exchange Commission on Public Policy Implications of Investment Company Growth*, H.R. 2337, 89th Cong., 2d sess., Dec. 2, 1966 (Washington, D.C.: Government Printing Office, 1966). Data for years 1940, 1950, 1955, 1960, and 1965 exclude, as far as possible, intercorporate holdings and investment company shares. The 1954 and 1961 data are in U.S., Congress, House, *Report of Special Study of the Securities Markets of the SEC*, H. Doc. 95, 88th Cong., 1963 (Washington, D.C.: Government Printing Office, 1963), Part 2, p. 970. The 1964, 1966, 1967, and 1968 (preliminary) data are in U.S., Securities and Exchange Commission, *Statistical Series*, Release No. 2358, dated May 1, 1969, Table 3, p. 6.

§Data from New York Stock Exchange, *New York Stock Exchange Fact Book* (New York: New York Stock Exchange, 1966). Issued annually; later years also consulted. The NYSE only total market value includes preferred stocks—both straight and convertible as follows:

1940	$ 6.3 billion
1950	8.1 billion
1960	8.0 billion
1965	6.8 billion
1967	14.9 billion
1968	24.5 billion
1969	22.6 billion

Other market value estimates that include NYSE data must include these amounts. All exchange market totals do not include over-the-counter market estimates of common stock as the Goldsmith, Friend, and the SEC net estimates do.

‖Data from U.S., Securities and Exchange Commission, *34th Annual Report* (Washington, D.C.: Government Printing Office, 1969).

TABLE 6

Size Distribution of Assets of Mutual Fund
Companies, 1952, 1958, and 1968 Year End

| Assets | 1952 | | 1958 | |
(In Millions)	Number	Percentage	Number	Percentage
Panel 1*				
Under $10	61	51.7	57	36.5
$10 to $50	39	33.1	49	31.4
$50 to $150	13	11.0	29	18.7
$150 to $300	3	2.5	12	7.7
$300 to $600	2	1.7	6	3.8
Over $600	0	0	3	1.9
Total	118	100.0	156	100.0

| | 1968 | |
	Number	Percentage
Panel 2†		
Under $10	219	40.6
$10 to $50	141	26.2
$50 to $200	115	21.3
$200 to $500	35	6.5
Over $500	29	5.4
Total	539	100.0

*Data from U.S., Congress, House, Committee on Interstate and Foreign Commerce, *A Study of Mutual Funds,* Report of the Committee on Interstate and Foreign Commerce, House, 89th Cong., Dec. 2, 1962 (prepared for the SEC by the Wharton School of Finance and Commerce and called the "Wharton Report"), p. 41.

† *Vickers Directory of Investment Companies,* Dec. 31, 1968.

TABLE 7

Concentration Ratios for Assets of Mutual Funds, 1952, 1958, and 1968
(Dollar Amounts in Millions)

Number of Companies*	December 31, 1952†		September 30, 1958†		December 31, 1968‡	
	Assets	Percentage of All Assets	Assets	Percentage of All Assets	Assets	Percentage of All Assets
1	$ 512	13.1	$ 1,295	10.6	$ 2,988	5.3
4	1,436	36.7	3,783	30.8	10,288	18.1
8	1,961	50.1	5,447	44.4	16,699	29.3
20	2,839	72.6	8,113	66.1	28,383	50.7
50	3,630	92.9	10,722	87.4	40,924	71.9
All mutual funds	$3,910	100.0	$12,271	100.0	$56,954	100.0

*Ranked from largest to smallest.

†Data from U.S., Congress, House, Committee on Interstate and Foreign Commerce, *A Study of Mutual Funds*, Report of the Committee on Interstate and Foreign Commerce, House, 89th Cong., Dec. 2, 1962 (prepared for the SEC by the Wharton School of Finance and Commerce and called the "Wharton Report"), p. 43.

‡Prepared by author from Arthur Wiesenberger, *Investment Companies, 1969* (New York: Arthur Wiesenberger and Co., 1969).

TABLE 8

Net Assets of Ten Largest Investment Company Complexes, 1950-68
(In Millions of Dollars)

Complex	Dec. 31 1950*	Dec. 31 1960*	Dec. 31 1965	June 30 1966†	Dec. 31 1968*
Investors Diversified Services					
Investors Mutual	$235.1	$1,599.2	$2,876.7	......	$2,988.0
Investors Selective Fund	6.6	28.5	46.1	......	36.0
Investors Stock Fund	18.7	713.1	1,801.2	......	2,340.8
Investors Variable Proprietary Fund	.....	166.1	469.2	......	1,182.7
IDS New Dimension Funds	.....	......	......	......	120.1
Total	$260.4	$2,506.9	$5,293.2	$5,172.5	$6,667.6
Massachusetts Investment Trust Group					
M.I. Growth Stock Fund	$362.3	$1,508.3	$2,251.6	......	$2,292.9
M.I.T.	24.3	403.4	898.0	......	1,263.5
Total	$386.6	$1,911.7	$3,140.6	$3,019.5	$3,556.4
Fidelity Management and Research Company					
Congress Street Fund	.....	......	$ 48.4	......	$ 51.3
Contrafund, Inc.	.....	......	......	......	......
Dow Theory Investment Fund, Inc.	.....	$ 1.1	81.0	......	157.6
Essex Fund, Inc.	.....	......	7.1	......	21.6
Everest Income Fund, Inc.	.....	......	......	......	10.1

*Data from Arthur Wiesenberger and Company, *Investment Companies* (New York: Arthur Wiesenberger and Co.), and Moody's Investors Service, Inc., *Moody's Bank and Finance Manual* (New York: Moody's Investors Service, Inc.).

†Data from U.S., Congress, House, Committee on Interstate and Foreign Commerce, *Report of the Securities and Exchange Commission on Public Policy Implications of Investment Company Growth*, H.R. 2337, 89th Cong., 2d sess., Dec. 2, 1966 (Washington, D.C.: Government Printing Office, 1966), pp. 48-49. The fund complexes and net assets for June 30, 1966, are used as reported in this source.

(*Continued*)

TABLE 8 (*Continued*)

Complex	Dec. 31 1950*	Dec. 31 1960*	Dec. 31 1965	June 30 1966†	Dec. 31 1968*
Fidelity Fund, Inc.	$ 43.4	$ 397.6	$ 636.5	......	$ 898.0
Fidelity Capital Fund, Inc.	.....	25.0	635.8	......	724.0
Fidelity Trend Fund, Inc.	.....	0.6	343.0	......	1,346.3
Magellan Fund, Inc.	.....	......	3.1‡	......	10.0‡
Memphis & Shelby County Medical Society, Inc., Investment Retirement Trust	.....	......	......	......	8.8‡
Puritan Fund, Inc.	0.2	85.5	490.1	......	825.4
Second Congress Street Fund	.....	......	42.2	......	48.0
Total	$ 43.6	$ 509.8	$2,284.1	$2,678.3	$4,092.3
Waddell and Reed, Inc.					
United Continental Fund	.....	$ 44.2	......	......	......
United Accumulative Fund	$ 3.0	411.1	$1,236.9	......	$1,460.3
United Bond Fund	.....	.....	......	......	3.8
United Funds Canada International, Ltd.	.....	......	13.5	......	10.2
United Income Fund	40.9	262.4	684.8	......	852.5
United Science Fund	4.6	145.9	296.9	......	471.2
Total	$ 89.4	$1,373.4	$2,232.1	$2,239.2	$2,798.0
Wellington Management Co.					
Exeter Fund, Inc.	.....	......	......	......	$ 40.2‡
Wellington Fund, Inc.	$154.5	$1,133.5	$2,047.6	......	1,754.3
Windsor Fund, Inc.	.....	51.0	91.8	......	211.4
Total	$154.5	$1,184.5	$2,139.4	$2,050.4	$2,005.9

*Data from Arthur Wiesenberger and Company, *Investment Companies* (New York: Arthur Wiesenberger and Co.), and Moody's Investors Service, Inc., *Moody's Bank and Finance Manual* (New York: Moody's Investors Service, Inc.).

†Data from U.S., Congress, House, Committee on Interstate and Foreign Commerce, *Report of the Securities and Exchange Commission on Public Policy Implications of Investment Company Growth*, H.R. 2337, 89th Cong., 2d sess., Dec. 2, 1966 (Washington, D.C.: Government Printing Office, 1966), pp. 48-49. The fund complexes and net assets for June 30, 1966, are used as reported in this source.

‡Letter dated July 8, 1969, from Fidelity Management and Research Company.

(*Continued*)

TABLE 8 (*Continued*)

Complex	Dec. 31 1950*	Dec. 31 1960*	Dec. 31 1965	June 30 1966†	Dec. 31 1968*
Investors Management Co., Inc.					
Total (five separate funds)	.....	$ 805.4	$1,484.3	$1,581.1	$2,265.3
Union Service Corporation §					
Total (four separate funds)	$126.7	$ 816.0	$1,490.1	$1,439.9	$1,915.4
Lord, Abbett & Co.					
Total (two separate funds)	$152.6	$ 658.1	$1,321.4	$1,282.3	$1,834.1
Keystone Custodian Funds (KCF)					
Total (thirteen separate funds)	$221.9	$ 546.7	$1,183.5	$1,194.4	$1,955.4
Putnam Management Fund, Inc.					
Total (five separate funds)	$ 44.9	$ 375.0	$1,218.0	$1,193.3	$1,812.6
Total of ten fund complexes	$1,480.6	$10,687.5	$21,795.7	$28,851.3	$28,903.0
All investment company assets	$3,324	$18,801	$37,741	....	$55,437
Percentage of ten fund complexes to total assets	48.2	56.9	57.5	....	52.2∥

*Data from Arthur Wiesenberger and Company, *Investment Companies* (New York: Arthur Wiesenberger and Co.), and Moody's Investors Service, Inc., *Moody's Bank and Finance Manual* (New York: Moody's Investors Service, Inc.).

†Data from U.S., Congress, House, Committee on Interstate and Foreign Commerce, *Report of the Securities and Exchange Commission on Public Policy Implications of Investment Company Growth*, H.R. 2337, 89th Cong., 2d sess., Dec. 2, 1966 (Washington, D.C.: Government Printing Office, 1966), pp. 48-49. The fund complexes and net assets for June 30, 1966, are used as reported in this source.

§No common internal management; service provided at cost to clients.

∥These ten complexes held 55 per cent of all mutual fund assets and 45 per cent of all investment company assets at this date according to Wiesenberger, *Investment Companies*, p. 48.

TABLE 9

Concentration Ratios of Mutual Fund Groups, 1952, 1958, and 1968
(Dollar Amounts in Millions)

Number of Groups*	December 31, 1952†		September 30, 1958†		December 31, 1968‡	
	Assets	Percentage of All Assets	Assets	Percentage of All Assets	Assets	Percentage of All Assets
1	$ 544	14.2	$ 1,807	14.7	$ 6,668	12.0
4	1,576	40.3	4,634	37.8	17,113	30.9
8	2,312	59.1	6,408	52.2	25,254	45.6
20	3,334	85.5	9,694	79.0	n.c.§	....
All mutual funds	$3,910	100.0	$12,271	100.0	$55,437	100.0

*Ranked from largest to smallest.

†Data from U.S., Congress, House, Committee on Interstate and Foreign Commerce, *A Study of Mutual Funds*, Report of the Committee on Interstate and Foreign Commerce, House, 89th Cong., Dec. 2, 1962 (prepared for the SEC by the Wharton School of Finance and Commerce and called the "Wharton Report").

‡Prepared by the author from Arthur Wiesenberger and Company, *Investment Companies* (New York: Arthur Wiesenberger and Co., 1969).

§n.c. = not calculated.

TABLE 10

Relationships between Investment Company Size and Potential Ownership of Portfolio Companies
(In Millions)

Size of Investment Company	5 Per Cent of Assets of Investment Company	Market Value of Common Stock of a Corporation in Which Amount Shown in Second Column Represents 10 Per Cent of Market Value
$ 100	$ 5	$ 50
500	25	250
1,000	50	500
2,000	100	1,000
5,000	250	2,500
10,000	500	5,000

TABLE 11

Portfolio Concentration for Largest Corporations at End of 1935*

Company	Percentage of Common Stock Held by Investment Trusts and Investment Companies	Comment
Allied Chemical and Dye	26.08	22.58 per cent owned by Solvoy American Investment Company.
American Gas and Electric	10.52	No single investment company owns more than 1 per cent.
American Water Works and Electric	20.52	14.66 per cent owned by Electric Power Associates, Inc.
Brooklyn Manhattan Transit	12.87	2.85 per cent owned by the Adams Express Company, and 2.72 per cent by the Lehman Corporation.
Chesapeake and Ohio Railway	49.15	47.67 per cent owned by Chesapeake Corporation.
Columbia Gas and Electric	22.04	20.66 per cent owned by the United Corporation.
Commonwealth and Southern	22.02	14.22 per cent owned by American Superpower Corporation (including 1,287,400 shares held by Bankers Trust Company to be sold), and 5.34 per cent by the United Corporation.
Consolidated Oil	16.94	11.32 per cent owned by Petroleum Corporation of America, and 4.62 per cent by Pierce Petroleum Corporation.
E. I. duPont de Nemours	29.59	27.60 per cent owned by Christiana Securities Company.

Erie Railroad	19.88	14.23 per cent owned by Alleghany Corporation and an additional 4.57 per cent by its subsidiary, the Chesapeake Corporation.
Missouri, Kansas and Texas Railroad	15.42	9.11 per cent owned by Selected Industries, Inc.
Missouri Pacific Railroad	63.17	63.12 per cent owned by Alleghany Corporation.
Niagara Hudson Power	34.98	21.19 per cent owned by the United Corporation and 12.46 per cent by Niagara Share Corporation of Maryland.
North American	23.85	18.32 per cent owned by 3 affiliated companies—American Cities Power and Light Corporation, Electric Shareholdings Corporation, and Central States Electric Corporation.
Public Service of New Jersey	21.39	17.96 per cent owned by the United Corporation.
United Gas Improvement	27.51	26.09 per cent owned by the United Corporation.
United Light and Power A (nonvoting)	12.74	6.97 per cent owned by American Superpower Corporation.
United Light and Power B (voting)	12.81	9.99 per cent owned by United States and International Securities Corporation. In January, 1936, the Chase National Bank sold 448,667 shares which had been deposited with it as collateral for a loan by Continental Shares, Inc., to six investment companies—American Cities Power and Light Corporation: Blue Ridge Corporation; the Chicago Corporation; Electric Shareholdings Corporation; Selected Industries, Inc.; and Tri-Continental Corporation.

*All 86 companies with $200,000,000 or more in assets at that time were studied. Concentrations of 10 per cent or more only are reproduced in this summary. Data for this table are from U.S., Congress, Senate, Committee on Banking and Currency, *Investment Trusts and Investment Companies, Hearings*, before the Subcommittee on Banking and Currency, Senate, 76th Cong., 3d sess. (Washington, D.C.: Government Printing Office, 1940), Part 4, pp. 725-27.

TABLE 12

Ranking of Thirty Portfolio Companies by Amount of Institutional Investment,* 1954, 1964, and 1968

Portfolio Company	Ranking			Market Value of Investments (In Millions)			Percentage of Portfolio Company Common Stock Owned		
	1954	1964	1968	1954	1964	1968	1954	1964	1968
International Business Machines	16	1	1	$102	$897	$2,026	8.5	5.8	5.7
Standard Oil of New Jersey	1	2	3	354	728	536	8.3	3.8	3.2
General Motors	4	3	9	154	676	408	1.9	2.4	1.8
Texaco	5	4	7	149	653	510	6.9	5.5	4.5
Royal Dutch Petroleum†	19	5	4	77	307	518	5.0	7.0	8.5
Ford Motor Company	...‡	6	38	...‡	278	182	...‡	4.6	3.1
Gulf Oil	6	7	12	134	268	401	8.9	4.4	4.5
Mobil Oil	15	8	20	102	260	264	6.1	5.4	4.4
Monsanto	35	9	...§	53	247	...§	11.4	9.6	...§
General Electric	2	10	17	210	245	282	5.5	2.9	3.3
International Nickel	70	11	41	33	245	180	4.6	9.9	6.2
Xerox	...‡	12	6	...‡	213	511	...‡	10.5	8.7
Eastman Kodak	23	13	14	69	204	375	6.6	3.7	3.2
International Telephone and Telegraph	...§	14	13	...§	203	387	...§	17.9	11.4
Continental Oil	14	15	28	108	197	213	15.6	12.0	10.6
Southern Company	73	16	...§	33	197	...§	10.1	12.7	...§
Amerada Petroleum	9	17	15	131	194	340	22.8	18.4	23.4

Company									
Chrysler Corporation	71	18	21	33	193	261	5.5	8.1	10.0
American Telephone and Telegraph	12	19	8	121	192	429	1.7	0.5	1.5
Union Carbide	7	20	78	133	181	127	5.5	4.7	4.6
Columbia Broadcasting System	92	21	...§	30	162	...§	16.7	20.3	...§
Avon Products	...‡	22	18	...‡	161	274	...‡	10.4	7.5
Standard Oil of California	8	23	23	132	160	246	6.1	3.0	4.2
General Telephone and Electronics	...//	24	77	...//	157	128	...//	4.8	3.1
Goodyear Tire and Rubber	54	25	35	38	157	187	10.3	9.7	9.3
Sears Roebuck & Company	21	26	30	74	152	208	4.2	1.6	2.2
Southern Pacific Company	64	27	66	34	150	136	8.4	14.4	11.3
DuPont (E.I.) de Nemours	3	28	31	190	138	204	2.9	1.4	2.7
Texas Utilities	31	29	...§	56	149	...§	17.0	9.6	...§
Central & South West Corp.	43	30	...§	44	142	...§	17.9	13.0	...§

*Ownership by corporate pension funds cannot be included because such information is not public. Data for 1954 are from U.S., Congress, Senate, *Factors Affecting the Stock Market*, Staff Report to the Committee on Banking and Currency, Senate, 84th Cong., 1st sess., July 30, 1955, p. 199. Data for 1964 are from U.S., Congress, House, Committee on Interstate and Foreign Commerce, *Report of the Securities and Exchange Commission on Public Policy Implications of Investment Company Growth*, H.R. 2337, 89th Cong., 2d sess., Dec. 2, 1966 (Washington, D.C.: Government Printing Office, 1966), p. 292. Data for 1968 are from *Vickers Favorite 50*, Dec. 31, 1968.

†Shell Oil Company.

‡Corporation was still closely held at this date.

§Not in first 80 at this date.

//Name adopted March 5, 1959, when Sylvania Eelctric Products merged with General Telephone.

TABLE 13

Increases in Portfolio Concentration Ratios for Holdings of
Investment Companies, 1952, 1958, and 1966*

Portfolio Concentration Ratios (Percentage)	Investment Companies			Investment Company Complexes		
	1952	1958	1966	1952	1958	1966 (Eight Largest Only)
1.0- 1.9	518	813	...	371	727	...
2.0- 2.9	196	357	...	166	315	...
3.0- 3.9	77	180	...	92	177	...
4.0- 4.9	38	96	...	49	101	...
5.0- 5.9	17	54	⎫	29	57	...
6.0- 7.9	12	58	⎬ 289†	17	64	n.c.‡
8.0- 9.9	16	29	⎭	11	29	n.c.‡
10.0-12.4 ⎫			73			...
12.5-14.9 ⎪	7	22	39	15	27	n.c.‡
15.0-17.4 ⎨			23			...
17.5-19.9 ⎭			7			...
20.0-24.9 ⎫			12			9
25.0-29.9 ⎪	1	2	8	2	6	3
30.0-34.9 ⎨			5			2
35.0-40.0 ⎭			1			1
Total	882	1,611	...	752	1,503	...
Total assets (in millions)	$4,909	$14,875	$37,247			
Open-end companies	3,931	13,242	34,829			
Close-end companies	978	1,633	2,418			

*Data for 1952 and 1958 are from U.S., Congress, House, Committee on Interstate and Foreign Commerce, *A Study of Mutual Funds,* Report of the Committee on Interstate and Foreign Commerce, House, 89th Cong., Dec. 2, 1962 (prepared for the SEC by the Wharton School of Finance and Commerce and called the "Wharton Report"), p. 408. Data for 1966 were prepared by the author for this study.

†There are many additional portfolio holdings by individual investment companies that would fall into this cell for which the computations were not completed.

‡Not calculated.

TABLE 14

Changes in Portfolio Concentration Percentages for Fifty Highly Concentrated Companies, 1950 through 1968

Companies	Number of Large Funds Owning in 1966	1966 Market Value of Company's Common Stock (In Millions)	\multicolumn{7}{c}{Percentages}						
			1950	1955	1960	1962	1964	1966	1968
Northwest Airlines	28	$ 791	4.9	....	17.2	31.1	33.3	34.4	29.8
Trans World Airlines	31	496	....	....	.8	1.3	....	24.1	12.3
American Airlines	28	645	2.4	6.2	10.1	19.5	27.1	21.4	16.3
Armstrong Rubber	5	78	....	6.9	4.8	8.5	6.8	25.1	12.8
General Instrument	7	227	....	....	....	.7	1.3	30.9	23.3
Gimbel Brothers	14	338	2.8	5.3	26.3	21.0	25.4	26.4	24.3
International Mining	9	278	....	18.6	26.8	8.0	16.6	32.5	8.3
National Airlines	19	290	2.3	1.4	6.2	2.7	14.9	32.4	25.8
Pabst Brewing	12	307	....	....	1.5	4.7	16.7	35.0	31.5
Vornado, Inc.	8	195	....	....	....	....	10.2	31.4	14.7
AMP, Inc.	12	456	....	....	14.3	12.9	14.2	13.7	13.7
Allegheny Ludlum	10	323	....	....	....	11.6	11.0	14.5	9.4
Arkansas-Louisiana Gas	19	388	....	....	....	21.3	18.6	21.2	14.3
Automatic Retailers	8	312	....	....	1.6	16.9	12.1	12.9	20.8
Burroughs Corp.	23	1,515	1.5	7.6	2.7	4.5	3.1	22.8	20.2

(*Continued*)

175

TABLE 14 (*Continued*)

Companies	Number of Large Funds Owning in 1966	1966 Market Value of Company's Common Stock (In Millions)	Percentages						
			1950	1955	1960	1962	1964	1966	1968
Capital Cities Broadcast	4	$127	....	....	....	14.9	15.5	20.1	20.3
Carpenter Steel*	6	164	....	....	1.1	3.6	4.6	12.6	10.8
Chicago & Great Western	2	29	....	....	5.3	8.8	8.8	27.3	....
Chicago & North Western	8	200	.9	2.9	2.5	6.4	10.2	25.1	....†
Collins Radio	5	293	....	2.4	2.1	3.3	2.0	16.4	14.2
Container Corp. of America	11	353	1.1	3.9	8.9	10.3	15.7	12.5	....‡
Copperweld Steel Company	3	55	....	.4	7.9	14.5	24.2	19.6	15.6
Cutler-Hammer	5	154	....	4.3	8.8	24.9	14.5	10.2	9.2
Delta Air Lines	20	653	3.5	2.3	7.3	24.0	22.8	21.3	18.2
Eastern Airlines	21	527	4.7	7.8	8.6	10.0	8.6	16.6	12.3
Gov. Emp. Life Insurance	6	9	....	1.8	3.3	4.0	7.1	26.6	4.6
Grumman Aircraft Engineering	16	263	2.5	1.0	1.0	7.4	14.8	18.3	23.8
Illinois Central Industries§	8	385	10.4	18.6	7.8	11.8	16.8	16.6	19.2
Kaiser Alum. & Chem.	19	826	.6	1.2	1.9	1.1	2.1	11.2	13.0
Kansas Gas & Electric	7	179	2.3	11.1	16.6	12.5	14.6	15.5	5.2
Kayser-Roth	12	169	....	....	....	2.0	24.2	19.4	17.2
Kerr-McGee	14	833	1.7	6.5	11.8	5.5	9.2	19.0	15.5
Macy (R.H.)	10	320	.6	3.3	9.4	1.1	10.4	15.6	13.9
Metro-Goldwyn-Mayer	8	268	....	....	12.3	13.7	15.7	20.8	20.1
Norfolk Southern R. R.	2	19	....	....	....	....	....	21.1	.01

176

Pacific Southwest Airlines	4	$ 79	....	....	....	3.6	21.8	8.6
Pan American World Airways	23	783	.8	1.8	6.5	10.4	14.9	9.5
Panhandle Eastern P. L.	7	445	5.2	2.8	9.3	11.4	11.6	10.3
Philip Morris	20	483	5.5	3.7	15.9	18.7	25.2	29.9
Polaroid Corp.	40	3,965	....	6.7	11.7	16.6	21.2	13.9
Raytheon Co.	14	669	.7	.8	1.8	.1	23.2	27.0
Reynolds Metals	25	838	.2	5.6	4.8	8.3	14.8	10.8
Scovill Mfg.	6	127	.6	2.7	3.7	22.4	12.1	17.2
Seaboard Airline R. R.	11	123	14.8	15.2	24.2	22.9	22.7	....//
Texas Instruments	23	1,173	....	8.1	9.7	10.6	12.2	4.6
Unilever N. V. Adr.#	5	358	....	.9	3.8	3.1	28.7	.01
United Air Lines	23	1,213	4.1	10.6	21.9	21.3	17.6	9.2
United Shoe Machinery	7	140	.1	8.1	4.7	8.8	18.2	16.3
Universal Oil Products	14	318	....	4.4	9.9	13.7	25.5	6.5
Western Air Lines	9	166	....	6.8	18.2	26.7	15.4	17.6

*Renamed Carpenter Technology in 1968.

†80 per cent of stock purchased by Northwest Industries

‡Container Corporation of America merged with Montgomery Ward to form Marcos.

§Figures are for Illinois Central Railroad for years 1950, 1955, 1960, and 1962.

//Merged with Atlantic Coast Line to form Seaboard Coast Line.

#American drawing receipts.

TABLE 15

Inner Structure of Portfolio Concentration Percentages for Large Investment Funds and Investment Fund Groups, 1966

Portfolio Company	Number of Investment Holding Companies	Percentage Held by All Investment Companies	Percentage Held by Largest Individual Funds				Percentage Held by Largest Fund Groups	
			Largest Fund	Four Largest Funds	Eight Largest Funds	Twelve Largest Funds	Four Largest Groups	Eight Largest Groups
	(1)	(2)	(3)	(4)	(5)	(6)	(7)	(8)
Northwest Airlines	28	34.4	7.4	16.0	22.3	26.7	17.7	22.3
Trans World Airlines	31	24.1	3.1	10.7	16.5	19.2	13.3	18.4
American Airlines	28	33.2	1.7	6.1	8.9	13.1	10.0	14.7
Armstrong Rubber	5	37.5	13.4	25.1	....	....	13.7	....
General Instrument	5	32.0	15.7	27.8	....	....	27.8	15.9
Gimbel Brothers	14	35.6	4.7	15.9	23.1	26.1	4.7	15.9
International Mining	9	32.5	6.2	27.2	32.5	....	27.2	32.5
Mid-American Pipeline	4	31.8	9.8	31.8	....	....	31.8	....
National Airlines	19	36.0	5.2	15.5	24.3	28.7	18.5	27.2
Papst Brewing	12	36.6	5.8	19.6	30.1	35.0	24.0	35.2
Vornado, Inc.	8	35.0	6.7	20.5	31.4	....	23.5	....
AMP, Inc.	23	13.7	4.3	9.3	12.4	13.7	10.4	13.6
Allegheny Ludlum	10	14.5	3.1	9.3	13.9	....	9.3	13.9
Arkansas-Louisiana Gas	19	21.2	3.8	10.4	16.1	18.7	15.4	21.4

Automatic Retailers	8	12.9	3.6	9.9	12.9	...	9.9
Burroughs Corp.	23	22.8	2.3	7.8	13.2	16.5	11.1
Capital Cities Broadcast	4	20.1	7.5	20.1	...	...	20.1
Carpenter Steel	6	12.6	4.7	11.4	...	...	11.4
Chicago & Great Western	2	27.3	18.6	...	...	...	...
Chicago & North Western	8	25.1	6.0	20.3	25.1	...	...
Collins Radio	5	16.4	8.1	16.1	...	...	...
Container Corp. of America	11	12.5	3.6	7.9	11.0	...	8.1
Copperweld Steel Company	3	19.6	9.9	19.6	...	...	...
Cutler-Hammer	5	10.2	4.5	10.0	...	...	10.0
Delta Air Lines	20	21.3	5.2	10.5	15.1	18.3	11.8
Eastern Airlines	21	16.6	2.6	8.2	11.6	14.0	9.3
Gov. Emp. Life Insurance	7	26.6	8.1	22.8	...	...	22.8
Grumman Aircraft Engineering	16	18.3	4.0	9.2	13.7	16.7	9.8
Illinois Central Industries	8	16.6	5.5	13.0	16.7	...	13.0
Kaiser Alum. & Chem.	19	11.2	1.8	5.9	8.7	10.3	6.23
Kansas Gas & Electric	7	15.5	4.2	12.4	...	...	15.0
Kayser-Roth	12	19.4	3.8	11.6	15.9	18.6	11.8
Kerr-McGee	14	19.0	4.9	12.6	17.3	18.9	15.5
Macy (R. H.)	10	15.6	4.5	10.2	14.9	...	11.7
Metro-Goldwyn-Mayer	8	20.8	8.3	17.7	20.8	...	19.5
Norfolk Southern R. R.*	2	21.1	18.3	...	...	...	...

12.9	12.9
17.1	
11.6	
16.5	
12.8	
14.2	
16.7	
9.0	
16.8	
18.8	

*Figures for shares outstanding based on 1965 data.

(Continued)

TABLE 15 (*Continued*)

Portfolio Company	Number of Investment Holding Companies (1)	Percentage Held by All Investment Companies (2)	Largest Fund (3)	Percentage Held by Largest Individual Funds			Percentage Held by Largest Fund Groups	
				Four Largest Funds (4)	Eight Largest Funds (5)	Twelve Largest Funds (6)	Four Largest Groups (7)	Eight Largest Groups (8)
Pacific Southwest Airlines	4	21.8	11.9	21.8	....	....	21.8	....
Pan American World Airways	23	14.9	2.6	8.1	11.7	13.3	10.7	12.9
Panhandle Eastern P. L.	7	11.6	3.0	9.4	....	....	11.6	....
Philip Morris	20	25.2	4.7	13.5	19.4	22.8	15.7	21.8
Polaroid Corp.	40	21.2	2.9	8.6	12.3	15.3	10.8	15.9
Raytheon Co.	14	23.2	5.6	12.5	19.2	22.5	15.7	22.0
Reynolds Metals	25	14.8	1.9	6.1	9.6	11.8	7.7	12.0
Scovill Mfg.	6	12.1	3.2	11.1	....	....	11.1	....
Seaboard Airline R. R.	11	22.7	7.2	14.4	20.3	....	14.4	20.3
Texas Instruments	23	12.2	2.1	6.4	9.1	10.7	6.8	9.5
Unilever N. V. Adr.†	5	28.7	12.7	27.7	....	....	28.7	....
United Air Lines	23	17.6	2.5	7.4	12.0	15.1	10.0	15.4
United Shoe Machinery	7	18.2	6.7	14.3	....	....	14.3	....
Universal Oil Products	14	25.5	4.2	13.6	21.9	25.0	14.5	22.7
Western Air Lines	9	15.4	4.3	10.3	14.8	....	10.3	14.8

†American drawing receipts.

TABLE 16

Detailed Structure of Ownership Concentration by Investment
Companies—Northwest Airlines
December 31, 1966

Rank	Investment Company	Percentage of Outstanding Shares Owned	Cumulative Percentage
1	Dreyfus Fund	7.38	7.38
2	Fidelity Trend Fund	3.50	.....
3	Investment Company of America	2.94	.....
4	Fundamental Investors	2.18	16.00
5	United Accumulative Fund	1.69	.....
6	Fidelity Fund	1.65	.....
7	Massachusetts Investors Growth Stock Fund	1.53	.....
8	State Street Investment Company	1.44	22.31
9	Television-Electronics Fund	1.21	.....
10	Fidelity Capital Fund	1.21	.....
11	Channing Growth Fund	.98	.....
12	Keystone Custodian Funds Series S-4	.98	26.69

Number of shares outstanding   9,149,626
Number of shares held by large investment companies   3,149,137
Number of investment companies   28
Concentration percentage   34.4

TABLE 17

Portfolio Concentration Percentages for Investment Company Complexes—1966

Investment Company Group	Portfolio Company	Percentage of Portfolio Company's Stock Held by Group
Fidelity Group	National Airlines	8.1
Massachusetts Investment Trust	International Mining	8.6
Keystone	Chicago Great Western	8.7
Fidelity Group	Vornado, Inc.	9.0
Fidelity Group	Metro-Goldwyn-Mayer	9.3
Fidelity Group	Raytheon Co.	9.4
Fidelity Group	Pabst Brewing	10.3
Keystone	Pacific Southwest Airlines	12.0
Fidelity Group	Chicago & North Western	12.9
Investors Diversified Services	Armstrong Rubber	13.7
Fidelity Group	Copperweld Steel Company	15.1
Investors Diversified Services	Norfolk Southern R. R.	18.3

TABLE 18

Assets of Noninsured Corporate Pension Funds
(Market Value in Millions of Dollars)

Year	Total	Corporate Stock	Corporate Bonds	Other Assets
Noninsured corporate pension funds				
1920	$ 50*	n.a.	n.a.	n.a.
1922	90*	n.a.	$ 55†	n.a.
1925	150*	n.a.	n.a.	n.a.
1929	500*	....	300	n.a.
1933	700*	$ 1†	420†	n.a.
1939	1,050*	12†	578†	n.a.
1940	1,000‡	100‡	n.a.	n.a.
1945	2,327	212†	663†	$1,452
1946	2,843	272	928	1,642
1947	3,436	367	1,223	1,846
1948	4,046	462	1,544	2,040
1949	4,695	586	1,863	2,246
1950	5,595	774	2,080	2,741
1951	7,042	1,194	2,171	3,677
1952	8,677	1,754	2,162	4,761
1953	10,491	2,203	2,297	5,991
1954	13,241	3,703	2,284	7,254
1955	16,066	5,305	2,536	8,225

*Data from Raymond W. Goldsmith, *A Study of Savings in the United States,* Vol. I (Princeton, N.J.: Princeton University Press, 1955), 468.

†Data from Raymond W. Goldsmith, Robert E. Lipsey, and Morris Mendelson, *Studies in the National Balance Sheet of the United States,* Vol. II (Princeton, N.J.: Princeton University Press, 1963); 1920-39 corporate stock data, 318-19; corporate bond data, 310; 1945-55 data, 180-81.

‡Data from U.S., Congress, House, Committee on Interstate and Foreign Commerce, *Report of the Securities and Exchange Commission on Public Policy Implications of Investment Company Growth,* H.R. 2337, 89th Cong., 2d sess., Dec. 2, 1966 (Washington, D.C.: Government Printing Office, 1966), p. 276.

(*Continued*)

TABLE 18 (*Continued*)

Year	Total	Corporate Stock	Corporate Bonds	Other Assets
1955	$16,670§	$ 5,666§	$ 7,289§	$3,715
1956	18,470	6,600	8,141	3,729
1957	20,913	7,027	10,139	3,747
1958	25,962	10,880	11,236	3,846
1959	29,841	13,723	11,794	4,324
1960	34,073	15,505	13,687	4,881
1961	41,629	21,559	14,815	5,258
1962	42,821	20,685	16,171	5,965
1963	50,068	26,103	17,327	6,638
1964	58,131	31,651	18,845	7,635
1965	65,550	37,514	19,652	8,384
1966	64,903	36,219	19,980	8,704
1967	......	......	......	.....
1968	......	......	......	.....
All private noninsured pension funds				
1958	$ 28.2	$11.6	......	.....
1959	32.4	14.5	......	.....
1960	37.1	16.5	......	.....
1961	45.8	22.9	......	.....
1962	46.7	21.9	......	.....
1963	54.6	27.7	......	.....
1964	63.4	33.6	......	.....
1965	71.4	39.7	......	.....
1966	71.0	38.6	......	.....
1967	82.7	49.5	......	.....
1968	92.7	59.6	......	.....

§Data from U.S., Securities and Exchange Commission, Division of Trading and Markets, *Corporate Pension Funds,* supplemental tables, July, 1964 (mimeographed), Table 2 for years 1955-63. For later years see U.S., Securities and Exchange Commission, *Statistical Series,* releases on private noninsured pension funds. The 1964 supplemental tables include book value data beginning with 1951.

TABLE 19

Corporate Stock Owned by Institutional Investors
(In Millions of Dollars)

Year	Noninsured Corporate Pension Funds*	Investment Companies	Life Insurance Companies†	Property and Casualty Insurance Companies	State and Local Pension Funds
1900	.....	.....	$ 95	$ 121‡	.....
1912	.....	.....	84	230‡	.....
1920	.....	.....	75	.....	.....
1922	.....	$ 69§	75	370‡	.....
1925	.....	.....	81	.....	.....
1929	.....	2,191§	352	1,511‡	.....
1930	.....	.....	519	.....	.....
1933	$ 1	1,006§	535	952‡	.....
1935	.....	.....	583	.....	.....
1939	12	1,216§	568	1,458‡	.....
1940	100	1,800∥	605	.....	.....
1945	212	2,910#	999	2,420‡	.....
1949	586	3,510#	.....	2,950‡	.....
1950	774	4,340#	2,103	3,600	.....
1952	1,754	6,580#	2,221	.....	.....
1955	5,666	12,750#	3,633	5,400∥	200**
1956	6,600	13,360#	3,503	.....	.....
1957	7,027	12,510#	3,391	.....	.....
1958	10,880	18,080#	4,109	.....	.....
1959	13,723	.....	4,561	.....	.....

(*Continued*)

TABLE 19 (*Continued*)

Year	Noninsured Corporate Pension Funds*	Investment Companies	Life Insurance Companies†	Property and Casualty Insurance Companies	State and Local Pension Funds
1960	$15,505	$20,500‖	$ 4,981	$ 7,500‖	$ 600**
1961	21,559	....	6,258	....	....
1962	20,685	....	6,302	....	....
1963	26,103	....	7,135	....	....
1964	31,651	34,600††	7,938	....	....
1965	37,514	41,200††	9,126	12,400‖	2,200‖
1966	36,219	37,400††	8,755	11,000††	2,800††
1967	....	51,000††	10,787	13,000††	4,200††
1968	....	59,600††	13,230	14,700††	4,800††

*See Table 18, pp. 183-84.

†Data from Institute of Life Insurance, *Life Insurance Fact Book, 1968* (New York: Institute of Life Insurance, 1969), p. 81.

‡Data from Raymond W. Goldsmith, Robert E. Lipsey, and Morris Mendelson, *Studies in the National Balance Sheet of the United States*, Vol. II (Princeton, N.J.: Princeton University Press, 1963), 318-19 and 176-77.

§Data from *ibid.*, 318-19.

‖Data from U.S., Congress, House, Committee on Interstate and Foreign Commerce, *Report of the Securities and Exchange Commission on Public Policy Implications of Investment Company Growth*, H.R. 2337, 89th Cong., 2d sess., Dec. 2, 1966 (Washington, D.C.: Government Printing Office, 1966), p. 276.

#Data from Goldsmith, Lipsey, and Mendelson, *Studies in the National Balance Sheet*, 168-69.

**Data from U.S., Congress, House, *Report on...Investment Company Growth*, p. 276.

††Data from U.S., Securities and Exchange Commission, *Statistical Series*, Release No. 2358, May 1, 1969, Table 3, p. 6.

TABLE 20

Historical and Projected Growth of Private Retirement Plans*

End of Year	Covered Active Employees (In Millions)	Beneficiaries (In Millions)	Benefit Payments (In Billions)	Pension Fund Reserves (Assets) (In Billions)		
				Insured Plans	Non-insured Plans	Total
Historical data						
1940	4.1	.16	$ .14	. . .	. . .	$ 2.4
1945	6.4	.31	.22	. . .	. . .	5.4
1950	9.8	.45	.37	$ 5.6	$ 6.5	12.1
1955	15.4	.99	.85	11.3	16.1	27.5
1960	21.2	1.78	1.75	18.8	33.1	52.0
1962	23.1	2.09	2.24	21.6	41.9	63.5
1964	27.0†	2.40	2.70	25.0	51.5	76.5
1967	31.1†	. . .	4.30‡	32.0†	71.8	103.8
1968	. . .	. . .	4.91‡	35.0†	80.3§	115.3
Projections						
1970	34.0	3.90	4.40	. . .	. . .	125.0
1975	38.7	5.20	6.50	. . .	. . .	175.0
1980	42.7	6.60	9.00	. . .	. . .	225.0

*Data from U.S., President's Committee on Corporate Pension Funds and Other Private Retirement and Welfare Programs, *Public Policy and Private Pension Programs,* a report to the President on private employee retirement plans (Washington, D.C.: Government Printing Office, 1965), Appendix A, Table 1. Historical data were brought together by the Office of the Actuary, Social Security Administration. Projections were based on estimates made by the Social Security Administration and the National Bureau of Economic Research.

†Data from Institute of Life Insurance, *Life Insurance Fact Book,* 1968 (New York: Institute of Life Insurance, 1968), pp. 39, 40.

‡Includes $910,000 paid to 935,000 persons under insured plans in 1967, and $1,030,000 under these plans in 1968. See sources listed above.

§ Data from U.S., Securities and Exchange Commission, *Statistical Series,* Release No. 2406, Dec. 12, 1969. Comparisons with SEC data indicate clearly that the book value series was used.

TABLE 21

Corporate Pension Fund Assets by Size of Fund
(Percentage of Total)

	1957*			1966†		
Size of Fund (In Thousands)	Number of Plans	Total Assets	Stock of Other Companies	Number of Plans	Total Assets	Common Stock
$100,000 and over	1.5	55.3	50.2	3.3	50.3	51.5
$20,000 to $99,999	5.0	18.1	19.7	13.5	33.3	33.1
$10,000 to $19,999	7.3	10.2	10.2	8.0	6.4	6.4
$5,000 to $9,999	9.1	6.0	7.4	13.0	5.2	4.8
$2,500 to $4,999	10.3	3.9	4.3	12.3	2.4	2.3
$1,000 to $2,499	15.2	3.0	3.6	16.8	1.6	1.3
$500 to $999	13.0	1.2	1.3	11.2	0.5	0.4
$0 to $499	38.6	2.3	3.3	21.9	0.3	0.2
Total	100.0	100.0	100.0	100.0	100.0	100.0

*Unpublished sample statistics of Securities and Exchange Commission, Oct., 1958, quoted by Victor L. Andrews, "Noninsured Corporate and State and Local Government Retirement Funds in the Financial Structure," in *Private Capital Markets,* ed. by Irwin Friend, Hyman P. Minsky, and Victor L. Andrews (Englewood Cliffs, N.J.: Prentice-Hall, Inc., 1964), Table III-A5, p. 525.

†Unpublished sample statistics prepared by the Branch of Capital Markets, Securities and Exchange Commission, Oct., 1967.

TABLE 22

Asset Size of Corporate Pension Funds Held by Firms
with Largest Assets Responding to 1967 Survey

Size of Fund (In Millions)	Number of Funds	
	Total Assets	Book Value of Common Stock
$1,000 and up	5	...
$500 to $999	1	3
$250 to $499	6	5
$100 to $249	26	7
$50 to $99	8	19
$25 to $49	1	13
Total	47	47

TABLE 23

Investment and Portfolio Concentration Practices and Rules for Noninsured Corporate Pension Funds

Practices and Rules	Number of Responses	Frequency Distribution Maximum Percentage										
		1	2	3	4	5	6	7	8	9	10	Above 10
Practice												
Largest percentage of investment in common stock in one portfolio company	11	1	1	...	1	...	2	2	...	1	...	3*
Largest percentage of portfolio company's stock	14	8	3	2	...	1	...	...	...	...	...	...
Rules												
Largest percentage of investment in common stock in one portfolio company	16	...	2	2	1	6†	1	...	...	...	4	...‡
Largest percentage of portfolio company's stock	15	3	1	2	...	8	...	...	...	...	1	...

*Of those holding an investment of over 10.0 per cent in common stock in one portfolio company, one held 11.0 per cent, one 12.8 per cent, and one 14.0 per cent.

†One fund added the qualification: except for a few small companies. Another fund stated that it was very concerned about exceptions.

‡One respondent said that his fund seldom went over 15 per cent.

TABLE 24

Attitudes of Corporate Pension Fund Administrators toward Portfolio Concentration Problems
(Number of Responses in Parentheses)

General Response	Amplification of Response Giving More Specific Reasons	Additional, Even More Detailed Reasons
No (serious and/or present) ownership concentration problem exists (26)	Because trustee has discretion in investment matters within limits of agreed upon general policy (9)	And corporation's concern is solely with investment performance (3)
	Because common stock portfolio is widely diversified and total investment relatively small (8)	
	Because institutional investors do not act in concert (1)	
	Because there is no desire to use pension funds to take over other businesses (1)	
	Because there is no public information about the portfolio holdings of other pension funds (1)	
	Because the banks as trustee usually limit ownership to 5 per cent of one issue (2)*	Because banks appear to have widely different and uncoordinated policies (1)
	Because case for serious concentration problem is not yet proved (2)	
	If a serious concentration problem exists it need not be unfavorable (3)	
	If a serious problem arose present legislation is adequate to deal with it (1)	

*Comments received from trust department officers of two banks that are among the ten largest in terms of the amount of pension funds administered.

(*Continued*)

TABLE 24 (*Continued*)

General Response	Amplification of Response Giving More Specific Reasons	Additional, Even More Detailed Reasons
Concern with ownership concentration (14)	Influence on management (6)	Administrators (trustees) usually vote with management (or seldom vote against management) (2)
		Usually through buying and selling shares (3)
		If a problem were to arise the solution should lie in professional integrity and existing governmental regulation (2)
		However, institutional investors' policies will differ so much that eventual governmental influence is inevitable (1)
		May be detrimental to small stockholders (1)
		Because of the possibility of a "takeover" (1)
	Influence on price (3)	Problem in disposing of large holdings (3)
		Institutional buying and holding can bid up prices of desirable stocks (1)
	Influence on trustee (1)	Trustee may fall heir to new and unwanted responsibilities, or to responsibilities that he is not qualified to handle (1)
		May lead to new legislation that restricts investment flexibility (1)
	But same problems exist for other institutional investors (2)	
	Problems may be serious where portfolio company is small (4)	But a commingled pension trust fund eases the problem (1)

Concern (more directly) with stock prices (13)

Problems may become serious for all pension trust funds considered as a whole (1)

Increases price instability or price risk (12)

Because of reduction of floating or market supply (4)

Because of uniformity of buying and selling decisions (4)

Because price instability affects portfolio company itself (2)

Because of extent of holdings of individual funds (or trustees) (2)

If fewer different stocks are held in an effort to improve performance (1)

If the number of outstanding shares is small (1)

Because of steady flow of funds into market (1)

Increases price stability (1)

Diversification is sought (or concentration avoided) to reduce market instability of investment (2)

TABLE 25

Assets Administered by Trust Departments of Commercial Banks
November 1 to December 31, 1967*
(Dollar Amounts in Millions)

Name of Bank	Employee Benefit Accounts		All Trust Assets			Stock Included in All Trust Assets			Percentage of All Trust Assets Held by Bank
	Amount	Percentage of Total	Rank by Size	Amount	Percentage of Total Assets	Rank by Size	Amount	Percentage of Total Stock	
Morgan Guaranty Trust	$ 9,655	13.34	1	$ 16,824	6.73	1	$ 11,361	7.09	67.53
Bankers Trust Company	7,685	10.62	3	11,091	4.43	3	6,807	4.25	61.37
Chase Manhattan Bank	6,513	9.00	2	13,644	5.45	2	9,426	5.89	69.09
First National City Bank (NYC)	4,706	6.50	4	10,872	4.35	4	6,481	4.05	59.61
Mellon National Bank (Pittsburgh)	3,289	4.55	6	7,630	3.05	5	5,552	3.47	72.77
First National Bank of Chicago	2,978	4.12	9	5,430	2.17	9	3,978	2.48	73.26
Manufacturers Hanover Trust Company	2,701	3.73	7	7,330	2.93	8	4,507	2.81	61.49
Continental Illinois National Bank	2,217	3.06	10	5,137	2.05	10	3,128	1.95	60.89
National Bank of Detroit	2,012	2.78	17	3,427	1.37	16	2,215	1.38	64.63
Chemical Bank New York	1,737	2.40	11	4,593	1.84	13	2,632	1.64	57.30
Ten-bank total	$43,493	60.10		$ 85,978	34.37		$ 56,087	35.01	
Total accounts†	$72,900	100.00		$253,300	100.00		$161,700	100.00	

*Data from U.S. Congress, House, Committee on Banking and Currency, *Commercial Banks and Their Trust Activities, Emerging Influence on the American Economy*, Vol. I, Staff Report for the Subcommittee on Domestic Finance, 90th Cong., 2d sess., July 8, 1968 (Washington, D.C.: Government Printing Office, 1968), 33-35 and 47-48. Percentages for individual banks except for those in the final column are given in the report itself.

†Data cover only trust departments with portfolio concentrations greater than 5 per cent.

TABLE 26

Distribution of Voting Rights in Common Stock Held by Trust Departments of Commercial Banks (Eight Selected Corporations)*

Corporation	Bank	Total of Shares Outstanding	Trustees' Voting Rights by Percentage		
			Sole Voting Rights	Partial Voting Rights	No Voting Rights
Ford Motor Company	Manufacturers National Bank (Detroit)	6.9	0.2	....	6.6
Gulf Oil Corporation	Mellon National Bank & Trust (Pittsburgh)	17.1	1.9	10.8	4.4
Boeing Company	Chase Manhattan Bank	8.7	7.2	1.3	0.2
General Dynamics	Bankers Trust Company	6.2	4.7	1.5	....
Trans World Airlines	State Street Bank & Trust (Boston)	6.2	....	....	6.2
Trans World Airlines	Chase Manhattan Bank	7.8	7.4	0.3	0.1
Trans World Airlines	Morgan Guaranty Trust	7.4	6.1	0.3	1.0
Northwest Airlines	Chase Manhattan Bank	11.0	9.9	0.9	0.2
Louisville & Nashville Railroad Company	Mercantile Safe Deposit & Trust (Baltimore)	33.9	0.6	0.1	33.2
Gimbel Brothers	State Street Bank & Trust	16.2	0.5	0.1	15.5

*Data from U.S., Congress, House, Committee on Banking and Currency, *Commercial Banks and Their Trust Activities: Emerging Influence on the American Economy*, Vol. I, Staff Report for the Subcommittee on Domestic Finance, 90th Cong., 2d sess., July 8, 1968 (Washington, D.C.: Government Printing Office, 1968), pp. 93-215.

TABLE 27

Frequency Distribution of Percentage of Common Stock Held in
Leading Corporations by Forty-Nine Large Banks*

Percentage	Number of Banks
15 or more	28
14.0 to 14.9	7
13.0 to 13.9	2
12.0 to 12.9	7
11.0 to 11.9	10
10.0 to 10.9	6
9.0 to 9.9	17
8.0 to 8.9	23
7.0 to 7.9	30
6.0 to 6.9	43
5.0 to 5.9	50
Total	223

*Data from U.S., Congress, House, Committee on Banking and Currency, *Commercial Banks and Their Trust Activities: Emerging Influence on the American Economy,* Vol. I, Staff Report for the Subcommittee on Domestic Finance, 90th Cong., 2d sess., July 8, 1968 (Washington, D.C.: Government Printing Office, 1968), pp. 93-215. Percentages of 5 or more only provided. Tabulation prepared by author.

TABLE 28

Stock and Total Assets of Life Insurance Companies*
(Dollar Amounts in Millions)

Year	Total Assets	Stock			Stock as a Percentage of Total Assets
		Preferred	Common	Total	
1890	$ 771	....	....	$ 30	3.9
1900	1,742	....	....	95	5.5
1910	3,876	....	....	130	3.3
1920	7,320	....	....	75	1.0
1925	11,538	....	....	81	0.7
1930	18,880	....	....	519	2.8
1935	23,216	$ 365	....	583	2.5
1940	30,802	417	....	605	2.0
1945	44,797	819	....	999	2.2
1950	64,020	1,454	$ 649	2,103	3.3
1955	90,432	1,744	1,889	3,633	4.0
1960	119,576	1,798	3,183	4,981	4.2
1961	126,816	2,035	4,223	6,258	4.9
1962	133,291	2,183	4,119	6,302	4.7
1963	141,121	2,315	4,820	7,135	5.0
1964	149,479	2,516	5,442	7,938	5.3
1965	158,884	2,863	6,263	9,126	5.7
1966	167,455	2,829	6,003	8,832	5.3
1967	177,832	3,067	7,810	10,877	6.1
1968	188,636	3,235	9,995	13,230	6.9

*Data from Institute of Life Insurance, *Life Insurance Fact Book*, 1969 (New York: Institute of Life Insurance, 1969), pp. 68 and 81; Houghton Bell and Harold G. Fraine, "Legal Framework, Trends, and Developments in Investment Practices of Life Insurance Companies," *Law and Contemporary Problems*, XVII (Winter, 1952–"Institutional Investments"), 55.

TABLE 29

Common Stock and Total Assets of Fifteen Largest Life Insurance Companies*
(Dollar Amounts in Millions)

Company	Year	Total Assets (Book Value)	Common Stock		Number of Stocks
			Amount	Valuation Basis	
Prudential Life	1967	$25,111	$1,068	Market	178
Metropolitan Life	1967	24,601	170	Market	156
Equitable Life Assurance (New York)	1966	12,576	416		128
New York Life	1966	9,196	308		106
John Hancock Mutual	1967	8,865	478	Book	99
Aetna Life Insurance	1966	6,244	107	Book	63
Northwestern Mutual	1968	5,229	160	Book	91
Travelers (Hartford)†	1966	5,094	188		137
Connecticut General (Hartford)	1967	3,634	83	Market	119
Massachusetts Mutual	1966	3,436	168	Market	151
Connecticut Mutual	1966	2,249	175	Market	96
Mutual of New York	1967	3,427	296	Market	100
New England Mutual Life Insurance	1966	2,981	207		...
Mutual Benefit Life	1967	2,333	43	Market	102
Penn Mutual (Philadelphia)	1967	2,203	55		70

*Data from annual reports, investment summaries of companies, and letters to the author.
†Includes property and casualty companies in Travelers group.

TABLE 30

Contributions of Highly Concentrated
Insurance Companies to Concentration Ratios*

Contribution to Concentration Ratio in Percentage Points	Number of Portfolio Companies in This Range
0.1 to 2.4	20
2.5 to 4.9	17
5.0 to 7.4	7
7.5 to 9.9	0
10.0 to 12.4	1
	45

*Table 43, pages 214-15, reports fifty companies with overall concentration ratios of 20 per cent or above in 1966.

TABLE 31

Stock and Total Assets of Property and Casualty Insurance Companies
(Dollar Amounts in Billions)

Year	Total Assets		Stocks		NYSE Listed Holdings Only*
	Estimate	Estimate	Estimate	Estimate	
1900	...	$ 0.5†	$ 0.1†	...	...
1912	...	1.0†	0.2†	...	...
1920	$ 2.5‡	...	...	$ 0.5‡	...
1925	3.6‡	...	...	0.9‡	...
1930	5.1‡	4.7† (1929)	1.5† (1929)	1.7‡	...
1935	4.0‡	3.5† (1933)	1.0† (1933)	1.2‡	...
1940	5.0‡	...	...	1.6‡	...
1945	7.6‡	7.7†	1.9†	2.4‡	...
1950	13.1‡§	...	3.6§	3.4‡	$ 1.7 (1949)
1955	21.7§	...	5.4§	...	4.5 (1956)
1960	29.4§	...	7.5§	...	6.0
1961	...	...	...	...	7.7
1962	...	...	...	...	7.1
1963	...	...	...	...	8.2
1964	...	...	...	11.4‖	9.5
1965	42.1§	...	12.4§	12.0‖	10.1
1966	...	...	...	11.0‖	9.2
1967	...	...	...	13.0‖	11.0
1968	...	...	...	14.7‖	12.6

*Data from New York Stock Exchange, "Institutional Holdings, of NYSE-Listed Stock–1968," *New York Stock Exchange Research Report,* Jan., 1969 (a two-page mimeographed release).

†Data from Raymond W. Goldsmith, *Financial Intermediaries in the American Economy Since 1900* (Princeton, N.J.: Princeton University Press, 1958), p. 225. Goldsmith has separate estimates for fire and marine insurance companies and for casualty and miscellaneous insurance companies, pp. 225, 375, and 378.

‡Data from Charles H. Schmidt and Eleanor J. Stockwell, "The Changing Importance of Institutional Investors in the American Capital Markets," *Law and Contemporary Problems,* XVII (Winter, 1952–"Institutional Investments"), 12.

§Data from U.S., Congress, House, Committee on Interstate and Foreign Commerce, *Report of the Securities and Exchange Commission on Public Policy Implications of Investment Company Growth,* H.R. 2337, 89th Cong., 2d sess., Dec. 2, 1966 (Washington, D.C.: Government Printing Office, 1966), p. 276.

‖Data from U.S., Securities and Exchange Commission, *Statistical Series,* Release No. 2358, May 1, 1969, Table 3, p. 6.

TABLE 32

Common Stock and Total Assets of Fifteen of the Largest
Property and Casualty Insurance Companies*

Company	Year	Total Assets (In Millions)	Common Stock	
			(In Millions)	Number of Stocks
Continental Insurance Company	1967	$2,075	$1,359	284
Insurance Company of North America	1967	1,604	628	212
Aetna Casualty and Surety	1967	1,538	480	164
Allstate Insurance Companies	1967	1,528	563	186
State Farm Insurance	1966	1,230	83	85
Liberty Mutual (combined companies)	1967	1,226	121	...
U.S. Fidelity and Guaranty	1967	1,125	449	150
Home Insurance	1967	1,019	361	133
Hartford Fire, Accident and others	1967	953	311	182
Continental Casualty Company	1967	865	187	156
Great American	1967	587	310	194
St. Paul Fire and Marine	1967	585	104	213
Reliance Insurance Company	1967	488	211	179
Maryland American General	1967	474	124	242
Nationwide Mutual Insurance Company	1968	399	26	60

*Data from annual reports, investment summaries, and letters to the author.

TABLE 33

State and Local Pension Funds

Year	Total Assets (In Millions)*†	Major Retirement Systems Only‡		
		Total Assets (In Millions)	Stock (In Millions)*//	Percentage of Stock to Total
1920	$ 49	...	...	...
1925	203	...	...	...
1930	494	...	...	...
1935	938	...	...	...
1940	1,629	...	...	...
1945	2,615	...	...	...
1950	5,300	...	...	...
1955	10,500	...	...	...
1960	19,300	...	...	...
1961	21,700	$13,234	$ 335	2.5
1962	24,300	...	...	...
1963	27,100	16,943	664	3.9
1964	30,200	...	...	...
1965	33,500	21,410	1,064	5.0

1966	37,300	...	...	...
1967	41,300	27,872	1,867	6.8
1968	45,800	...	...	...
1971§	55,200	...	...	...
1976§	83,400	...	...	...
1981§	124,600	...	...	...

*Data from Raymond W. Goldsmith, *A Study of Savings in the United States*, Vol. I (Princeton, N.J.: Princeton University Press, 1955), 1063, years 1920-45.

†Data from U.S., Securities and Exchange Commission, various releases for 1950-68.

‡Data from Investment Bankers Association of America, *State and Local Pension Funds: 1968*, prepared by Thomas M. Adams (Washington, D.C.: Investment Bankers Assoc., 1968), p. 7.

§Data from Daniel M. Holland, *Private Pension Funds: Projected Growth*, National Bureau of Business and Economic Research, Occasional Paper 97 (New York: Columbia University Press, 1966), p. 143.

∥Two other estimates (in millions of dollars) for the stock held are as follows:

	NYSE Listed Stocks Only	State and Local Trust Funds
1960	$0.5	n.a.
1964	1.5	$1.7
1965	2.0	2.4
1966	2.2	2.8
1967	3.6	4.2
1968	5.4	4.8 (preliminary)

Data for the NYSE stock are from "Institutional Holdings of NYSE-Listed Stock—1968," *New York Stock Exchange Research Report*, Jan., 1969 (a two-page mimeographed release). Data for state and local trust funds are from U.S., Securities and Exchange Commission, *Statistical Series*, Release No. 2358, May 1, 1969, Table 3, p. 6.

TABLE 34

Stock and Total Assets of Fifteen Largest State and Local Pension Funds,* 1967

State or Area	Number of Separate Systems	Total Assets (In Millions)	Stock		Legal Maximum Authorized Percentage
			Millions of Dollars	Percentage of Total Assets	
New York City	5	$4,920	$ 86.8	1.8	20†
State of New York	2	4,801	295.1	6.1	20†
California	2	3,938	....	0.0	25
Ohio	4	2,459	55.3	13.0	25
Pennsylvania	2	2,092	....	0.0	0
New Jersey	6	1,819	33.6	2.5	10
Texas	2	1,276	228.8	17.9	50
Los Angeles	1	1,031	1.1	.1	25
Wisconsin	24	876	178.1	20.3	35
Illinois	3	672	68.1	10.1	10
Minnesota	7	653	146.5	22.4	35
Michigan	2	640	20.4	3.2	10
Louisiana	2	601	3.7	0.7	No limit
North Carolina	1	587	42.5	7.2	15
Florida	4	558	....	0.0	10

*Data from Investment Bankers Association of America, *State and Local Pension Funds: 1968*, prepared by Thomas M. Adams (Washington, D.C.: Investment Bankers Assoc., 1968).

†This limit has been raised to 50 per cent according to the following source: George W. Cloos, "Pension Funds and Capital Markets," *Business Conditions,* a publication of the Federal Reserve Bank of Chicago, Aug., 1969, p. 12.

TABLE 35

Frequency Distribution of Common Stock Maximum
Percentages Authorized for State Pension Funds*

Maximum Percentage of Assets	Number of States
0	9
10	12
12	1
15	2
20	5
25	5
35	3
40	1
50	4
No maximum specified	7
Not available	1
Total	50

*Data from Investment Bankers Association of America, *State and Local Pension Funds: 1968*, prepared by Thomas M. Adams (Washington, D.C.: Investment Bankers Assoc., 1968). Summary by Soldofsky from state-by-state information included in this publication.

TABLE 36

Common Stock and Total Assets of Nine Large Foundations*
(Dollar Amounts in Millions)

Foundation	Year	Total Assets (Book Value)	Common Stock		
			Book Value	Market Value	Number of Stocks
Ford Foundation	1967	$3,121	$541†	n.a.†	164
Rockefeller Foundation	1964	287	253	$865	45‖
Carnegie Foundation	1967	n.a.	109	208	63
Alfred P. Sloan Foundation	1967	n.a.	204	326	47
John A. Hartford Foundation	1967	186#	...‡	...‡	...‡
Duke Endowment	1966	167	108	619	...§
Commonwealth Foundation	1966	95	26	77	50
Lilly Endowment	1967	30	29	394	...
Danforth Foundation	1967	27 (203)#	...	...	...

*Data from annual reports of the foundations and financial supplements when available.

†Excludes Ford Motor Company Nonvoting Common Stock of $1,398,830,248.

‡No information given on stock holdings, but it is very likely to be predominantly that of the Greater Atlantic and Pacific Tea Company.

§Includes 13,035,100 shares of Duke Power which had a book value of $95,141,000 and market value of $532,810,000.

‖1965 figure.

#Market value.

TABLE 37

Common Stocks and Total Assets of Seven Large University Endowment Funds*
(Dollar Amounts in Millions)

University	Date	Total Assets	Common Stock		
			Book Value	Market Value	Number of Shares
Harvard University	6/30/67	$1,038	$593	n.a.	194
Yale University	6/30/67	409	230	n.a.	113
Massachusetts Institute of Technology	6/30/67	231	51	$149	n.a.
Princeton University	6/30/67	186	103	351	161
University of Chicago	5/31/68	n.a.	175	n.a.	88
Cornell University	3/31/68	173	103	146	111
University of California	6/30/67	132	51	n.a.	122

*Data from correspondence with university officials. Also see Armon Glenn, "Degree of Risk; Common Stocks Now Constitute Nearly 58% of College Endowment Funds," *Barron's*, March 25, 1968, pp. 5 and 15. The University of Chicago's principal endowment is stated in this article to be $287 million. The endowments in some instances differ from those given in the table.

TABLE 38

Gross National Product Projections—Total and Per Capita

Gross National Product	Year			
	1975	1985	2000	2020
Total GNP in billions of dollars:				
Projected GNP in 1965 prices*				
Low (3.4 per cent growth rate)	$ 918	$1,285	$ 2,177	$4,008
High (4.9 per cent growth rate)	1,062	1,713	3,628	8,947
GNP adjusted for price increases				
2 percent annual increase†				
Low	$1,119	$1,910	$ 4,354	....
High	1,295	2,546	7,356	....
4 per cent annual increase†				
Low	$1,359	$2,815	$ 8,590	....
High	1,572	3,753	14,316	....
Per capita GNP in dollars:				
Projected GNP in 1965 prices*				
Low	$4,150	$5,000	$ 6,850	....
High	4,800	6,650	11,550	....
Adjusted for 2 per cent annual price increase†				
Low	$5,059	$7,430	$13,700	....
High	5,851	9,882	23,100	....

*Data from Herman Kahn and Anthony J. Wiener, *The Year 2000: A Framework for Speculation on the Next Thirty-three Years* (New York: Macmillan Co., 1967), p. 168.

†Prepared by Soldofsky.

TABLE 39

Projected Market Values for Stock Holdings of Financial Institutions

Financial Institution	Market Value (In Billions)			Percentage of Total Market Value			Growth Rates (Percentage per Year)	
	1968*	1980	2000	1968	1980	2000	1968-80	1981-2000
Noninsured corporate pension funds	$ 56.0	$ 269	$2,362	7.3	13.7	25.8	14.0	11.5
Investment companies	59.6	258	1,730	7.8	13.1	18.9	13.0	10.0
State and local pension funds	4.8	37	357	0.6	1.9	3.9	17.0	12.0
Life insurance companies	12.8	46	171	1.7	2.3	1.8	13.5	6.8
Property and casualty insurance companies	14.7	37	118	1.9	1.9	1.3	8.0	6.0
University and college endowments	9.0	28	190	1.2	1.4	2.1	10.0	10.0
Foundations	15.8	28	74	2.1	1.4	0.8	5.0	5.0
Common trust funds	4.4	11	53	0.6	0.6	0.6	9.0	8.0
Total institutional holdings	$177.1	$ 714	$5,055	23.2	36.3	55.2	12.3	10.3
Market value of all outstanding stock†	$761.3	$1,966	$9,161				8.0	8.0

*Data from U.S., Securities and Exchange Commission, *Statistical Series*, Release No. 2358, May 1, 1969, p. 5, Table 3.

†For widely held companies only includes both common and preferred stocks.

TABLE 40

Stock Diversification Patterns by Type of Financial Intermediary and Size Class

Financial Intermediaries			Number of Stocks in Portfolio							
Type	Number	Average Numbers of Stocks Held	Under 50	50-74	75-99	100-124	125-149	150-174	175-199	200 or more
$1 billion or more										
Investment companies	7	119.7	...	...	1	3	2	1	...	...
Corporate pension funds	0	...	...	...	...	...	...	...	...	...
Life insurance companies	1	178.0	...	...	...	...	...	...	1	...
Property and casualty insurance companies	1	284.0	...	...	...	...	...	...	...	1
$250 million to $1 billion										
Investment companies	23	91.0	...	5	10	7	1	...	...	...
Corporate pension funds	7	185.1	...	...	...	1	1	1	...	4
Life insurance companies	4	108.2	...	...	1	2	1	...	...	...
Property and casualty insurance companies	7	174.4	...	...	...	...	1	2	3	1

$100 million to $250 million

Investment companies	29	75.3	6	13	5	4	...	...	1
Corporate pension funds	8	142.4	...	1	1	2	1	1	2
Life insurance companies	9	118.1	...	1	3	1	1	3	...
Property and casualty insurance companies	6	169.5	...	1	...	...	...	2	1	2

$50 million to $100 million

Investment companies	28	63.8	8	11	7	2	...	...	...
Corporate pension funds	17	102.6	...	3	5	5	2	2	...
Life insurance companies	14	88.8	...	5	4	4	1	...	...
Property and casualty insurance companies	5	120.8	...	1	2	1	1	...	...

$25 million to $50 million

Investment companies	24	68.1	6	10	5	1	2	...	...
Corporate pension funds	13	104.2	...	2	4	3	2	2	...
Life insurance companies	5	75.4	1	1	2	1	...	...	...
Property and casualty insurance companies*	...	.....	...	...	...	...	...	...	...

*Too few respondents to merit calculations.

TABLE 41

Companies Cross-classified by Market Value of Common Stock and Portfolio Concentration Percentage
December 31, 1966

Dollar-Size Class	Market Value of Common Stock by Company (In Millions)	Number of Firms	Distribution by Portfolio Concentration Percentage									
			0-2.49	2.50-4.99	5.0-9.99	10.0-14.99	15.0-19.99	20.0-24.99	25.0-29.99	30.0-34.99	35.0+
I	$2.29 to $63.38	28	11	2	5	3	2	1	4	...	...
II	$64.08 to $100.18	23	9	5	4	2	1	1	...	...	1
III	$100.36 to $138.14	44	11	3	5	13	8	3	1	...	...
IV	$139.64 to $191.68	37	3	9	5	9	5	5	1	...	...
V	$191.96 to $277.74	44	7	2	7	13	9	2	2	2	...
VI	$279.26 to $370.98	39	6	5	6	9	3	3	4	...	3
VII	$371.41 to $527.43	44	4	3	9	15	6	3	3	...	1
VIII	$529.04 to $756.86	35	4	2	11	9	6	2	...	1	...
IX	$760.10 to $1,291.10	41	4	8	6	7	10	5	...	...	1
X	$1,296.84 to $35,132.06	30	5	4	8	9	2	1	1	...	...
	Total	365	64	43	66	89	52	26	16	3	6

TABLE 42

Portfolio Concentration Multiple Regression Experiments, 1966 Known Portfolio Concentration Ratios*
[Regression Coefficients (t values)]

		With Population Split at the 10 Per Cent Portfolio Concentration Level†				Whole Population in Terms of Portfolio Concentration Levels	
		Five Largest Size Classes Only‡		All Size Classes‡		5 Largest Size Classes‡	All Size Classes‡
	Symbol	Below 10 Per Cent	Above 10 Per Cent	Below 10 Per Cent	Above 10 Per Cent		
Regression Coefficients							
Constant term	a	2.94 (3.046)§	23.78 (9.96)∥	27.90 (5.044)∥	15.50 (14.32)∥	12.15 (6.241)∥	8.99 (10.51)∥
Growth rate (percentage)	g	.480 (6.897)∥	.857 (5.999)∥	.247 (-4.815)∥	.380 (3.913)∥	.446 (3.711)∥	.263 (3.582)∥
Size (in millions of dollars)	$\frac{s}{\sqrt[3]{s}}$ $\sqrt[4]{s}$	-.0402 ...... (-2.176)#	...... -2.328 (-6.121)∥	.0000509 ...... (-.784)	-.001130 ...... (-1.571)	...... -.4795 (-3.154)§	...... .00319 (-2.100)§
Coefficient of Multiple Determination	R^2	.345	.445	.108	.0879	.110	.0447
Partial correlation for growth	$R13.2$	.569	.55	.325	.291	.263	.184
Partial correlation for size	$R12.3$	-.216	-.562	-.0558	-.121	-.226	-.109
Overall F test of R^2		26.57§	32.49§	11.95§	8.001§	11.409§	8.578§
Number of observations		104	84	200	170	188	370

*Portfolio concentration data for trust departments of commercial banks are for the period November-December, 1967.
†The split is in fact just above the 10 per cent level which accounts for any discrepancy noticed between the figures here and those in Table 41.
‡Size class refers to dollar-size classes as shown on Table 41.
§Significant at the .01 level.
∥Significant at the .001 level.
#Significant at the .05 level.

TABLE 43

Known Portfolio Concentration Ratios above 20 Per Cent Resulting from Stock Holdings of Financial Intermediaries, 1966*

Name of Business Institution	Number of Investment Companies Owning	Market Value of Common Stock (In Millions)	Total (1)†	Investment Companies (2)‡	Insurance Companies (3)§	Trust Departments of Commercial Banks‖		
						Percentage of Shares Outstanding Held (4A)	Percentage of Sole Vote (4B)	Percentage of Partial Vote (4C)
40 Per Cent and Up								
Northwest Airlines	28	$ 791	46.0	34.4	1.7	11.0	9.9	0.9
Trans World Airlines	31	496	40.1	24.1	2.5	15.2	13.5	0.6
30 Per Cent to 40 Per Cent								
Armstrong Rubber	5	78	37.5	25.1	7.0	5.6	5.4	0.1
General Instrument	5	227	32.0	30.9	1.1	....	....	....
Gimbel Brothers	14	337	35.6	26.4	8.7	16.2	0.5	0.1
International Minerals and Chemical	9	278	32.5	32.5	....	....	....	....
Mid-American Pipeline	4	24	31.8	31.8	....	....	....	....
National Airlines	19	290	36.0	32.4	3.6	....	....	....
Pabst Brewing	12	307	36.6	35.0	1.6	....	....	....
Vornado, Inc.	8	195	34.9	31.4	3.5	....	....	....
20 Per Cent to 30 Per Cent								
American Airlines	28	665	26.8	21.4	5.4	7.5	....	0.3
AMP, Inc.	12	456	23.3	13.7	5.0	7.5	4.6	1.0
Allegheny Ludlum	10	323	23.6	14.5	1.5	10.3	7.6	0.7
Arkansas-Louisiana Gas	19	389	24.4	21.2	3.2	....	....	....
Automatic Retailers	8	312	23.9	12.9	5.5	10.9	5.5	0.2
Burroughs Corp.	22	1,515	23.1	22.8	0.3	....	....	....
Capital Cities Broadcast	4	127	20.5	20.1	0.4	....	....	....
Carpenter Steel	6	164	23.8	12.6	1.1	19.4	11.2	2.2
Chicago & Great Western	2	29	27.4	27.3	0.1	....	....	....
Chicago & North Western	8	200	26.4	25.1	1.2	13.8	0.1	....
Collins Radio	5	292	27.6	16.4	0.8	12.1	10.4	0.4
Container Corp. of America	11	353	20.7	12.5	3.5	7.7	4.7	1.6
Copperweld Steel Company	3	55	26.0	19.6	6.4	....	....	....

214

Company							
Cutler-Hammer	5	154	22.9	10.2	2.8	17.6	9.9	0.9
Delta Air Lines	20	652	23.8	21.3	2.5	...	...	...
Eastern Airlines	21	527	25.2	16.6	2.5	6.4	6.1	0.2
Gov. Emp. Life Insurance	6	9	26.8	26.6	0.2	...	...	...
Grumman Aircraft Engineering	16	263	20.9	18.3	2.5	7.8	0.1	...
Illinois Central Industries	8	385	29.9	16.6	4.5	9.5	8.8	0.7
Kaiser Alum. & Chem.	19	826	20.4	11.2	3.5	6.6	5.7	0.3
Kansas Gas & Electric	7	179	21.5	15.5	6.0	...	...	...
Kayser-Roth	12	169	22.8	19.4	3.4	...	...	...
Kerr-McGee	14	833	21.8	19.0	2.5	10.1	0.3	...
Macy (R.H.)	10	320	26.0	15.6	10.4	...	...	...
Metro-Goldwyn-Mayer	8	268	21.0	20.8	0.2	...	...	...
Norfolk Southern R.R.	2	19	21.1	21.1	...	...	...	...
Pacific Southwest Airlines	4	78	21.8	21.8	...	...	...	...
Pan American World Airways	23	445	23.9	14.9	2.6	6.7	6.4	0.2
Panhandle Eastern P. L.	7	783	24.1	11.6	3.5	11.4	9.0	0.8
Philip Morris	20	483	26.2	25.2	1.0	...	...	...
Polaroid Corp.	40	3,965	26.5	21.2	0.7	10.5	4.6	0.4
Raytheon Co.	14	669	24.4	23.2	1.2	...	...	...
Reynolds Metals	25	838	21.6	14.8	1.5	5.5	5.3	0.1
Scovill Mfg.	6	127	21.6	12.1	2.7	11.5	6.8	1.6
Seaboard Airline R.R.	11	123	22.7	22.7	...	...	...	...
Texas Instruments	23	1,172	21.5	12.2	1.8	8.9	7.5	1.2
United Air Lines	23	1,213	-24.6	17.6	.9	15.0	6.1	0.4
United Shoe Machinery	7	140	22.0	18.2	3.4	6.3	0.4	0.1
Universal Oil Products	14	318	27.5	25.5	2.0	...	...	...
Western Air Lines	9	166	25.3	15.4	3.7	6.7	6.2	0.3

*Arthur Wiesenberger and Company, *Investment Companies—1967* (27th ed.; New York: Arthur Wiesenberger and Co., 1967) contains 1966 year-end information.

†Total of columns (2), (3), and (4B). The shares held by bank trust departments over which they have only partial voting rights or no voting rights according to the Staff Report for the Subcommittee on Domestic Finance are excluded.

‡Only the common stocks of 89 of the largest investment companies were used in these tabulations but these companies accounted for about 90 per cent of the industry's assets.

§United Statistical Associates, *Stocks*, Vol. I of *Corporate Holdings of Insurance Companies* (New York: United Statistical Assoc., 1968) contains 1967 year-end data.

‖Data from U.S., Congress, House, Committee on Banking and Currency, *Commercial Banks and Their Trust Activities, Emerging Influence on the American Economy*, Vol. I, Staff Report for the Subcommittee on Domestic Finance, 90th Cong., 2d sess., July 8, 1968 (Washington, D.C.: Government Printing Office, 1968). Data are for November and December, 1967.

TABLE 44

Known Concentrated Holdings of Airline Common Stock by Financial Intermediaries—1966
(Percentage of Common Stock Owned by Financial Intermediaries)

Financial Intermediary		North-west Airlines	Trans World Airlines	American Airlines	National Airlines	Eastern Airlines	Delta Airlines	Pacific Southwest Airlines	Pan American World Airways	United Air Lines	Western Air Lines
(Percentage of total identified concentration)		(46.0)	(40.1)	(26.6)	(36.0)	(25.2)	(23.8)	(21.8)	(23.9)	(24.6)	(25.3)
Trust department of commercial banks*											
Chase Manhattan Bank		9.9	7.4	.....	.....	6.1	.....	.....	6.4	6.0	6.2
Morgan Guaranty Trust		.....	6.1	6.4	.....	.....	.....	.....	.....	.....	.....
Investment companies (or groups)†											
Investors Diversified	(3)	.....	1.6	3.2	3.6	2.3	5.2+	4.0	2.6	3.2	.....
Massachusetts Investment Trust	(2)	1.5	2.3	.....	.....	.....	2.4	.....	4.3	2.5	.....
Fidelity Group	(5)	6.6	3.1	1.2	8.1	3.7	1.1	.....	1.5	2.7	2.0
Waddell and Reed	(3)	2.3	4.9	.....	4.3	.....	2.9	.....	2.4	0.9	.....
Wellington Management	(3)	.....	1.5	.....	.....	.....	.....	.....	.....	0.9	.....
Keystone	(5)	1.3	1.0	.....	1.9	.....	.....	12.0	.....	1.1	.....
Putnam Management	(4)	1.0	.....	.....	.....	.....	.....	3.8	.....	1.7	.....

Channing	(2)	1.0	.....	1.2	2.4	.....	.....	.....
Fundamental Investors	(2)	2.2	.....	.....	.....	1.1	.....	.....
Broadstreet	(3)	.....	.....	3.1	.....	.....	.....	.....
American Mutual, et al.	(3)	2.9	.....	1.1	2.2	1.2	.....	1.4
Lehman-One William Street	(2)	.....	.....	.....	.....	.....	.....	.....
Axe-Houghton	(1)	.....	.....	.....	.....	.....	3.7	.....
American Investors	(1)	.....	.....	.....	.....	.....	2.3	.....
Hamilton Fund	(1)	.....	.....	.....	.....	.....	.....	4.3
Lord, Abbett	(2)	.....	.....	.....	.....	.....	.....	2.3
Dreyfus Fund	(1)	.....	.....	.....	.....	.....	.....	1.4
American Investors	(1)	.....	.....	.....	.....	.....	.....	1.7
Insurance companies‡								
Prudential Life (Newark)		.....	1.6	4.7	.....	.....	2.6	3.1
Insurance Company of North America (Philadelphia)		.....	.....	.....	1.8	1.0	.....	.....
Total in named intermediaries		28.7	29.5	20.9	24.3	14.9	21.8	20.1	19.0	22.4
Market value of common stock, 12/31/66 (in millions)		$791	$496	$665	$290	$527	$652	$78	$445	$1,213	$166

*Data from U.S., Congress, House, Committee on Banking and Currency, *Commercial Banks and Their Trust Activities, Emerging Influence on the American Economy*, Vol. I, Staff Report for the Subcommittee on Domestic Finance, 90th Cong., 2d sess., July 8, 1968 (Washington, D.C.: Government Printing Office, 1968).

†Data from United Statistical Associates, *Stocks*, Vol. I of *Corporate Holdings of Insurance Companies* (New York: United Statistical Assoc., 1968).

‡Data from Arthur Wiesenberger and Company, *Investment Companies—1967* (27th ed.; New York: Arthur Wiesenberger and Co., 1967).

TABLE 45

Demonstration of Difference between Overall Market Percentage of Total Investment and Portfolio Concentration Ratios
(Dollar Values in Millions)

Company	Market Value	Portfolio Concentration Pattern			
		A		B	
		Investment	Portfolio Concentration (Percentage)	Investment	Portfolio Concentration (Percentage)
A	$10,000	$1,500	15	$1,165.8	11.7
B	900	153	17	135.0	15.0
C	600	120	20	180.0	30.0
D	400	100	25	200.0	50.0
E	300	90	30	180.0	60.0
F	250	63	25	125.0	50.0
G	150	30	20	52.5	35.0
H	125	19	15	31.2	25.0
I	80	8	10	12.0	15.0
J	25	1	4	2.5	10.0
	$11,870	$2,084		$2,084.0	
Overall market percentage of total investment		17.6		17.6	
Average of individual portfolio concentration ratios			18.1		30.2

218

TABLE 46

Stockholder Pyramids for Two Very Large Corporations*

Number of Shares Held by Stockholder	Number of Stockholders	Percentage of Stockholders		Number of Shares Held	Percentage of Shares Held	
		By Class	Cumulative	By Class	By Class	Cumulative
Corporation A:						
1 to 10	117,585	48.9	48.9	581,181	1.3	1.3
11 to 25	44,600	18.5	67.4	848,235	1.8	3.1
26 to 50	33,600	14.0	81.4	1,376,458	3.0	6.1
51 to 100	23,493	9.8	91.2	1,987,490	4.3	10.4
101 to 200	10,471	4.4	95.6	1,664,860	3.6	14.0
201 to 500	6,528	2.7	98.3	2,165,257	4.7	18.7
501 to 1,000	1,981	0.8	99.1	1,445,288	3.2	21.9
1,001 to 5,000	1,561	0.7	99.8	3,380,114	7.3	29.2
Over 5,000	581	0.2	100.0	32,626,899	70.8	100.0
Total	240,535	100.0		46,075,782	100.0	
Corporation B:						
1 to 49	22,562	35.2	35.2	418,897	1.2	1.2
50 to 99	9,663	15.1	50.3	642,220	1.8	3.0
100 to 499	23,395	36.5	86.8	4,948,831	13.8	16.8
500 to 999	4,447	6.9	93.7	3,101,831	8.7	25.5
1,000 and over	4,049	6.3	100.0	26,708,314	74.5	100.0
Total	64,116	100.0		35,820,093	100.0	

*The corporate secretaries requested that the names of their respective corporations be kept anonymous. The letters are in the author's files.

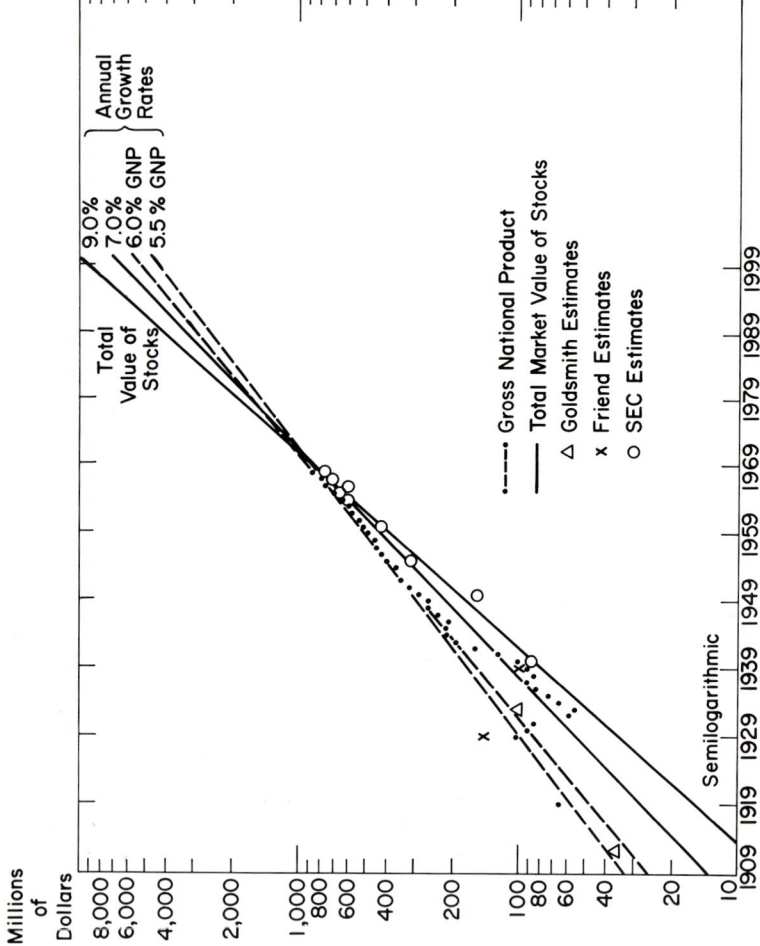

Fig. 1: Growth of GNP and total market value of stocks (1909-2000).

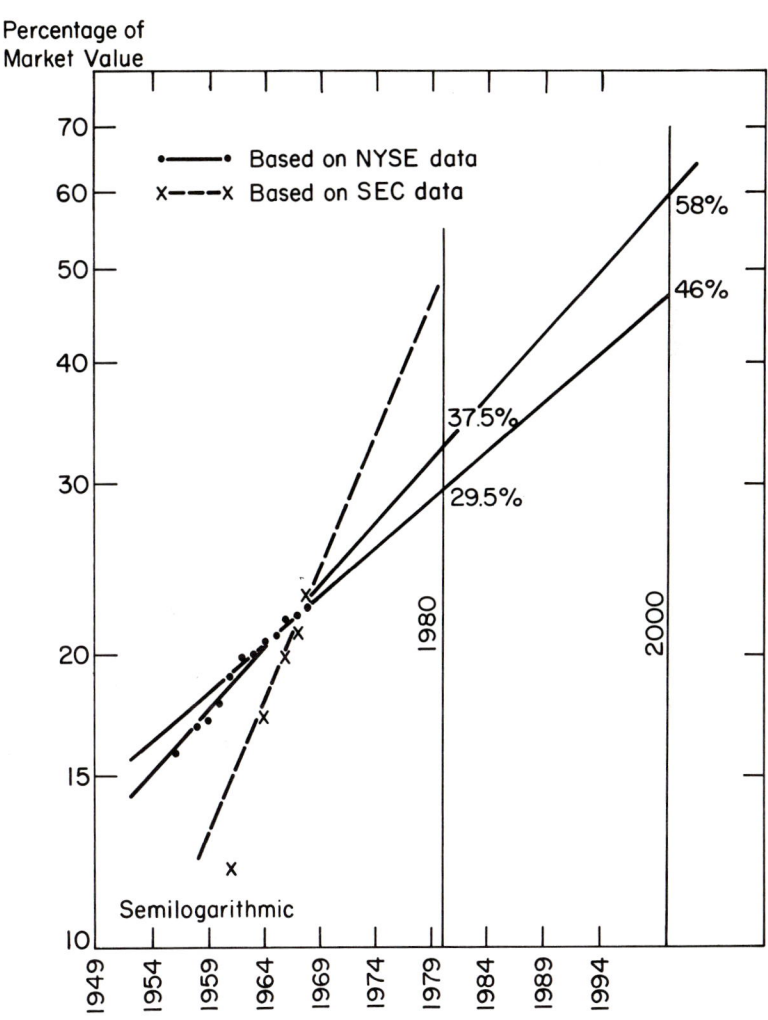

Fig. 2: Stock holdings of financial intermediaries relative to total market value of stock.

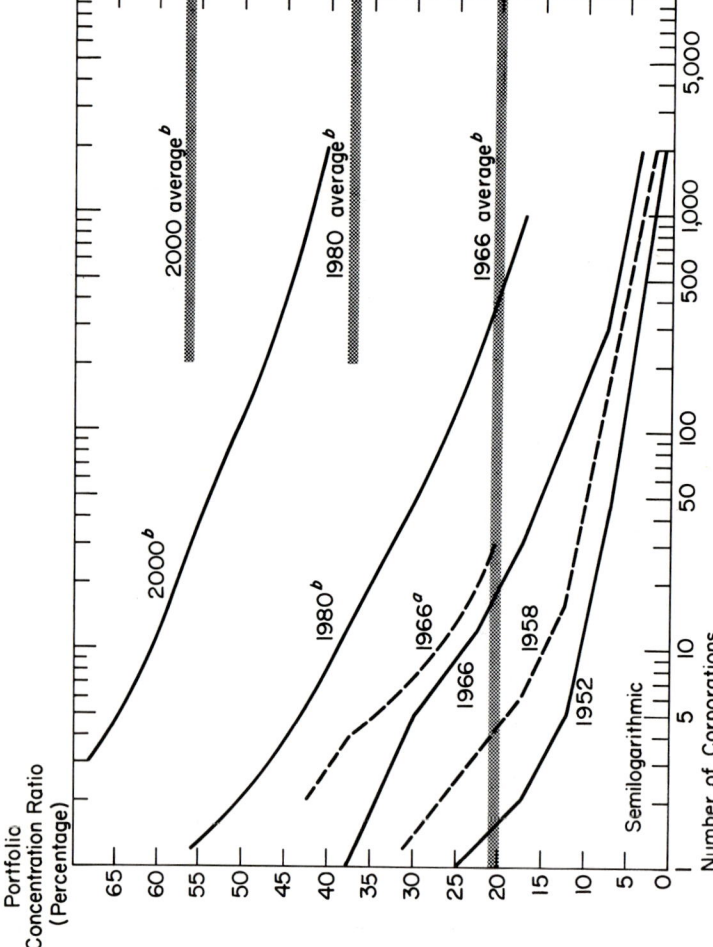

Fig. 3: Portfolio concentrations: 1952-2000; *a* includes what is known about commercial banks' trust department holdings of common stock; *b* designates projected figures.

INDEX

Accounting, public: public acceptance of, 1; history and growth of profession, 1, 3-5, 6; licensing laws, 4

Actuarial profession: its emergence, 3; growth and history, 5

Actuarial Society of America: establishment and early growth, 5; merges into Society of Actuaries, 8

Airline industry: financial intermediaries' stock holdings in, 96-97; **high portfolio concentration ratio**, 94—reasons for, 97

American Airlines stock, 96; concentration ratio, 28

American Express Co.: establishes first private pension plan, 37

American Finance Association, 6

American Gas & Electric Co., 35*n30*

American Institute of Actuaries, 5

American Telephone and Telegraph Co.: assets in 1968, 9*n1*; number of stock holders, 115; mentioned 35*n30*, 58

Appleton Rule, 55, 57

Armstrong Committee: 1905 investigation of life insurance industry, 2, 151*n62*

Armstrong Rubber Co.: ownership structure, 30, 108; mentioned, 94

Arnold, Thurman (Attorney General): and trust busting, 2

Atchison, Topeka & Santa Fe Railway Co., 35*n30*

Bank of America: assets in 1968, 9*n1*

Banking Act (1933), 148*n33*

Banks (commercial) and corporate customers: complex relationship with, 118-19; power over, 129

Banks, trust departments of: and portfolio companies, 31; administer corporate pension funds, 36, 47-48, 129; and state and local pension funds, 126; mentioned, 1, 7, and *passim*; **and portfolio concentrations of stock**, 48-50, 109—desirability of information, 49-50; and airline stock, 96; internal rules limiting, 109-10; author's suggestions for limiting, 110-11

Bechtel Corp.: annual sales of, 146*n12*

Behrens, Charles, 65

Berle, Adolph A.: Estimates pension fund assets, 51; mentioned, 113-16, 121, 146*n16*, 147*n22, 24, 25,* and *passim*

Alfred M. Best Co., 60

"Blue Sky" law, 9*n4*, 146*n15*

Boston Fund: compilation of "favorite stocks" of universities, 69

Bullock, Hugh (president of Galvin Bullock): and Investment Company Act, 17, 18, 22, 107

Bunker, Arthur, 107

Burroughs Corp., 35*n33*, 95

Cabot, Paul C.: letter to author, 15; mentioned, 14, 32*n1*

Casualty Actuarial Society: establishment of, 5

Cargill, Inc.: annual sales of, 146*n12*

Carnegie Corp., 69

Cartwright, Dorwin, 115, 117

Chase Manhattan Bank: assets in 1968, 9*n1*; and airline stock, 96; mentioned, 31

Clayton Act (1914), 2

Coca-Cola stock: and universities, 69

Common stock. *See* **Stock**

Communications Satellite Corp.: board of directors of, 152*n72*

Companies, joint stock, 122

Companies, regulated: described by Adam Smith, 122

Conglomerate mergers. *See* **Mergers**

Consolidated Edison Co. of N.Y., 35*n30*

Continental Grain Merchants: annual sales of, 146*n12*

Continental Insurance Co.: structure of stock portfolio, 60, 61

Corporate financial reports: publication of, 4, 6

Corporation, modern: development of, 122-24

Cowan, Geoffrey: and "Campaign GM," 126

Currency system: U.S. history of, 3

Dahl, Robert A., 115, 117

Danforth Foundation: and Ralston Purina stock, 68

Duke Endowment, 68

Duke Power stock, 68

E.I. du Pont de Nemours, 35*n30*

Durkheim, Emile, 106, 146*n16*

Eastman Kodak stock, 69

East India Company, 122

Employee benefit accounts: administered by banks, 25

Equitable Life Assurance Co.: assets in 1968, 9*n1*

Federal Home Loan Bank System: board of directors of, 152*n72*

Federal National Mortgage Association: board of directors of, 152*n72*

Federal Reserve System: 1897 forerunner of, 3; established 1913, 3

Fidelity Group: and investment concentration, 108; mentioned, 30

Financial analysts, 6

Financial intermediaries: and portfolio turnover, 7; comparison of stock holdings of, 21-22; comparison of stock ownership and market value structures, 31; portfolio diversification by size of intermediary, 85-86; and airline stock, 96-97; projections for stock ownership, 98; ratio of total market value owned, 98; concerned with return not control, 124, 129-30; concentration of stock ownership, *passim*; **and voting control of stock,** 114-15—and election of corporate directors, 120; future limitations on, 133-35; **power through stock ownership,** 117—legitimacy of, 121, 124

First National City Bank: assets in 1968, 9*n1*

Ford Foundation: assets, 68

Ford Motor stock: and Ford Foundation, 68; and Rockefeller Foundation, 69; and universities, 69; public offering of, 75; mentioned, 72*n21*

Foundations: stock ownership structure, 68; assets of, 68; probable decrease in growth of, 83-84

Friend, Irwin: stock market series, 20

Gardiner, William Tuder, 14, 32*n1*

General American Investors Co., 17

General Electric Co.: reports asset value of pension fund annually, 41

General Motors Corp.: assets in 1968, 9*n1*; stock, 58, 69; and "Campaign GM," 126-27; mentioned 34*n30*

Gimbel Brothers: concentration ratio, 28

GNP. *See* **Gross national product**

Goldsmith, Raymond: stock market series, 20

The Great American Co.: stock holdings of, 61

Griswold, Merrill: and tax problems of mutual funds, 14; and Investment Company Act, 17, 18; mentioned, 32*n1*, 108

INDEX

Gross national product: historic growth rate, 74; projections to 2000, 74-77

Gulf Oil stock: and universities, 69

Harbrecht, Fr. Paul, S.J., 116; and projections of pension fund assets, 51

Harvard University: stock holdings of, 69

Holland, Daniel: projections for pension funds, 51, 62

Housing and Urban Development Act, 152n72

Hudson Institute, 74

Hughes, Charles Evans: and Armstrong investigations, 55

IBM stock, 61, 69

Income Tax Amendment to Constitution (1913): effect on laws licensing public accountants, 4

Incorporated Investors: started 1925, 13

Inland Steel decision, 38

Insurance companies, fire: Merritt Committee investigations, 59

Insurance companies, life: 1905 investigation by Armstrong Committee, 3, 55, 59, 151n62; different from casualty insurance, 54; stock ownership permitted in New York, 55; and New York Life Insurance Code, 55, 56, 57-58; separate pension accounts, 56, 81; entering investment company activities, 82; **and stock ownership**—holdings of, 21; increase in, 54-56, 81; history of, 54-56; limitations on and regulations, 55, 56, 57, 87; publication of, 58; decline in growth rate, 81

Insurance companies, property and casualty: Merritt Committee investigation of, 3; growth of assets, 59, 82; structure of asset ownership, 60; diversity of activities, 60; **stock holdings of**, 59-63—legal restrictions on and diversification, 60-61; growth of, 83; projections for, 83

Internal Revenue Code: and diversification of investment companies, 12; and 5-10 rule, 15; and employee benefit plans, 38; mentioned, 11, 52n3

Internal Revenue Service, 40

International Nickel of Canada, 35n30

Interstate Commerce Act (1887), 2

Investment companies and complexes: closed end, 11; diversification of, 11; mutual funds, 11, 22-23; and tax provisions, 12; history and growth, 13-15, 20, 21-25, 78-79; SEC investigations, 13, 25-26, 151n62; most aggressive stock investors, 86; and airline stock, 96-97; consulted by their portfolio companies, 117-18, 128; future limitations on voting of stock, 133; **diversification rules**, 12, 108—recommendations, 109; **portfolio concentrations**, 13, 25-30, 133—projections for, 79

Investment Company Act (1940): and growth of insurance company assets, 12; and 5-10 rule, 12, 15, 22, 108; Senate hearings, 16-19, 108; final form, 19; suggestions for changes, 109; mentioned, 19, 21, 30, 110

Investment Company Institute: data published by, 20

Investors Diversified Services, 30; and Armstrong Rubber stock, 94; **assets**, 24, 25—growth of, 23

Investors Mutual, Inc.: assets of, 22

Investors Variable Payment Fund, 24

Iowa Board of Regents: and "Campaign GM," 127

Iowa-Illinois Gas & Electric Co., 125-26

Iowa Power & Light Co., 125

Iowa Public Employees Retirement System, 125; and "Campaign GM," 127

Kahn, Herman: projection for GNP, 74

Kentucky Fried Chicken, 61

Kerr-Mills Act (1960), 150n60

Keystone Custodian Funds, 23

King, Willford I., 74

Labor Management Relations Act: and employee pension plans, 38

Landis, James (Chairman of SEC), 14

Eli Lilly stock, 68

Lilly Endowment, 68

Lindsay, John (Mayor of New York): and "Campaign GM," 126

Lord, Abbett and Co., 23

McGrath, Raymond D.: and Investment Company Act, 17

Marshall, Alfred, 146$n16$

Massachusetts Institute of Technology: and "Campaign GM," 127

Massachusetts Investors Trust: started 1924, 13; assets, 22; mentioned, 108

Means, Gardiner C., 113, 115, 146$n16$

Medicare and Medicaid, 131

Mergers: history of, 2; and corporate financial reporting, 6; and investment company influence, 128; compared to concentrations of stock ownership, 151$n63$

Merritt Committee: investigations of insurance companies, 3, 59

Metropolitan Life Insurance Co.: assets in 1968, 9$n1$; stock holdings of, 58; mentioned, 60

Mid-America Pipeline Co., 94

Money supply: and National Banking Act (1863), 3

Money Trust: investigated 1912 by Pujo Committee, 3

Morgan Guaranty Trust: and employee benefit accounts, 25, 47; and airline stock, 96

Nader, Ralph: and "Campaign GM," 126-27

National Association of Securities Dealers, 6

National Banking Act (1863): and money supply, 3

National Bureau of Business and Economic Research: projections of pension funds, 51

National Monetary Commission: established 1908, 3

Natrella, Vito: and SEC survey of pension funds, 51

New York Life Insurance Code, 55, 56, 57-58

New York State Employees Retirement System: assets of, 63; portfolio regulation, 66

New York State Teachers Retirement System: assets of, 63; portfolio regulation, 66

New York Stock Exchange: asks corporations to publish statements, 4; tries to set accounting standards, 4; mentioned *passim*

North American Securities Administrators, 6

Northwest Airlines: ownership structure, 29, 30, 31; stock, 96; mentioned, 35$n33$

NYSE. *See* **New York Stock Exchange**

NYSE listed stock. *See* **Stock**

Parsons, Talcott, 106, 121, 130-31, 146$n16$

Patman Committee (1968), 47, 48, 49, 51, 57, 98

University of Pennsylvania: and "Campaign GM," 127

Pension funds, corporate: and increase in number of actuaries, 5; administered by banks; insured versus uninsured plans, 39-40; accounting problems, 40, 53$n10$; and retirement age, 52$n8$; percentage of assets in common stock, 101$n7$; contribute to power of banks, 129; **history and growth,** 37-41—Labor Management Relations Act (1947), 38; Revenue Act (1928), 38; and income tax relief, 38-39; 1965 Report of President's committee, 39; **portfolio concentrations,** 43-47—paucity of information, 41; attitude of corporation officials to, 44-47; **growth of stock ownership,** 42, 80—projections for, 80; **growth of assets,** 79—projections for, 51, 80

Pension funds, state and local: independence of systems, 62; funding and asset size, 101$n8$; problems of voting stock, 125-26; use of bank trust departments, 126; **growth of,** 63—reasons for, 62; projections of, 62-63; **assets of systems,** 63—growth and projections of, 80; **stock holdings of,** 63-67—portfolio regulation, 63-64, 66, 87-88; reasons for investments, 65; growth of, 66-67; projections for, 80-81

Pensions, old-age, 150$n59$

Philip Morris, 35$n33$

Polaroid Corp., 35$n33$, 95

Portfolio churning: by financial intermediaries, 7

Postal fraud laws (1909), 146$n15$; and fraudulent sale of securities, 9$n4$

Pound, Roscoe: and legal history of property, 123

Property, private: theories of, 122-24

Prudential Life Insurance Co.: assets in 1968, 9$n1$; stock holdings, 57; airlines' stock, 96, 97; mentioned, 60

Public accounting. See Accounting, public

Pujo Committee: investigations of Money Trust, 3

Putnam Management Co., 23

Railroads: populist reaction to power of, 2; audited statements required, 4

Ralston Purina stock: owned by Danforth Foundation, 68

Ratheon Corp., 35$n33$

Resources for the Future, Inc.: and projections of GNP, 74

Retirement benefits: formulas for, 101$n8$

Revenue Act (1928): and private pension plans, 38

Revenue Act (1936): and investment company income, 12; and undistributed profit tax, 14; Senate Finance Committee debate, 14; defines "mutual investment company," 14; Paul Cabot's opinion, 15; mentioned, 19

Ripley, William Z. (economist), 4, 114, 147$n22$

Rockefeller Foundation: stock holdings of, 69; and "Campaign GM," 127

Roosevelt, Franklin D.: economic recovery measures, 13-14

Rubinaw, Isaac M., 5, 10$n8$

Savings, monetary: effect on stock prices, 76

Schenker, David: and Investment Company Act, 16-17

Sears, Roebuck & Co.: assets of profit-sharing pension plan, 53$n13$; stock, 69; Savings and Profit Sharing Fund, 149$n37$

SEC. See Securities and Exchange Commission

Securities Act (1933), 6, 114

Securities and Exchange Act (1934), 6, 114

Securities and Exchange Commission: and publication of corporate financial statements, 4, 6; and development of public accounting, 6; investigations of investment companies, 13, 16, 25-26, 151$n62$; mentioned *passim*; creation of, 6—background to, 131

Security analysts. See Financial analysts

Senate Finance Committee: and Revenue Act (1936), 14

Sherman Anti-Trust Act (1880), 2

Simon, Herbert A., 115

Smelser, Neil J., 130-31, 146$n16$

Smith, Adam, 122

Social Security Act (1935), 131

Society of Actuaries: formation of, 5

Standard Oil Co.: assets in 1909, 2

Standard Oil of New Jersey: assets in 1968, 9$n1$; stock, 58, 69; mentioned, 35$n30$

State Farm Insurance Co.: stock investment policy, 61

State Street Investment Corp.: started 1924, 13

State Street Research and Management Corp., 69

State Teachers Retirement System of Ohio, 65

Stock: changes in ownership structures, 77-78; attractiveness of different corporations, 90; and rights of private property, 123-24; differentiation of ownership and control, 131-32; future separation of, 132-33; future limitations on financial intermediaries, 133-35; **concentration of stock ownership**—growing public awareness of, 1; society's options to shape, 7; by financial intermediaries, 1, 2, 7; compared to corporate mergers, 115n63; **holdings of financial intermediaries**—comparison between, 21-22; projections for, 84, 98; **portfolio concentrations of**, 26-31—NYSE lists misleading for analysis of, 31; by size of financial intermediary, 85-86; legal restrictions, 87-88; and risk, 88; unnecessary diversification of, 89; and size of corporations, 90-93, 94; projections for, 91-93, 95-96, 107; "ceiling" on, 111-12; **market value of**—growth rate of, 75; projections for, 75, 107; effects of institutional ownership on, 76; **voting control of**—and financial intermediaries, 112, 115; and proxies, 113, 114; power of owners, 115-17; development of one vote per share, 122; **and "stockholders voting council,"** 135-44—social background to establishment of, 136-37; election of members, 138; results of, 138-39; votes transferred by financial intermediaries, 139-40; costs and fees, 141; compared to Federal Reserve Banks, 142

Stock market: current concern about organization of, 7; effect of institutional investment on, 26

Temporary National Economic Committee: investigations, 2

Texaco stock, 61, 69

Tilove, Robert, 116
Trans World Airlines stock, 96
Tri-Continental Corp.: assets in 1968, 22
Truth-in-Securities Act (1933), 131
Unilever, 108
Union Carbide and Carbon, 34n30
United States Steel Corp.: assets in 1909, 2; reports asset value of pension fund annually, 41
Universities: size of stock holdings, 69; and voting of stock, 69; projections for endowment growth rate, 83

Waddell & Reed: and TWA stock, 96
Walsh, Senator: and Revenue Act of 1936, 14
Weber, Max, 106, 166n16
Welfare and Pension Plans Disclosure Act (1958): and corporate pension plans, 41; abuses before, 53n11
Wellington Management Co.: and Armstrong Rubber stock, 94; mentioned, 30
Wharton, Joseph, 3
Wharton School of Finance and Economy: establishment of 1881, 3
Wiener, Anthony J.: projections for GNP, 74
Wisconsin Investment Board, 64

Xerox stock, 69

Selectric IBM Composition
by
Monique Snitchler
Bureau of Business Research
Graduate School of Business Administration
The University of Michigan
Ann Arbor, Michigan

DATE DUE

JUL 2 8 1972			
~~DEC 1 5 1973~~			
~~OCT 2 7 1977~~			
~~DEC 1 5 1987~~			
~~DEC 1 4 1988~~			
GAYLORD			PRINTED IN U.S.A.